Marlene Calvin

Diasporic Lives

Afrika und ihre Diaspora

herausgegeben von

Manfred Kremser und Werner Zips
(Institut für Kultur- und Sozialanthropologie
der Universität Wien)

Band 9

LIT

Marlene Calvin

DIASPORIC LIVES

Alienation and Violence
as Themes in African American
and Jamaican Cultural Texts

LIT

Cover photo: from the Film *The Harder They Come* by Perry Henzell
With kind permission from Justine Henzell
Graphic design: Carmen Mankel

This book has been generously supported with grants from Heinrich-Heine-Universität Düsseldorf - Graduiertenförderung and Düsseldorf Entrepreneurs Foundation

D 61

Dissertation Heinrich-Heine-Universität Düsseldorf 2007

Gedruckt auf alterungsbeständigem Werkdruckpapier entsprechend
ANSI Z3948   DIN ISO 9706

Bibliographic information published by the Deutsche Nationalbibliothek
The Deutsche Nationalbibliothek lists this publication in the Deutsche Nationalbibliografie; detailed bibliographic data are available in the Internet at http://dnb.d-nb.de.

ISBN 978-3-643-10574-5
Zugl.: Düsseldorf, Univ., Diss., 2008

A catalogue record for this book is available from the British Library

©LIT VERLAG Dr. W. Hopf Berlin 2010
Fresnostr. 2   D-48159 Münster
Tel. +49 (0) 2 51-620 320   Fax +49 (0) 2 51-922 60 99
e-Mail: lit@lit-verlag.de   http://www.lit-verlag.de

Distribution:
In Germany: LIT Verlag Fresnostr. 2, D-48159 Münster
Tel. +49 (0) 2 51-620 32 22, Fax +49 (0) 2 51-922 60 99, e-mail: vertrieb@lit-verlag.de

In Austria: Medienlogistik Pichler-ÖBZ, e-mail: mlo@medien-logistik.at

In Switzerland: B + M Buch- und Medienvertrieb, e-mail: order@buch-medien.ch

In the UK: Global Book Marketing, e-mail: mo@centralbooks.com

In North America by:

Transaction Publishers
Rutgers University
35 Berrue Circle
Piscataway, NJ 08854

Phone: +1 (732) 445 - 2280
Fax: + 1 (732) 445 - 3138
for orders (U. S. only):
toll free (888) 999 - 6778
e-mail: orders@transactionpub.com

Livication

To my mother & father Daisy Lee Calvin & Cleveland Calvin,
My daughter Chea Neneh, my favorite aunt Lillian Lee,
All the family in the small district of Bachelors Hall in Western Jamaica,
And the rest of the family in the United States yu don knows.
Jah Guidance!

Table of Contents

Preface and Acknowledgements

Give thanks to Jah Rastafari! And all the other sources that kept me going in the last few years.

I would like to thank my doctor father Prof. Dr. Herwig Friedl for his support throughout the whole project, for giving me the chance to present different chapters of the thesis during his doctoral colloquium and for reading and making vital suggestions for the final draft of the thesis.

My study has been made possible with the financial support of two scholarships: One from the Heinrich-Heine-University Düsseldorf as part of the 'Graduiertenförderung', which supported me for a period of two years. In the final phase of my research, I was awarded a one-year fellowship from the 'Düsseldorf Entrepreneurs Foundation'. Without both scholarships the work would not have been possible at this time, so I would like to thank both the University and the Foundation for their generous financial support.

I would like to say a very big 'thank you' to Dr. Rainer Holtei for the final proofreading of the thesis, but naturally I take full responsibility for any mistakes remaining in the thesis.

Thanks to Christoph Hollender for all his help during the whole project and for formatting the thesis, thank you very very much.

Thanks to Professor Carolyn Cooper at the University of the West Indies, Mona for granting me access to Dr. Imani Tafari's study on violence, when I told her about my aims for the doctoral thesis; for taking time out of her busy schedule, and for offering me a place to stay or suggesting where I could stay whenever I was in Kingston on research work. Thank you very much.

I would like to thank Professor Barry Chevannes, dean of the Faculty of Social Sciences at the University of the West Indies, Mona for taking time out of his busy schedules to give me an interview on the sociological developments in Jamaica in the last few years. And also for just taking the time and showing interest in a fellow Jamaican.

I am also grateful to Professor Werner Zips of the University of Vienna for his invitation to have my book published in the series "Afrika und ihre Diaspora". Respect!

Thanks to Dr. Imani Tafari-Ama for allowing me to use her dissertation and for offering me a place to stay while I was in Kingston doing research work at the University of the West Indies.

I would also like to thank Susan Coye and the rest of the Coye family for their warm support. Ellen Köhlings and Pete Lilly, thank you both for being such good friends and my daughter's godparents 'big up'.

Thanks to Bettina Lantz-Okoye and the Lantz-Okoye family, Chantal Turri, Holger Haas, Karin Oettel, Carmen Mankel, Melanie Tilstra, Imgard Müller, Jean Racsanji, and all the other friends who occasionally took care of my daughter Neneh for a few hours, so that I could work on the thesis or just rest. I am forever grateful for your help and support.

My biggest thanks go to my daughter Chea Neneh for just being the best daughter that any mother could wish for, Sweetie you are just wonderful.

Special thanks to my parents and the rest of the family and friends in Jamaica and America, 'one love'!

And also to all the people that listened and gave their support over the years, once again thank you.

A very special thank you to Dr. Elisabeth Schäfer-Wünsche, one of my best teachers, advisers and a very supportive friend in the end, thank you so much!

Marlene Calvin

So we come a long way from the chains and the fields
A long way from the back o' the bus
Shoulda brought along a little map for the travelling
Seems we've come a long way from us
Squander our money waiting for reparation,
never make plans for retirement day
Who's to be blamed for our lack of preparation
now we done spent every dime of our pay
On big pimping, flossing every dollar we've got on the much less fortunate
Small thinking got us bound tighter than the chains that we try to forget

Tell me now Malcolm, do we hurt your pride?
Can you hear me now Rosa, was it worth the ride?
Can you see me now Marcus, we're still not unified, no we're not.
So tell me now Martin, is this why you died. (…)

(Tanya Stephens, *Rebelution*, 2006)

1 Introduction

The concepts of alienation and violence are as old as human existence. In almost all human cultural history there is some sort of manifestation of violence and alienation. In my thesis *Diasporic Lives: Alienation and Violence as Themes in African American and Jamaican Cultural Texts*, I will show how the Africans' arrival in the so-called New World cultures of the United States and the British owned colony of Jamaica were determined by slavery and its socio-economic, political and historical aspects. I will emphasize that alienation and violence confronting African American and Jamaican cultures today have their seeds planted in the forced dispersion and enslavement of the Africans in both cultures, bearing in mind that the Africans were not only violently removed from their homelands, but also suffered enslavement, and were forced to toil on cotton and sugar plantations in the American South and in Jamaica.

My interest in examining both cultures comes from my experiences of living in both Jamaica and the United States. I was born in Jamaica but when I was thirteen my parents migrated to the United States. After living in New York City for about the same period of time as in Jamaica I moved to Germany. Because my family and relatives are still in the United States and Jamaica I am a frequent visitor to both countries. It was after my attendance at *Stone Love 30th Anniversary Show* (2002) in Kingston, which turned violent that I decided to concentrate on the theme of violence in both cultures. Before the *Stone Love Show* I was only going to examine Jamaican culture focusing on the theme of alienation, but after the show I asked myself why is it that whenever I visit my parents in East Brooklyn or families in Jamaica that I keep hearing gun shots. I wanted to 'get to the bottom of the whole thing' as Jamaicans sometimes say. I am aware that alienation and violence can be found in almost all cultures. One just needs to turn on the radio or television, the news is full of violence, but I was curious to know the particular circumstances causing the violence in African American and Jamaican cultures. I also wanted to see if there were similarities in the types of violence and alienation. Being aware of the negative stereotypes, which are very often used to describe African diasporic cultures, and the possible danger of my study aiding to reinforce these stereotypes, I was still interested to know what was causing this violence. It was also clear that with themes such as alienation and violence I would have to use an inter-disciplinary theoretical framework even though I was working mostly with fictional texts. Claiming that alienation and violence cannot be separated from their social, and historical cultural context, there was a demand to examine and keep in mind the sociological developments of both cultures in order to fully understand these subjects. This is what I will attempt to do in my dissertation, not only give a close reading and interpretation of the texts, but also tie elements of alienation and violence into sociological developments of both cultures.

The Europeans and their descendants in the Americas constructed diverse ethical explanations and discourses to justify the inhuman treatment of Afri-cans. They professed that Africans were either not totally human, or if they were human beings they were primitive folks that needed the 'enlightenment' of the Christian monotheistic beliefs instead of their own polytheistic religious traditions. The new scientific study of 'man' supported the European cultural bias that Africans were not human in the same way as Europeans or other peoples. Empirical studies of African somatic features along with measure-ments of their skulls were compared with ancient Greek sculptures, which the Europeans and their descendants agreed were the ideal. The Europeans also defined the ideal human skin color. Africans with their dark skin color and thick hair texture became the "Other" against which the European concepts of humanity and beauty were measured. The Europeans also considered their tradition of a written culture the epitome of human civilization. African cul-tures with their oral traditions were seen as the lowest human stage, close to animality. These cultural discourses on human species by Europeans and their descendants in the eighteenth and nineteenth centuries have influenced and are continually influencing the way Africans and their descendants are represented in the so-called New World cultures of the United States and Jamaica. The concept of race developed in the nineteenth century plus the stereotypes created and reinforced by popular American culture have fixed certain images of African identity in the United States. In the Jamaican culture the subject of race and its European pseudo-scientific definitions were camouflaged by the British influenced discourse of class in the colonial and post-colonial society, even though the concept of race played and is continuing to play a germane role in the Jamaican society. In my thesis I will illustrate how European artistic and cultural ideals as well as the 'scientific' definition of race have contributed to experiences of alienation and violence in the cultural development of African Americans and Jamaican societies as represented in their cultural texts.

The experiences of forced dispersal and the trans-atlantic slave trade have formed the foundation of African American and African Jamaican cultural histories in the both the United States and Jamaica. The sociologist Orlando Patterson in his comparative study *Slavery and Social Death* points out that an enslaved person is inevitably confronted with alienation and violence. He also claims that in all slave societies there has to be some visible mark on the slave that shows his or her status of servitude. In the trans-atlantic slave societies the dark pigmentation of the African skin became a symbol of slavery. The legacy of making African skin color and somatic features symbols of slavery has lead to traumatic experiences for some African descendants in the so-called New World.

According to Ron Eyerman arguments on cultural trauma slavery became traumatic for African Americans after the failure of emancipation to truly liberate the former slaves. The 19th century popular culture of minstrelsy with its stereotype images and visual arts reinforced the myth of the "happy slave", and experiences of slavery where seen as beneficial to African Americans as well as European Americans (Eyerman 2001). This distortion of African American cultural history has forced African Americans up to this day to struggle over their representation in American society. The somatic definition of race and the stereotype images along with the blackface make-up created for minstrelsy popular culture has continued to influence some media images of African Americans today.

According to Henry Louis Gates African descendants are the only enslaved group of people to have created a genre of literature. The autobiography was the first genre of literature that African descendent slaves used to voice their experiences of slavery and to assert themselves against the alienating slave system. The fugitive slave narrative was a way for the runaway slaves to testify against the oppressive slave system and their in-human treatments. In my analysis of African American cultural texts I will interpret two autobiographical works, a novel, and one film. For my interpretation of Jamaican cultural texts I have chosen three films and two novels, one of the novels being a novelization of one of the films. Compared with African American culture African Jamaicans have a very limited literary tradition but the cultural productions of films in Jamaica have captured the difficulties of African Jamaican urban life experiences in the post-colonial era.

There is no study on the combination of diaspora, alienation and violence on African American or Jamaican cultural representations. Even though the subject of African diaspora has been thematized by different scholars, they mostly analyzed it under the aspects of nation and identity, as Paul Gilroy's *The Black Atlantic*. My study presents a unique approach to literary and film criticism by combining the concept of diaspora with alienation and violence and questioning the effect of race on experiences of alienation and violence in both cultural representations.

Organization of the Study

Starting with a genealogy of the concept diaspora, paying close attention as to how and when the term entered into Black cultural studies, and bearing in mind according to Paul Gilroy the implication of violence in the term diaspora I use the term to examine and compare two different examples of African descendent peoples' societies in the so-called New World.

Next I show how the concept of race as empirically defined in eighteenth and nineteenth centuries was conditioned by Euro-centric artistic ideals (West 1999) and demonstrate that the legacies of European cultural subjectivity in scholarly studies are still confronting the African diaspora cultures in the form of the stereotype images of African people in their diasporas.

I then continue my study with a brief look at race in the Jamaican culture. Due to the fact that the majority of the Jamaican population are of African descent class is often times used to avoid clear discourse of race (Gunst 1995). According to Laurie Gunst partially Jamaicans still have a preference for "'bright' skin and 'good' hair and white featured faces" (Gunst 1995).

I proceed by introducing Patterson's main sociological arguments regarding the alienation and violence which he claims inevitably confronts any enslaved person. The daily use of violence in a given slave society is inevitable due to the low motivation of slaves regarding work (Patterson 1982).

Afterwards I present Ron Eyerman's arguments on cultural trauma where he points out that slavery became traumatic for African Americans after the failure of emancipation to truly liberate the former slaves. It was only after the Civil War, which was re-narrated as the 'civilized war' through which European American North and South were reunited and African Americans were articulated as separated social groups that experiences of slavery became traumatic for African Americans and there descendants (Eyerman 2001).

Continuing with a short genealogy of the concept alienation, which was first used by Georg Wilhelm Hegel in a *geistige* mode. Karl Marx took up Hegel's meaning of the term and turned it upside down when he focused his interest on material working conditions. For Marx alienation is economically grounded and can only be changed with the changing of the production mode. Marx's definition is very influential for conditions of sociological and psychological alienation in the cultural texts to be analysed later in my study.

Then I introduce Frantz Fanon's work *Les damnés de la terre – The Wretched of the Earth* focusing on Fanon's situating of violence as liberating factor. Then I will question how the subject of violence as a liberating factor is thematically dealt with in African diasporic cultural texts. I will also examine Fanon's arguments on alienation in his text *Black Skin White Masks* (1967) paying close attention to his arguments on how small children in colonized societies are taught very early to scorn their own mother language – the Creole. I will use Fanon's arguments for my analysis of Wright's, Patterson's, and Henzell's cultural texts.

Afterwards I present some of Imani Tafari Ama's sociological arguments on contemporary violence in a Jamaican inner-city community. Tafari connects the excessive violence in Jamaican urban centers with the political economy of the country, her arguments are relevant for my analysis of the films *Dancehall Queen* and *Third World Cop*.

I also refer to Tafari's argument on gender pointing to her reference of the male quality of violence in Jamaica today. I will refer again to Tafari's arguments when I interpret the Jamaican cultural texts.

Next I present some of Patterson's main arguments regarding African American gender relationships. Patterson argues that the problematic gender relationships between African Americans were accepted as a fact long before it became the "de rigueur" for academic and other supports of African American cultures to "deny behavioural and cultural problems" (Patterson 1998). Patterson's arguments are crucial when I examine different gender conflicts in the cultural texts of both diasporic societies.

I then analyse Fredrick Douglass' autobiography, where he describes the physical violence committed on him and his fellow slaves and also his representation of his displaced family relationship due to the system of slavery. His representations are vital for my arguments that violence and alienation affect all facets of the slave's life.

Richard Wright's autobiographical text *Black Boy* (1945) is a personal documentation of Wright's experiences of growing up in Jim Crow ruled South, but at the same time Wright shows the effects of racial oppression on African

Americans in general. The cultural autobiographical quality of both Douglass' and Wright's texts and the importance of the autobiographical expression in African American literary tradition are the reasons why I choose to begin my interpretation with their texts.

To continue my analysis of themes of alienation of violence in African American cultural texts I use Toni Morrison's third novel *Song of Solomon* (1977). Morrison fictionalizes a number of racial violent experiences of African Americans in her text. The representation of domestic violence and the alienating internal class conflicts among African Americans are some of the reasons why I chose Morrison's novel.

The last African American cultural text that I analyse is Spike Lee's film *Bamboozled.* In his film Lee questions how African Americans are represented today in the American media; and he also re-examines the stereotype representations of African Americans in the minstrel culture. Lee's attention to the historical and contemporary images of African Americans in the United States are important for my arguments on alienation and violence in both diaspora cultures.

Before turning my attention to the interpretation of Jamaican cultural texts I present a historical overview of Jamaica paying close attention to the fact how the Spaniards brutaly wiped out most of the Indian population under their rule on the island. The number of slave rebellions that took place in Jamaica after the British took over the island from Spain is to show that violence has been a part of the society since its inception. After the historical overview I proceed with a short summary of Marcus Garvey and Rastafarian cultural influences in the Jamaican society due to their relevance for my analysis of the Jamaican film and novel *The Harder They Come.*

I then for another theoretical line of thought on Jamaican cultural texts use two essays by Albert Camus, *Absurdity and Suicide* taken from *An Absurd Reasoning* and the essay *The Myth of Sisyphus* (Camus 1959). I present Camus' arguments on absurdity and point out how his reading of absurdity can be used to analyse some moments of alienation that I focus on in Patterson's novel.

The first film that I analyse is Perry Henzell's film *The Harder They Come* (1972). My reading of the film includes an interpretation of the different songs from the soundtrack. Here I show how the lyrics help to support the story line of the film. After that I present an analysis of the different moments of alienation and violence that the main character Ivan suffers. This is followed by an interpretation of the novel with the same title written by Michael Thelwell. An interpretation that will also include an excursus on how the author came to do a "novelization" of the film. I point to the difference between the film and the novel and then focus on modes of alienation and violence I see expressed in the novel. Here I concentrate on those elements of alienation and violence that I did not refer to in my reading of the film.

Next I will analyse Orlando Patterson first novel *The Children of Sisyphus* (1964). Patterson's sociological descriptions of characters and their life circumstances are some of the reasons why I choose the novel. The subject of violence among women is also another reason for choosing the novel.

Following my analysis of Patterson's novel I interpret the film *Dancehall Queen* (1997). Before commencing with the reading of the film I define the concepts of *rude boy, dancehall,* and the *dancehall costume.* These three terms are used to support my reading of alienation and violence in the film. An important part will be the role of the informer in the film representation of Jamaican society to show that violence is used to silent people accused of informing. I question the sociological implication of such use of violence.

The last Jamaican cultural text is the film *Third World Cop* (2000) directed by Christopher Browne. The concepts of *deportee, don* and *shotta* will be defined for my interpretation, followed by aspects of police violence shown in the film; connecting the excessive use of violence by the Jamaican police to the type of policing and the original reasons why the Jamaica Police Force was created.

My aim is to show how various aspects of alienation and violence in both African diasporic cultures are embedded in the historical, political, and socio-economic developments of the United States and Jamaica.

2   Tracing Genealogies

2.1. Diaspora

In my analysis of *Alienation and Violence as Themes in African American and Jamaican Cultural Texts* I use the concept of diaspora to connect both cultures; being aware of the differences between both cultures, I am claiming that the concept of diaspora can still be used to demonstrate certain similarities between both cultures.

The concept of the diaspora is an ancient one, which has its origin in the Hebrew religious culture as represented in the biblical narratives of the Old Testament. The Babylonian exile of the Jewish people in the 8th century B.C., and the dispersion of the Jews among the Gentiles, after their period of exile in 538 B.C., represent the religious root of the Jewish diaspora. The term was initially used to describe the Jewish communities outside of Palestine (Klein 1967).

Since the 19th century and the beginning of the modern Zionist movement, the concept of diaspora has acquired a broader and more secular meaning. Paul Gilroy, professor of sociology and African American studies, who has focused parts of his studies on the issues of race, culture, nation and identity (Gilroy 1987, 1993, 2000), has illustrated how the concept of diaspora entered Black cultural history. He points to the shared aspirations and rhetoric of late 19th century Zionism and Black Nationalist movements (Gilroy 1993: 207). According to Gilroy, Pan-Africanist Edward Wilmot Blyden, a scholar from the former Danish colony of St. Thomas, is credited with importing the Jewish concept of diaspora into Black cultural history.

> The precise genealogy of diaspora concept in black cultural history remains obscure, but George Shepperson, who comes closest to providing it has pointed to the fundamental impact of Blyden's Pan-African formulation on legitimising the importation of the term and to the significance of the *Presence Africane* project in making it credible. The link between these phases of modern black Atlantic political culture is supplied by Negritude, something that Leopold Sedar Senghor, one of its founders has also connected to Blyden's influence. (Gilroy 1993: 211)

In the mid 1950s and early 1960s Black writers and intellectuals started using the terms 'African diaspora' or 'Black diaspora'. The trend continued in the 1960s by educated Blacks in Britain and the United States. (Mayrhofer took up the ideas referring to Shepperson 1982 and Drake 1982 in Zips 2000: 53.)[1] Today the term that was

> (A)ssociated primarily with the historical exodus of the Jewish people from the biblical Israel (…), now finds application and acceptance as a reference to the massive movement and world-wide dispersal of many other peoples. Each of these people share a common origin, separation from a shared homeland, and the yearning to retain, reclaim or return to that land or the traditional culture, history, symbols or creed specifically identified with it – as their own. (Mayrhofer in Zips 2003: 57)

Gilroy points out that the concept implies elements of violence and displacement:

> As the biographies of Equiano and Wheatley suggest, life itself is at stake in the way the word connotes flight following the threat of violence rather than freely chosen experiences of displacement. Slavery, pogroms, indenture, genocide, and other unnameable terrors have all figured in the constitution of diasporas and the reproduction of diaspora consciousness in which identity is focused, less on the equalizing, pre-democratic force of sovereign territory and more on the social dynamics of remembrance and commemoration defined by a strong sense of the dangers involved in forgetting the location of origin and the tearful process of dispersal. (Gilroy 2000: 123)

Considering the fact that both African American and Jamaican history begin with the forced dispersion of Africans in the so-called New World, the concept of diaspora is appropriate to describe both cultures. The African diaspora is not contained within the boundaries of any nation state. Instead "(C)onsciousness of diaspora affiliation stands opposed to the distinctively modern structures and modes of power orchestrated by the institutional complexity of nation-states" (Gilroy 2000: 124). The contrariety to the single nation state that is implied in the concept of diaspora enables me to use the term in my research on *Alienation and Violence in African American and African Jamaican cultures*. Even though both African American and African Jamaican societies are shaped and influenced by their different political, economic and cultural environments,

---

[1] The collection *Afrikanische Diaspora: Out of Africa Into New Worlds* edited by anthropology professor Werner Zips is the result of over twenty years of research conducted by the Vienna Institute for Ethnology, Culture and Social Anthropology. One of the major focuses of the Institute is the Caribbean. Zips points out in his introduction to the collection that one goal of the scientific studies is to break with the Eurocentric paradigm of historical anthropology and historical ethnology. A second aim of the project is to deconstruct certain stereotypical constructions about Africa, African culture, and people of African descent. The essays in the collection were collected from a wide spectrum of master theses, dissertations, and papers presented at the conferences organized by the Vienna Institute over the last twenty years.

their shared experience of historical dispersion connects both societies. Both cultures are part of the African diaspora, "(D)iaspora identification exists outside of and sometimes in opposition to the political forms and codes of modern citizenship" (Gilroy 2000: 124). One has to keep in mind that

> (T)he African diaspora is both a process and pattern of relations intricately linked to the larger global or international system of political, economic, and social relationships. Therefore, a macro-level analysis of major historical junctures, events, and social forces that transcend the development of particular societies is central to the paradigm. (Mayrhofer quoted in Simm Hamilton 1990: 17 in Zips 2003: 63)

Even though the concept of diaspora has its genealogy in the Jewish cultural history, it is well appropriated to express the diverse experiences of slavery and indenture endured by the people of African descent in the so-called New World. The shared longing to know and reclaim traditional cultural histories and identities in African American and African Jamaican cultures makes the concept of diaspora appropriate to study these two cultures. I will further assert that the representations of alienation and violence in the cultural texts of both societies can most productively be compared and analysed in a diasporic mode, because of the underlying dispersed experience forming the inception of both cultural histories in the so-called New World.

Do you still Care

Where Bubba grew up, kept his tobacco chewed up
And when they used to hang ropes they always kept two up
Had crosses burning all night like the church blew up
And if you didn't look like them they fuck you up
Time passed Bubba turned 40 years old
And all them Jack Daniels started taking a toll
Seem like Bubba was about to make a final bow
None of his friends from the clan couldn't help him now
Family gathered at his bedside ready to sing the blues
When the doctor walked in and said, "I've got some news!
The good news is, Bubba, I've found you a liver.
Only bad news is it belongs to a nigger."

Do you care bout the texture of his hair or the cocoa brown color of his skin?
Do you still care? Do you still give a damm now you're in the predicament you're in?
Do you still care…does it still mean a lot now you're the one who's needing the help?
Do you still care?

(Tanya Stephens, *Rebelution*, 2006)

2.2. Race

In my analysis of *Alienation and Violence in African Diaspora Cultural Texts*, the concept of race is essential. Given the importance of the term in creating separate cultural lives in America for African Americans and European Americans, and separate social and economic conditions in Jamaica for people of African and European descent, it is relevant to point out how the concept of race was defined and used by a number of artists, writers, scholars, anthropologists, naturalists and other scientists of European descent to support oppression of people of African descent in the so-called New World and on the African continent. It is also important for my analysis to demonstrate how the concept of race as defined in an Euro-centric, White supremacy mode, contributes to various forms of *Violence and Alienation* in both cultures.

When one examines the late seventeenth to late eighteenth century European culture (1688–1789) a number of distinctive features seem to characterize this period. They show the re-emergence of celebrating and appropriating ancient Greek artistic and cultural heritage, the emergence of nation states, and the increasing acceptance of the authority of science (West 1999). The concept of "race" with its somatic description also gained prominence during this period.

The Random House Dictionary (1987) defines "race" as an arbitrary classification of modern humans, formerly based on any or a combination of various physical characteristics such as skin colour, facial form or eye shape.

The African American philosopher and scholar Cornel West in his essay *Race and Modernity* (West 1999) illustrated how White supremacy, racism and Euro-centrism condition the origin of their so called scientific studies and theories on "race" during the 'Age of Enlightenment'. I have chosen to follow the structural order and arguments of West's genealogical study put forth in his essay. His genealogy with its emphasis on Euro-centrism and racism is pertinent for this very study. The emergence of racism, White supremacy and Euro-centrism in the European discourse is important due to their historical significances. I am asserting that racism, White supremacy and Euro-centrism helped to reinforce the violent and alienating socio-political conditions of the African slaves and their descendants in America and Jamaica.

West points out that the French physician François Bernier was the first to use mainly skin colour for his category of "race" in 1684. Even though Bernier was maybe the first to use mainly skin colour in his classification of "race" the main arguments of proving "race" scientifically has its origin in the late eighteenth century.

Paul Gilroy in his text, *Against Race*, states that

(T)he history of scientific writing about "race" has involved a long and meandering sequence of discourses on physical morphology. Bones, skulls, hair, lips, noses, eyes, feet, genitals, and other somatic markers of "race" have a special place in the discursive regimes that produced the truth of "race" and repeatedly discovered it lodged in and on the body. (Gilroy 2000: 35)

During the eighteenth century many artists, writers, and scholars demonstrated a renewed enthusiasm for ancient Greek artistic and cultural heritage (West 1999). The idealized Greek sculptures became the prototype for European standards of beauty, as well as the archetype for all humankind. People who fell short of this idealized type were considered less human and inferior. Even though the Greek idealized facial and bodily proportions were recognized, appreciated and recommended for artistic use, many natural scientists appropriated these idealized measurements categories for the classifying of humankind (West 1999).

J. J. Winckelmann's *History of Ancient Art* became very influential for establishing rules of aesthetic values of beauty. According to West, "(h)e laid down rules – in art and aesthetics – that should govern the size of eyes and eyebrows, collarbones, hands, feet and especially noses" (West 1999: 76). Various artists and naturalists in their paintings and grouping of humankind would later use Winckelmann's aesthetic rules.

After François Bernier's somatic classification of humans in the 17th century, one of the first authoritative texts on racial division was the *Natural System* (1735) by the naturalist Carolus Linnaeus (West 1999). According to West, Linnaeus claimed that there were four different "races", Homo Europaeus, Homo Asiaticus, Homo Afer, Homo Americanus.

The next important text that stresses Euro-centric description of humankind was the *Natural History of Man* (1778) by Georges Louis Leclerc de Buffon. According to West, Buffon accepted Linnaeus' theory of "race". Buffon claimed that the natural colour of man was white, and that "(B)lack people and other races were variations of this natural color (…)" (West 1999: 78). Buffon did not see racial diversity as caused by differences in species. Instead he attributed the dark skin colour to the hot climate. Even though he did not recognize Africans as separate species, he claimed that African people had very "little genius".

John Friedrich Blumenbach credited with being one of the founders of modern anthropology, celebrated the anatomical proportion of ancient Greek sculpture; even though he accepted that all humans belong to the same species, he claims according to West, that moderate climate had something to do with the somatic beauty of humankind. According to Blumenbach the more moderate the climate the more beautiful the face. "The net result was that since Black people were farthest from the Greek ideal and located in extremely hot climates, they were, by implication, inferior in beauty to Europeans" (West 1999: 79).

The Dutch anatomist Pieter Camper's facial studies of ancient Greek sculpture also became very influential in establishing a White supremacy, Euro-centric stand in the study of humankind. Even though Camper stressed that his interest in establishing facial measurements were for the purpose of art, his idealized measurements for the facial structures was appropriated by various natural scientists. According to West, "Camper claimed that the 'facial angle' – a measure of prognathism – permitted a comparison of heads of human bodies by way of cranial and facial measurements" (West 1999: 79). The 100-degree "facial angle" of the ancient Greek sculpture became Camper's ideal facial measurement. European measuring counts 97 degree, while the "facial angle" of Africans measures 70 to 60 degree. Camper concluded that the measurement of Africans were closer to dogs and apes than human beings. Many natural scientists were willing to readily accept Camper's "facial angles" (West 1999).

The idealized ancient Greek prototype of beauty would become even more important with the introduction of phrenological and physiognomical studies.

> The idea of white supremacy as an object of modern discourse primarily occurred in the rise of phrenology (the reading of skull) and physiognomy (the reading of faces). These new disciplines – closely connected with anthropology – served as an open platform for the propagation of the idea of white supremacy not principally because they were pseudosciences, but more important, because these disciplines acknowledge the European value-laden character was based on classical aesthetic and cultural ideals. (West 1999: 79)

Johann Kasper Lavater is credited with being the father of physiognomy. "This new discipline links particular visible characteristics of human bodies, especially those of the face, to the character and capacities of human beings" (West 1999: 80). Lavater idealized that the human form has its aesthetic representation in ancient Greek sculpture. "His descriptions of the desirable specimen – blue eyes, horizontal forehead, bent back, round chin and short brown hair – resemble the beautiful person by Camper" (West 1999: 80).

One can see that a clear ideal had been established out of cultural preference. The European modernist culture with its admiration for ancient Greek sculptures, created their so-called scientific theories which reinforced Euro-centric ideals.

According to West another element in the eighteenth century "race" theories with White supremacy tendency was the study of phrenology. In 1796 the German physician Franz Joseph Gall argued that the shape of the skull could influence or determine how the brain works. "For example, he associated an arched forehead with a penchant for meta-physical speculation, a skull arched at the rear with love of fame and a skull large at the base with a criminal disposition" (West 1999: 80).

These diverse concepts of "race" with reference to somatic characteristics were used to differentiate and justify the enslavement, colonization and further inhuman treatment of Africans and their descent, along with other non-European peoples. As Gilroy states

> (W)e cannot remind ourselves too often that the concept of "race" as it is used in common-sense, everyday language to signify connectedness and common characteristics in relation to type and descent is a relatively recent and absolutely modern invention. Though it would be foolish to suggest that evil, brutality, and terror commence with the arrival of scientific racism towards the end of the eighteenth century (…). (Gilroy 2000: 31)

2.3. Race in the Jamaican Cultures

> My opponents say I am against white and fair-skinned people. This is not so. I am against the class system here which keeps the poor man down, and the poor mostly black people (…). (Marcus Mosiah Garvey in Sherlock and Bennett 1998: 362)

According to the prominent cultural critic and former Chancellor of the University of the West Indies, Mona (Jamaica), Professor Rex Nettleford, the subject of race and ethnicity in Jamaica is complex and ambivalent. In his *Mirror Mirror: Identity, Race and Protest in Jamaica* (rev. ed. 1998), Nettleford points to the continuing ambivalence and complexity which the theme of race is dealt with in Jamaica today; he claims that even though Jamaica is a predominantly 'Black' nation, the national motto *Out of Many One People* is often taken as a reality instead of the aspiration that it is. In the introduction Nettleford examines diverse debates regarding race in the academic discourse and local newspapers since his first publication of his text *Mirror Mirror* in 1970. He points to the continuing relevance of the subject of race in contemporary Jamaican society. He states that the subjects of race and identity in Jamaica are more complex than the mere sight of skin color: He connects the "institutional racism" in Jamaica to the trans-atlantic slave trade. He writes that

> (I)nstitutional racism, rooted in the Trans-Atlantic Slave Trade, is one of those "old institutions". It is more than skin-deep in its all pervasive thrust into power relations and social interaction; and the diagnostic efforts by academics and other who have produced field reports of all kinds, do attest to the fact that however ambiguous the play of race on social structure, economic organisation etc, the race factor exists, or is perceived to persist, with determined tenacity. (Nettleford 1998: xxxiv)

I will point out below in my analysis the ambiguous play of race regarding the characters Marcia and Olivine in the film *Dancehall Queen* (1997). Nettleford also states in his discourse that any claim for dignity by Afro-Jamaicans is taken to be isolationistic (Nettleford 1998: ix). He further states that "(I)n the minds of many Jamaicans, it is still a poor-black, a middle-class and privileged brown man, and a rich or wealthy white man" (Nettleford 1998: 24). Even though there are no White men or Brown men in the film *Dancehall Queen* I am asserting that this statement is still relevant when one examines the character of Olivine, which will be demonstrated later in my analysis.

Nettleford is not the only cultural critic to point to the complexity of Jamaican racial consciousness. Laurie Gunst, in her text *Born fi Dead,* a study of the connection between Jamaican politicians and notorious inner-city gunmen, points out that Jamaican racial consciousness is highly complex. She writes that

> I realized that class itself, not color, is one of the safe categories in which Jamaicans frame discussion about the gap between the skin shades. Because the overwhelming majority is black, point-blank discourse about race is often too threatening to the fragile order of Jamaica's establishment and its prevailing fiction of a plural society. So the bitter fact that color itself is what most often consigns many people to poverty is obscured by polite British-inspired talk about the evils of the class system. And the illusory ease with which lovers choose partners of a different shade simply masks a deeper racism; these couplings are possible not because race is not an issue, but for exactly the opposite reason: the darker partner knows that the child born of a union with a light-skinned lover or spouse will have a better chance in life. Jamaicans have not relinquished their preference for 'bright' skin, 'good' hair, and white featured faces. (Gunst 1995: 27)

3   Violence, Trauma, Alienation: Terminologies and Frameworks

3.1. Orlando Patterson's *Slavery and Social Death*

Orlando Patterson calls attention to the unique form of domination of the slave by his master, which is grounded in specific power relations. He points out that power has three facets. One is social and involves the use or threat of violence in the control of one person by another. The second facet of power is of psychological influence, the capacity to persuade another person to change the way he perceives his interests and his circumstances. The third facet of power is the cultural, "the means of transforming force into right, and obedience into duty" (Patterson 1982: 1). Using the works of the Marxist scholar on slavery, Elisabeth Welskopf, Patterson explains more specifically the first facet of power. Welskopf refers to the naked might-violence that is essential for the creation of slave systems. She argues that because one had to keep introducing new persons to the status of slavery one had to keep repeating the direct violence. This act of violence forms the prehistory of all stratified societies and the current history of slavery. Violence was not only used when a new person was introduced to the status, but also on a daily basis due to the low motivation of the slave regarding work (Patterson 1982). In my analysis of the *Narrative of the Life of Frederick Douglass* I will point to his representations of the various uses of violence in the slave society of the United States.

According to Patterson the person who is forcefully removed from his own social community loses his connection with his ancestral community and any legitimate social order besides his master. This contributes to the enslaved person's feelings of alienation.

> Slaves differed from other human beings in that they were not allowed freely to integrate the experience of their ancestors into their lives, to inform their understanding of social reality with the inherited meanings of their natural forebears, or to anchor the living present in any conscious community of memory. (Patterson 1982: 5)

I will show that because the African slaves could not freely integrate experiences of their ancestors in their lives, they became alienated. I will also assert in my study that the fracturing of the African slaves' nuclear family relationships contributed to the feeling and state of alienation endured by the slaves in the so-called New World slave societies.

Patterson continues his arguments on power stating that all power strives for authority. Even though he acknowledges that Max Weber is usually the accepted expert on the theme of authority, Patterson turns to the scholars of symbolic anthropology who criticized Weber's concept of authority. He states, "(T)hose who exercise power, if they are able to transform it into a 'right', a norm, a usual part of the order things, must first control (or at least be in a position to manipulate) appropriate symbolic instruments" (Patterson 1982: 37). The symbolic process has two aspects, one social and the other intellectual. Patterson states, "On the intellectual level symbolic thought attempts to explain in the language of symbols a given area of actual experience" (Patterson 1982: 37). The social aspect of authority concerns ritual processes in which symbolic ideas are acted out in real human interaction. I will show that the changing of the enslaved African names to European names demonstrated one area of the symbolic aspect of authority. As Patterson points out "(T)here are several reasons for the change of name. The changing of a name is almost universally a symbolic act of stripping a person of his former identity (…)" (Patterson 1982: 55). I will assert that the loss of identity which the slave undergoes every time a new slave master changes his name intensely contributes to the state of aliena-tion. In his arguments on power and its influence on the slave society Patterson further explains that power has two idioms: one social and the other concep-tual. He then classifies these two idioms as personalistic and materialistic. The personalistic idiom of power can be identified in the fictive kinship relationship between some masters and their slaves. Here power is clear and humanized but not mystified according to Patterson. The role of kinship or fictive kinship is important in asserting the domination of one person over another. I will show that in US and Jamaican slave societies fictive kinship was used to discipline the enslaved and to justify morally a system of exploitation.

Another aspect of slavery that Patterson mentions is the imposition of some visible marks on the slave to show his status of servitude. I will show that in the slave societies of the United States and Jamaica skin color combined with spe-cific African somatic features became the symbol of servitude. The consequence of coupling specific African somatic features with servitude in the so-called New World slave societies are negative legacies of slavery that are still affecting some people of the African diasporic cultures of Jamaica and the United States today.

Patterson states that the special character of violence and familial alienation aid in producing dishonor, a third constituent element of slavery. Examining the concept of honor in the slave society of the United States, Patterson analyses the ideology of the stereotypical "Sambo" character and the role he played for the concept of honor. Patterson quotes Stanley Elkins regarding the specific stereotype of "Sambo" in the slave culture of the South:

> Sambo, the typical plantation slave, was docile but irresponsible, loyal but lazy, humble but chronically given to lying and stealing; his behavior was full of infantile silliness and his talk inflated with childish exaggeration. His relationship with his master was one of utter dependence and childlike attachment: it was indeed this childlike quality that was the very key to his being (…). (Patterson 1982: 96)

The stereotype of the lazy, docile, irresponsible, lying and stealing slave, Patterson explains, could also be found in the Jamaican slave culture, and actually in almost all slave societies. It is an ideological argument of all slave systems (Patterson 1982: 96). The negative stereotypes were also used after slavery and emancipation to describe certain sections of African diaspora communities. I will point out where I see this happening in the cultural texts *Black Boy*, *Bamboozled*, *The Children of Sisyphus*, and *The Harder They Come*.

3.2. Ron Eyerman's *Cultural Trauma*

In his text *Cultural Trauma: Slavery and the Formation of African American Identity* (2001), the sociologist Ron Eyerman demonstrates how African American experiences of slavery aided in creating a cultural trauma for generations of African Americans. He points out that slavery became traumatic in retrospect for African Americans, explaining that it was only after the failure of emancipation to truly liberate the former slaves, as well as the failure of reconstruction that the experience of slavery became traumatic. Eyerman draws attention to the raised expectations engendered by emancipation and Reconstruction, when they failed to produce a progressive step African Americans were forced to re-examine their past, present and future in the American society (Eyerman 2001: 20). He also mentions that many Blacks as well as Whites had hoped that with emancipation the significance of race would diminish and the former slaves would be integrated into the dominant society. The fact that there was emancipation, but no real liberation for the manumitted, forced the freedmen and freedwomen along with their descendants to re-evaluate their past and present in the United States. African Americans were not the only ones re-evaluating their social status in America in the late 19th century. European Americans were also re-evaluating their past. According to Eyerman for the dominant American society by the 1880s the Civil War became the "civilized war" where European Americans both North and South could be reunited, reconciled and see the war as creating a new modern South. African Americans were made invisible and punished; they became the object of hate, the 'Other'. This rejection and punishment substantially contributed to make the memory of slavery traumatic for the manumitted. Eyerman states that it was after the re-narrating of the Civil War that Whites and Blacks were articulated as separate social groups. All Whites then could be identified with Western civilization, which was equated with civilization per se, while Blacks became associated with Africa and are thereby the "uncivilized". According to Eyerman the creation of a number of paintings in the 19th century reinforced the belief of the "happy slave", plus the popular culture of minstrelsy 'took-for-granted' that slavery was justified, necessary and beneficial to everyone concerned. The misrepresentation of the memory of slavery by mainstream American society has forced African Americans up to this day to struggle over their representation in American society. Eyerman claims that this struggle took place in literary, visual and political forms, and included the question as to who would define what is seen and heard. African Americans now confronted with "false" representations of their past and present in the United States were forced to produce a counter history. He states, "(W)ithout the means to influence public memory, Blacks were left to form and maintain their own collective memory, with slavery as an ever-shifting recon-structed reference point" (Eyerman 2001: 18). Ron Eyerman is not the first socio-logist to recognize the pertinence of memory and history in African American diasporic culture. David Blight in his essay *W.E.B. DuBois and the Struggle for American Historical Memory*,[2] points to the sheer passion and violence that can sometimes be produced in the cultural conflict over memory. He refers to the first prominent African American sociologist W.E.B. DuBois, and his awareness of the distorted and contradictory nature of history. Citing Dubois, Blight writes: "With sufficient general agreement among the dominant classes (…) the truth of history may be utterly distorted and contradicted and changed to any convenient fairy tale that the masters of men wish" (in Fabre and O'Meally 1994: 51).

The conflictive debate over the meaning of slavery by different generations of African Americans calls attention to the traumatic effect that the history of slavery and the failure of emancipation have had on African American society. Eyerman explains that in cultural trauma there is always an engagement in a "meaning struggle," the grappling with an event, which involves identifying the nature of the pain, the nature of the victim and attribution of responsibilities (Eyerman 2001: 3). As Blight points out in his reference to DuBois's astonish-ment over European American historians and their false representation of African American cultural history,

> (…) the study of historical memory might therefore be defined as the study of cultural struggle, of contested truths, of moments, events, or even texts in history that thresh out rival versions of the past which are in turn put to service of the present. (Fabre and O'Melly 1994: 46)

It was the misrepresentation of African American cultural history, and failing to recognize the effect of slavery on African Americans, plus the unwillingness of the dominant society to accept responsibilities for the institution of slavery, that contributed to make the experiences of slavery traumatic for African Ameri-cans. According to Eyerman in the psychoanalytical theory it is not necessarily the experience which produces trauma; it is rather the effect and remembrance of the experience, which causes trauma. In his reading of Cathy Caruth's psychoanalytic theory of trauma, he points out that there is always a time lapse between the event and the experience in which forgetting is peculiar. He states that "(a)s a reflective process, trauma links past to present through representa-tion and imagination" (Eyerman 2001: 3). Eyerman also explains that experience

---

[2] Taken from the book *History and Memory in African American Culture* edited by Genevieve Fabre and Robert O'Meally.

of trauma is usually mediated through newspapers, radio or television, and involves a certain amount of time and distance between the event and its experience. He states that it is through time delayed, and negotiated recollection of the event that cultural trauma is experienced (Eyerman 2001: 12). Representation plays a major role in how an event is remembered and depicted, and the media also plays a crucial role in bridging the gap between individual occurrences and their recollection (Eyerman 1982: 12). Slavery thus forms the root of an emergent collective identity for all African Americans. Eyerman states that

> making this memory collective is central to the process of cultural trauma, a process in which collective memory will be formative of collective identity, as recognizable victims and perpetrators are named and acknowledged, marking a membership group off against those outside. (Eyerman 2001: 70)

He draws attention to the link between collective memory and Durkheim's notion of collective consciousness. He writes that here collective memory is seen as shared past

> "that are retained by members of a group, large or small, that experience it" (…) and passed on either in an ongoing process of what might be called public commemoration, in which officially sanctioned rituals are engaged to establish a shared past, or through discourses more specific to a particular group or collective. (Eyerman 2001: 5)

He also refers to Maurice Halbwachs who conceived of individual memory in relation to the group, seeing each individual, as deriving from some form of collective be it family and community. In Halbwachs' classical notion the collective memory is germane for a group notion of itself (Eyerman 2001). The influence of linguistic and comparative literary theories on the concept of collective memory is important in the sense that the collective is conceived "within the discourse of people talking together about the past" (Eyerman 1982). Eyerman makes a clear distinction between collective memory and history, stressing that as an academic discipline history aims at something broader, more objective and universal than group memory. He also draws attention to ethnocentrism that can sometimes influence the writings of history. The fact that the history of slavery was written after emancipation, and Reconstruction and slavery were seen as mutually beneficial social systems for the former slaves as well as their former masters forced – as pointed out above – African Americans to produce a counter-history. This counter-history attempted to tell the history of slavery from the perspective and experiences of African Americans. In this counter-history slavery became a focal point for diverse generations of disfranchised African American and African diasporic communities in the so-called New World. I use the term collective memory as defined by Ron Eyerman even though I am aware of the diverse opinions on the validity of the concept. In her book, *Regarding the Pain of Other*, the American author Susan Sontag claims that there is no such thing as collective memory, but collective instructions (Sontag 2003: 85), and David Blight in his essay on DuBois's struggle for a truthful representation of African Americans in American history also points out that collective memory is a constructed and reconstructive process. I will refer again to these diverse arguments pertaining to collective memory in my analysis of African diasporic cultural texts. The diversity of African American communities has sometimes produced conflicts as to how slavery should be seen and commemorated. Eyerman further calls attention to the fact that when one reviews the latest literature on slavery such as George Fredrickson, slavery still is a skeleton in the American closet. Eyerman quotes Fredrickson, who states that after more than a hundred and thirty-five years African Americans appear to have diverse opinions still as to how they should remember slavery. Should the memory of slavery be suppressed as unpleasant, dispiriting, or commemorated the way the Jews remember the Holocaust? Fredrickson states that while African Americans have different opinions as to how slavery should be remembered, some European Americans feel less responsibility for slavery or its effect on African Americans (Eyerman 2001: 18). According to Eyerman there are three major patterns in which one sees African Americans working to liberate themselves. One is the struggle for civil rights which began after Reconstruction, a second pattern for liberation was through cultural and political nationalism, and a third pattern, according to Eyerman, was through the coupling of political nationalism with emigration. In my study I will demonstrate how effects of cultural trauma are represented in Richard Wright's *Black Boy*, Toni Morrison's novel *Song of Solomon*, and Spike Lee's film *Bamboozled*.

3.3. Genealogy of the Term 'Alienation'

The concept of alienation may be as old as human history. In general it describes the process in which whatsoever belongs to the individual human being becomes alien to the same human being (Hügli 1991: 157). Since Karl Marx was the first to systematically define and analyze the term alienation, I will take a closer look at his use of the term.

Especially in his early works Marx coined the term alienation grounding his argument in Georg Wilhelm Friedrich Hegel's use of the term. According to Hegel, alienation is always self-alienation. "The recognition of the self as a distinct and separate entity within a larger and frequently antagonistic society is the basis of alienation" (Childers and Hentzi 1995: 7). It is crucial that Hegel sees alienation as a process of the *Geist*: It has to become alienated from itself in order to develop a clear understanding of itself.

Marx takes up Hegel's definition and turns it upside down when he focuses his interest on material working conditions (Israel 1972: 14). Whereas Hegel is concerned with the *Geist*, Marx moves away from the *geistige* world to the material world, so that the human being in Marx's analysis becomes alienated through the working process. In the ideal work situation the human being produces/creates a product and thereby steps out of himself. This means the worker puts his efforts, his life into the product and thereby makes nature, that he shapes, his own (Hügli 1991: 157). This ideal state of production is ruptured by alienation. As soon as the product and the means of production belong to someone else other than the worker, the product turns into a foreign/alien object for the worker. The product thus exists outside of the producer; it is independent and alien to him. Through his state of being separated from the product, the product he has produced then controls the worker and his own work turns against him (see Lotter, Meiners, Treptow 1984: 93). The process of alienation becomes a social one, when human beings become alienated from each other, then human beings only interact with each other through alien products. Since, according to Marx, alienation is economically grounded it can only be eliminated by changing the conditions of production (Hügli 1991: 157).

Marx was maybe the first to use the term alienation in a sociological way instead of – as it was used before – in a philosophical context. Today the term alienation is used in two major fields: alienation as a psychological condition and alienation as a sociological problem. Existentialist philosophers of the twentieth century, however, are also concerned with the meaning of alienation. Jean-Paul Sartre used the term to describe the division between selfhood and the institutions of society. Sartre and the Existentialist philosophers are not too far from the Marxist interpretation of the term.

3.4. Psychological Alienation in the Theoretical Works of Frantz Fanon

In his work *Black Skin White Masks* that first appeared under the title *Peau Noire Masques Blancs* in 1952, Frantz Fanon used different examples to illustrate psychic alienation in colonial societies. As indicated in the introduction I will give a detailed analysis of Fanon's discourse/theory, but will use it to describe alienation as a direct consequence of colonialism as shown in post-colonial film and literature. Homi Bhabba who intensely relies on Fanon's work in his own analysis states:

> It is one of the original and disturbing qualities of *Black Skin White Masks* that it rarely historicizes the colonial experience. There is no master narrative or realist perspective that provides a background of social historical facts against which emerge the problems of the individual or collective psyche. (Bhabha 1994: 42)

This lack of specific history makes it possible for Fanon's thoughts on colonial societies in general to be used for situated interpretations of Jamaican post-colonial film and literature. For example, when Fanon shows in "The Negro and Language" how the language of the oppressor, which is taught in schools in the colonies, is used to alienate small children from the very beginning, this situation can be applied to the conditions in Jamaica as represented in the novel *The Children of Sisyphus*. Fanon states that the school children from Martinique are taught to scorn the dialect. The dialect, or rather the Creole of Martinique, as in other colonial and post-colonial societies, is the mother tongue. The middle-class's fear of their children speaking the dialect has to do with the wish to avoid anything that could connect one with the condition of the colonized or with an African past. They believe that the native "will come closer to being a real human being in direct ratio to his mastery of the French language"[3] (Fanon 1967: 18). For a lot of children the official education system represents one of the first moments of alienation they face in the colonial or post-colonial situation. This moment of alienation will perpetuate itself with those children who are unable to master the master's system of education. They will have to contend with social and economic hardships. On the other hand, those children who do master the master's system are alienated because they get drawn away from their own cultural achievements, language being one of them.

---

[3] French Language can be substituted by any colonial language such as English.

Fanon stated that the goal of *Black Skin White Masks* is the disalienation of the Black man.[4] His work is a psychological analysis of the situation, which he sees as the major cause of the alienated psyche of the colonized: the double process of social and economic realities, which are suffered by the colonized people. This can be demonstrated by the poverty and the lack of education and upward mobility among people of African descent in Jamaica as represented in the cultural texts.

In his influential work The *Wretched of the Earth* Frantz Fanon demonstrates how a colonial society may use violence to shake off their colonial oppressors. Even though Fanon's analysis is grounded in a colonial society that uses violence to shake off the colonial oppressors, a great deal of Fanon's arguments also illustrate the colonial and post-colonial conditions of Jamaica. Moreover Fanon's thought may also be applied to pre- and post-Civil Rights African American culture. I will assert that even though African Americans represent a minority culture in the United States their political, economic, and social conditions up to the time of the Civil Rights Movement were more closely identifiable with the position of the natives in the colonies.

Fanon asserted that the first encounter of the native with the settler was marked by violence, and that the exploitation of the native by the settlers was accomplished with the aid of bayonets and cannons. Comparing the conditions of African Americans prior to the Civil Rights Movement to that of the natives in the colonies, I will point to the use of violence in the exploitation of African Americans by European Americans. As cultural texts I will choose Richard Wright's *Black Boy* and Toni Morrison's *Song of Solomon*.

Fanon bases his study on the French-Algerian war in which he actively took part, joining the Algerian Nationalist Movement. He demonstrates the different steps that have to be taken before colonized people reach the state where they decide to use violence in order to achieve their freedom.

1. The oppressed people turn against themselves – they use internal violence, unable to take out their aggression on the oppressor.

2. The oppressed person is treated as an inferior, but is not totally convinced of his inferiority.

3. When the oppressed people fight against each other the knife is often used. This knife the oppressed person would rather use on the oppressor, yet, in that moment, the one using the knife takes the place of the oppressor.

An essential aspect of Fanon's argument is the Manichean division of the colonized world, spatialised as the native's and the settler's area. The colonizer paints the colonized as the essence of evil, including their traditions, myths, and

---

[4] Fanon indeed restricts his analyses mostly to the psyche of colonized men.

their way of life. He thinks that all his own values and beauty will become poisoned when the colonized uses them, since the natives are lacking ethical and moral values. "The town belonging to the colonized people, or at least the native town, the Negro village, the medina, the reservation, is a place of ill fame, peopled by men of evil repute (…). The native town is a hungry town, starved of bread, of meat, of shoes, of coal, of light" (Fanon 1963: 39). In contrast, "(t)he settler's town is a strongly build town, all made of stone and steel (…) the streets are covered with asphalt, and the garbage cans swallow all the leavings, unseen, unknown and hardly thought about" (Fanon 1963: 39). I will demonstrate with my reading of the cultural texts *The Harder They Come*, *The Children of Sisyphus* and *Black Boy*, where I see the Manichean order being represented in the colonial and post-colonial Jamaican society.

I will show that the Manichean order of the colonial world could also be found in the United States prior to the Civil Rights Movement. I will also assert that there is a certain element of the Manichean world order to be found today in urban African diasporic cultures. Finally I will demonstrate how certain sections of urban diasporic cultures continue to represent the "native" (for example inner-city communities that are referred to as "ghettos", or the dichotomy of uptown and downtown) in the post-colonial and post Civil Rights world of the United States and Jamaica.

As with Fanon's *Black Skin White Masks*, I will not give a detailed summary of *The Wretched of the Earth*, an analysis grounded in a colonial society as shown above that uses violence to shake off the colonial oppressors. Even though many of Fanon's arguments also illustrate the post-colonial condition of Jamaican society, there are also facts that are not relevant for my study. I will use both works of Fanon whenever the situation allows it, because, according to Bhabha, the "demand for a psychoanalytic explanation emerges from the perverse reflections of civil virtue in the alienating acts of colonial governance" (Bhabha 1994: 43).

3.5. Tafari's *Blood, Bullets and Bodies* – Violence in Urban Jamaican Space

In her doctoral thesis, *Blood, Bullets and Bodies: Sexual Politics Below the Poverty Line – The Political Economy of Violence, Power, Gender and Embodiment in Jamaica's Inner-City* (2002), the sociologist Imani Tafari Ama analyses the theme of violence in Kingston, the Jamaican capital city, focusing on the discourse of violence in the inner-city community of Southside. Tafari claims that her use of a hybrid combination of theoretical and methodological approaches to address the issue presents a unique attempt to analyze the topic of inner-city violence. She uses theoretical arguments and her skills as a researcher and journalist to analyze the problems of inner-city violence in Jamaica. Tafari also utilizes cultural communications such as music, dance, poetry and theatre as research tools to gather relevant information about and from the community which she studied. She writes:

> (O)n the one hand, cultural communications involves the use of cultural expressions like music, dance, theatre, poetry etc. as teaching tools on an individual level and ultimately as tools for community mobilization. That is the usual usage. On the other hand, cultural communications can also be used as a research tool to gather relevant data from the same individuals (…) or community, which was the novel usage that I employed in this instance. (Tafari 2002: 2)

Tafari points out that although inner-city violence is topical in the international literature it is usually analysed in the uni-dimensional framework of the prevailing political economy (Tafari 2002: 1). She utilizes the concepts of political economy, race/class, power, patriarchy, gender and the body together with a multi-media and multi-method research to demonstrate

> that the crisis of inner-city violence in Jamaica is an outcome of the peculiar style of bourgeois democracy practiced in the post-plantation society (…) and reflects the race/colour and class contradictions that are inherent in the wider society. (Tafari 2002: 1)

Tafari further claims that the theoretical tapestry which she is weaving should be comprehended as a hybrid set of connections. She states that she is using the concept hybrid "as the product of combining complementary but also contentious theoretical tools and research methods to explain a social problem" (Tafari 2002: 29). Tafari regards violence and poverty as dialectical partners in the political economy of Jamaica, and explains that inner-city violence has become an international motif for poverty and violence. She states that "(I)t is an established fact that state-controlled structures of power facilitate social injustice resulting in these indicators of urban marginality" (Tafari 2002: 8). I will demonstrate in my analysis of Jamaican cultural texts the relation of urban violence to the political economy in the Jamaican society.

Tafari continues her argument drawing attention to the antagonistic power relation in Jamaica between the state and the majority of the population which are linked to the political economy of the country (Tafari 2002: 36). She refers to the elite, which controls the economy of the country stating

> (T)he elite in Jamaica has its roots in plantation society (…), a mode of production which served to construct power in an idiom that positioned the White man as the highest symbol of social authority. Conversely, Black women, men and boys and girls are located at the lowest rung of this hierarchy. (Tafari 2002: 70)

Examining the role of class and race in the Jamaican society today Tafari connects both concepts with the historical background of the Island State.

> The Jamaican social system has been characterized as a colour and class system in which people rank each other, both conceptually and practically (as in hiring practices and marriage preferences), according to skin colour. This system grew out of slavery and colonialism. The social structures can be visualized as a pyramid in which a small white elite at the top is supported by a large base of blacks. Brown-skinned individuals of mixed European and African ancestry are generally in the middle. Although a few light-skinned and more than a few brown-skinned people are members of the lower class, darkness of colour, 'African' traditions, and low status are positively correlated and assigned a place at society's base. (Tafari 2002: 66)

Even though ideologies of race and class appear to be hereditary in the Jamaican society, Tafari quoting from Carl Stone indicates the importance of material affluence and income in determining one social position (Tafari 2002: 99). I will demonstrate the pertinence of race in my analysis of the Jamaican cultural texts, *The Harder They Come* and *The Children of Sisyphus* and *Dancehall Queen*.

Another element that Tafari examines in her discourse is the excessive use of violence by the Jamaican legal security forces. She states that

> (T)he legal security forces are also active agents in this scenario of violence. In fact, there is a general perception among the security forces that their primary role is to eliminate the inner-city gunmen. As the executive arm of the state, the individual policemen and soldiers in this social body (security force) recognize that the establishment of violence as a resource of symbolic and material capital by gun-powered inner-city Dons has seriously undermined their state sponsored authority. (Tafari 2002: 46)

Tafari also connects the power relation of the Jamaican security force today with the past colonial system. She states: "(…) we can view untenable tensions that attend the operations of the security forces today, as a relation of the power relations that were characteristic of colonial society" (Tafari 2002: 116). She further contends that although most of the security forces might be coming from oppressed lower classes, they professionally serve the privileged (Tafari 2002: 115). She claims that those who control the state and their institutional apparatus, for example, the security forces have played an active role in the violence in the inner-city communities (Tafari 2002: 124). Even though the violence of the gunmen is feared in the inner-city communities, residents are also afraid of the violence of the legal security forces.

> On the other hand, while several people said that they fear what unscrupulous gunmen may do, some also strongly expressed perceptions that the persecution of inner-city civilian by the police and associated security forces, is an even more deadly form of violence than that executed by the gunmen.(Tafari 2002: 145)

The moment where the legal security force demonstrates its primary role of eliminating the inner-city gunmen is reflected in several scenes in the film *Third World Cop*. I will draw attention to this moment in my interpretation of the film later.

Another element that plays a major role in the discourse of violence in the inner-city communities is the unwritten rule that informers will not be tolerated by the gunmen.

> An unwritten but very well understood code of ethical behavior is that those who have *knowledge* of criminal activities should remain silent or face the consequences of being identified as (police) informers. Those men, women or children who transgress this code virtually sign their own death warrants. (Tafari 2002: 229)

What also makes informing a deadly pastime is that some of the security forces are involved or connected to the gunmen themselves, so when innocent residents complain to the police, the police might inform the gunmen themselves of the informer. I will show the grave danger of informing in my analysis of the films *Dancehall Queen* and *Third World Cop*.

Examining the geographical location of Jamaica Tafari explains that its location between North and South America undermines the development potential of Jamaica. She mentions that Jamaica and other Caribbean countries due to their location serve as trans-shipment zones for drugs leaving South America for North and then again for transporting guns from North to South America and Jamaica itself.

In political and economic terms, its geographical positioning between North and South America has also undermined the development potential of Jamaica and indeed the Caribbean Basin as a whole. The region serves as a trans-shipment zone for drugs leaving South America for the North American market and equally for transporting guns from North to South. Jamaica has predictably become a fertile absorption ground for the high-powered weaponry used to fuel the ongoing violent conflicts that ensue not only between gangs and political factions, but also between the gunmen and the security forces. Furthermore, the use of force by those who control the state, also influences the development of ideological connotations of male power in the wider society. (Tafari 2002: 15)

In my analysis of diverse scenes from the film *Third World Cop* I will illustrate where I see Jamaica's geographical location in relation to North and South America reflecting the influence of violence in Jamaican urban communities. I will also show in my study of Jamaican cultural texts, *Third World Cop* and *The Harder They Come* how the idea of Jamaica has a fertile ground for high power weaponry from North America, and also for the message broadcast on the North American media of mass communication. According to Tafari

(T)here is a clear connection between violence-as-entertainment, a fundamental message broadcast on the North America media of mass communication, and the Jamaican inner-city expression of hegemonic masculinity in the idiom of violence. Of course, this is not the sole contributing factor but it is certainly a significant one. (Tafari 2002: 14)

Another factor that contributes to the violence in the inner-cities is the disparity between rich and poor. Tafari states that

(T)he sharp disparity between rich and poor in Jamaica, which is vulgarly displayed in the proximity of material wealth to penury, has also been cited as one of the fundamental factors that fuels the violence of the inner-city fractions. These experiences of systematic social exclusion inevitably result in the vulnerability of the poor to manipulation, or else propel them to make desperate choices in order to construct identity and survival strategies within the limited scope of available options. (Tafari 2002: 139)

In my analysis of the film *The Harder They Come* I'll show how the disparity between rich and poor leading to alienation is represented in the film.

3.5.1. Tafari's Gender Concept

Tafari claims that her analysis is informed by a 'Black Feminist' approach, and this gives her a wider lens through which she can highlight the contradictions of race, class, and gender, that she sees as inherent to political and social relationships in Jamaica (Tafari 2001: 41). According to Patricia Hill Collins in her *Black Feminist Thought: Knowledge, Consciousness and the Politics of Empowerment* (2000) 'Black feminist thoughts' have been informed by four basic traditions. She points out that these components are "its thematic content, its interpretive frameworks, its epistemological approaches, and its significance for empowerment" (Hill Collins 2000: 17). Tafari uses gender to indicate the construction of socio-political arguments which show the difference between men and women, boys and girls as normative or natural (Tafari 2002: 75). She also points out that she is using the concept of gender as an analytical tool for examing the power relations between men and women and other gendered groups in the society. She writes:

> (…) an analytical tool for analyzing the (power) relations between women and men, as well as other gendered groups in society. Gender operationalises the power mechanism of constructing binary oppositions as part and parcel of matrices of domination and is thus fundamental to my occupation and identity politics. (Tafari 2002: 73)

Tafari demonstrates the male gender quality of violence in the Jamaican society, but at the same time she states that there are women who are involved in the discourse of violence. "Some women have internalized the dominant discourse of violence as evidenced by the conflicts that exist among some inner-city women and the harmful methods that have been used to resolve these disputes" (Tafari 2002: 12). She further calls attention to the fact that some women form alliances with men who subscribed to violence, due to the benefits that comes from such relationships (Tafari 2002: 1). I will show in my analysis of the Jamaican cultural texts *The Children of Sisyphus* and the novel *The Harder They Come*, where I see the female gender quality of violence taking place. In her continued discourse of gender Tafari examines some of the methods used by inner-city women to subverted bourgeois determined stereotypes of beauty. Using the 'Dancehall Queen' as an emblematic type, even though she is aware of the diversity, Tafari points out in her reception of Carolyn Cooper and Brian Meek's analyses that these women represent subaltern subversive femininities, which might unsettle the uptown bourgeois prescriptions of morality (Tafari 2002: 305). Quoting from Fairweather-Wilson in Brian Meek's work:

Our genuine dance hall women leaders who originate from downtown, typically, have a measure of economic power and independence. Some achieve this through lucrative activities as informal commercial importers. Some have become successful by way of dressmaking and other business concerns. These women can afford to buy themselves the most fabulous finery, successfully competing with the well-kept women of dons. They often go out by themselves, in posses, dressed in their garments of liberation. They can certainly afford to pay their own bar bills. This level of economic independence has implications for the men-women relationship. It seems to me that the ongoing power struggle between men and women has taken on some new dimension in dance-hall culture. (Meek in Tafari 2002: 309)

Tafari further mentions the cultural rebellious stance of the 'Dancehall Queens' seen in their practices of 'elaborate undressing' and their parodies of bourgeois perception of fashion (Tafari 2002: 309). She also refers to the ambiguity of the 'elaborate undressing' by women in the dancehall culture, pointing out that for some women their ways of dressing are designed to support their self esteem, while some men claim that with the 'elaborate undressing' they are able to appreciate 'the merchandise', thereby objectifying the Dancehall Queens as sexual commodities (Tafari 2002: 308). I will demonstrate the relevance of examining the symbol of the Dancehall Queen in my analysis of the Jamaican film with the same title.

3.5.2. Patterson's Gender Concept

After presenting the historical sociologist Orlando Patterson's basic analysis of the embedded alienation and violence that appears to constitute any given slave society (see above), I would like now to present his arguments concerning the effects of slavery on African American gender relationship. In the second volume of his trilogy, *Rituals of Blood: Consequences of Slavery on the Gender Relationship Among African Americans* (1998), Patterson examines the gender relationship among African Americans today, and how African American males are represented and conceptualized in the American media today. In the first of his three interlocking essays, *Broken Bloodlines: Gender Relations and the Crisis of Marriage and Families Among Afro-Americans*, Patterson scrutinizes the male/female relationship between African Americans connecting different aspects of their relationship to the history of slavery in America. He states that he is using "the term *gender* in its broad sociological sense to include all aspects of human relations involving people's identities, attitudes, and behaviors as males and as females" (Patterson 1998: IX). He refers to the prolonged gender problems between African Americans of all classes stating that this crisis was widely acknowledged in the past "(B)efore it became de rigueur for academic and other

advocates of Afro-Americans to deny behavioral and cultural problems (...)"
(Patterson 1998: X). Patterson claims that although one has to pay close attention to the effects of current social and economic factors on African American
gender relations, he strongly argues that the root of the problem can be traced
back to the two and a half centuries of slavery and its aftermath, neo-slavery of
Jim Crow (Patterson 1998: XII). Patterson mentions that he is aware that he is
going against the 1970s revisionist literatures, which emerged in reaction to
earlier scholarship that stressed the destructive impact of slavery on the institutions of African Americans. He argues that certain Revisionists in their efforts to
demonstrate that slaves even under the domination of the masters could and
did exercise some agency came close to writing the slave masters out of the
story (Patterson 1998: 29). Patterson asserts that some of the Revisionists went
looking for what they called "the family" and when they found something close
to their model they claimed that the institution of slavery did not have much
effects on "the family". He states that

> (U)pon finding something that looked vaguely like "the family unit" to which they
> were accustomed, they emerged triumphant with the academic news that slavery
> had had no damaging impact on the Afro-American family, that indeed the Afro-
> Americans had emerged from two and a half centuries of powerlessness, sexual de-
> gradation, male emasculation, childhood neglect, legal nonexistence (in which being
> raped by anyone Euro-American was not a crime), and general racist oppression with
> their nuclear families intact, their gender relations unsullied, and their communities
> tightly knit and harmonious. (Patterson 1998: 29)

Patterson postulates that what Robert William Fogel and Stanley Engerman in
their revisionist work *Time on the Cross* found, was the *reproduction unit*, which
he explains was facilitated by slave masters who wanted their slaves to breed as
many children as possible (Patterson 1998: 30). He also criticizes the revisionist
works of Herbert Gutman and Eugene Genovese for concentrating mainly on
large slave plantations, which kept better records. Patterson draws attention to
the fact that slaves toiled on small, medium and large plantations, he also
criticizes other Revisionists for not taking into account regional diversities
(Patterson 1998: 30).

   In his study Patterson argues that without steady and lasting relationship
between men and women and without a supportive framework within which
children can grow up any group of people will face difficulties (Patterson 1998:
3). He makes it clear that he is aware of the negative effects of urban inner-city
life, but he still points to the peculiar history of slavery having a devastating
impact on their gender relationships.

Something else must be at play. Something that runs deep into the peculiarities of the Afro-Americans' own past. In searching for it, we are inevitably led back to the centuries-long holocaust of slavery and what was its most devastating impact: the ethnocidal assault on gender roles, especially those of father and husband, leaving deep scars in the relations between Afro-American men and women. (Patterson 1998: 25)

Patterson refers to the West African origins of most slaves in the United States and the Americas pointing to the kindred base of these societies, and the role of the father in training children for adulthood and determining their status in the society (Patterson 2001: 26). He claims that after the Middle Passage what would most likely have survived is the value of kin as expression of important relationships and ranking. In another work Patterson substantiates the strength of kinship relations. He states:

(O)ne experience did take place on the middle passage which was of lasting importance, and paradoxically, of great subsequent comfort to the slave. It was the formation of the strong bonds of friendship between all the slaves on the slave ship. These friends became known in the West Indies as "shipmates" and their love and affection for each other was proverbial (...) It was customary for children to call their parents' shipmates "uncle" or "aunt". So strong were the bonds between shipmates that sexual intercourse between them, in the view of one observer, was considered incestuous. (Patterson 1967: 150)

Furthermore Patterson refers to the devastation of the role of the father and husband during slavery.

Hence, the status and role of husband could not exist under slavery, since it meant having independent rights in another person and, in both the U.S. South and West Africa, some authority over her. Fatherhood could also not exist, since this meant owning one's children, having parental power and authority over them. Both infringed upon the power of the master and were therefore denied in law and made meaningless in practice. (Patterson 1998: 27)

In my analysis of the cultural texts *Dancehall Queen* and *Black Boy* I will demonstrate where I see the theme of African diasporic men having children without being able or willing to support them. I will show that the unwillingness of some African diasporic men to support their children leads to certain forms of alienation for the children and their mothers as represented in the cultural texts. Patterson further demonstrates the ravaged (destruction) of the role of the father and husband by asking a number of questions; he asks whether the male slave could protect his mate from being brutalized and physically punished by other men? Could he prevent her from being sold away? Could he provide for her materially or protect her from sexual predation of other men? Or could he monopolize his partner's sexual services? "If the answer to any of these questions is 'No', the role of husband did not exist. If the slave could do none of these things, then the role of husband had been devastated" (Patterson 2001: 32). He also examines the high mortality rate of slave children arguing that such factors plus the absence of any other meaningful ways for enslaved African men to express manhood that would contribute to the progenitor acquiring special values. He states that

> (S)ince they either could not secure a regular mate or could not be sure that the children of their partners on other plantations were their own, their best hope of satisfying the fundamental biological need to leave some progeny in the world would have been to plant their seed whenever and wherever they could. This was not promiscuity! Under the severe environmental exigencies of slavery, it would have been supremely rational male reproduction behavior. The fact that some masters persistently, and nearly all masters at some time, actively encouraged young unattached male slaves to act as human studs would simply have reinforced this reproduction strategy. (Patterson 1998: 43)

Patterson continues his arguments by pointing out that in all societies primitive and advanced the decision to become father is connected to the male ability to provide for his offspring. He writes:

> After two and a half centuries in which this linkage was forcibly severed, however, Afro-American males, and their descendants, *like male slaves and their descendants all over the Americas,* developed a reproductive strategy in which these two aspects of life were no longer necessarily or normatively linked. Bringing a child into the world became a virtual obligation of manhood and of ethnic survival that did not entail any consideration of the means, whereby one would support it. Afro-American, and American society at large (like Afro-Caribbean and Afro-Latin societies), are still living with the devastating consequences of this male attitude toward reproduction. (Patterson 1998: 43)

Patterson substantiates the effects of slavery on African American family structures by pointing to the distinctive pattern of sharecropping that emerged in rural South, which encouraged African American couples to produce many children. Even though African Americans had a limited amount of choice in the rural South, he suggests that maybe one of the reasons why so many African American got caught in the system was because this system fitted with the past. With sharecropping young African Americans couples had about eight children, but not the economic means to support them (Patterson 1998: 47). Patterson also connects the high proportion of African American female-headed households with the reproduction patterns of slavery. He states that

(S)lavery is important not only for our understanding of the high proportion of female-headed households resulting from fragile unions and male abandonment of their spouses and children but also for any explanation of other gender and familial patterns, including those that form the "family unit" perspective may seem to have been stable two-parent households. Nowhere is this more true than in our attempts to make sense of the patterns that evolved under the impact of the sharecropping farms where the great majority of Afro-Americans were to be found for the first four decades of the present century. (Patterson 1998: 47)

Another aspect of African American gender relation that Patterson examines is the distrust that slavery breeds. He explains that one of the main reasons for marriages over the world is to be sure that children of your partner are your own, but during slavery African American men could not be sure that their partners' children were their own. He writes that

(S)lavery almost certainly bred distrust in gender relations, especially on the part of men. One of the main reasons for marriage all over the world is that it provides security to men that their partner's children are in fact their own biological offspring. In the absence of any legally recognized marriage rights in his partner; and in the presence of both predatory Euro-American men, who could rape or otherwise sexually manipulate slave women with impunity, and a large minority of other young, unattached slave men; and further, with severe restrictions placed on his ability to conduct a mate search that would lead to the selection of someone he felt he could trust, the male slave was placed in an impossible situation, one bound to reduce him to a state of chronic jealousy and insecurity about women. (Patterson 1998: 35)

Patterson refers to the domestic violence among slaves, citing Ann Patton Malone who studied slave families in Louisiana. He quotes

"reports of domestic violence in planters' records" involving slave men against their wives and attributed them to the "overwhelming sense of powerlessness and impotence which threatened the male's concept of his manhood and fatherhood." She could also have attributed them to the brutality and pervasive violence of slavery itself (…). (Patterson 1998: 37)

He further refers to the traumatic impact of slavery on African American women, indicating to the double burden of women as worker and reproducer. He cites Deborah Gray White's study in which she demonstrates that "giving birth was life affirming for women" (Patterson 1998: 32). Patterson draws attention to the value place on mothering even today among African American women, which he claims appears to be out of tune with their highly modern gender views. He claims that one can explain this in terms of long years of struggle during and after slavery (Patterson 1998: 38). He also refers to White's arguments that demonstrate that slaveholders encouraged the primacy of mother-child relation above marriage (Patterson 1998: 38). The African American feminist writer Patricia Hill Collins in her prominent book *Black Feminist Thought: Knowledge, Consciousness, and the Politics of Empowerment,* also refers to White's arguments that

> (T)echniques such as assigning pregnant women lighter workloads, giving pregnant women more attention and rations, and rewarding prolific women with bonuses were all used to increase Black women's reproduction. Punitive measures were also used. Infertile women could expect to be treated "like barren sows and be passed from one unsuspecting buyer to the next". (Hill Collins 2000: 51)

Even though I agree with Patterson's point of view regarding the negative effects of slavery on some African diasporic male reproduction patterns today, I share the view of Patricia Hill Collins regarding African American male responsibility for their conduct towards their families. "They *can* be held accountable, no matter how badly treated they may be under racial oppression, for how they treat Black women, children, and each other" (Hill Collins 2000: 156). In the following study I will demonstrate in my interpretation of the cultural texts *Black Boy* and *Dancehall Queen* how I see negative influences of slavery concerning the gender relationship among African diasporians being thematized. I will also point out how the problematic gender relations contribute to alienation and violence as represented in various cultural texts.

4 Inflicting Pain on Minds and Bodies: African American Literary Texts

4.1. Frederick Douglass' *The Narrative of the Life of Frederick Douglass an American Slave Written by Himself* (1845)

The Narrative of the Life of Frederick Douglass an American Slave Written by Himself contains two verifications as to the honesty of the writer's identity. A preface written by Lloyd Garrison, a prominent Massachusetts Anti-Slavery thinker and publisher of *The Liberator,* an abolitionist newspaper first published in 1831. Garrison points out that he first met Douglass at an Anti-Slavery meeting in Nantucket where Douglass spoke openly about his experiences of slavery for the first time. Garrison vouches for Douglass' honesty in his representation of slavery, stating that as proof Douglass has given the names and places of his encounter with slavery. Garrison claims that he had never hated slavery as much as he hated it when he listened to Douglass' telling of his experiences of slavery.

The second confirmation of the sincerity of Douglass' text is a personal letter written by Wendell Phillips, a prominent abolitionist speaker, crusading lawyer and judge. The letter starts with the reference to the fable of *The Man and the Lion,* where the lion complains that he would not be misrepresented if he were able to write his history or (his story). Phillips is pleased that the slave is finally able to write about his experiences of slavery. He refers to how happy he was to learn how early slave children awake to a sense of their rights and of the injustice done to them. He emphasizes the fact that Douglass made his experiences of slavery in that part of the country where slavery was supposed to be mild compared with the 'Deep South', which he collates to the shadow of death. He contends that Douglass did not seem to have chosen any unfair or rare specimens of cruelty, but rather gives a fair representation of his treatment of slavery. He also draws attention to the danger Douglass placed himself in by giving all information concerning his ownership and his life and experiences of slavery.

The narrative of Douglass' life is rendered in eleven short chapters and written in the first person. At the end is an appendix where Douglass defends his representation of religious slaveholders pointing to the evil of a man "who wields the blood-clotted cowskin during the week and then fills the pulpit on

Sunday." He explains that the man who sells his sister into prostitution is the same one that "(…) stands forth as the pious advocate of purity" (Douglass 1845 in Gates 1987: 327)[5]. For Douglass the slaveholders who committed evil on their slaves during the week, but then on Sundays pretend to be pure and pious are nothing but hypocrites.

Orlando Patterson states that Frederick Douglass is maybe one of the most articulate slaves to have ever expressed his experiences of slavery (Patterson 1982). Frederick Douglass was born a slave in Tuckahoe near Hillsborough County in Maryland in February 1818. His mother Harriet Bailey was a slave of Captain Anthony, and it was rumoured that his mother's owner was his father. Douglass spends the first six years of his life with his material grandparents, Betsey Bailey, a slave of Captain Anthony, and Isaac Bailey, a manumitted slave. The Baileys lived in a log cabin on the banks of the Tuckahoe creek. Douglass enjoyed the love and kindness of his grandparents up to the age of six. Then he was taken to Captain Anthony's house twelve miles away from his grandparents. Here Douglass was assigned household duties, cleaning the yard and keeping chicken out of the garden, running errands for Lucretia, his master's daughter. Douglass and all the slave children who were too young to work in the fields were placed in the care of the slave Aunt Katy. Douglass refers to his suffering along with lack of food at his master's house. Captain Anthony was chief overseer of Colonel Lloyd's plantation; Colonel Lloyd owned over one thousand slaves on various plantations.

In 1825 Douglass was sent to Baltimore to live with Hugh Auld and his wife Sophia, and took care of their two-year-old son Thomas. Hugh Auld was the brother-in-law of Lucretia, Captain Anthony's daughter.

Sophia Auld had never owned a slave before Douglass went to live with her family; she was very kind and even began to teach him the letters of the alphabet. This was put to a stop when Hugh Auld found out about this. Hugh objected to teaching a slave to read, because this would "spoil" even the best slave, and it would make him discontented and unhappy. Sophia Auld followed her husband's order, but it was too late, Douglass found other means to continue with his learning.

About one year after Douglass went to live in Baltimore his master died, and he was sent back to Tuckahoe to be valued with the rest of the property. After the valuation in which Douglass fell into the possession of Lucretia, he was allowed to return to Baltimore. In 1832 Douglass left Baltimore to live with his master Thomas Auld at St. Michael, Lucretia and her brother had died a few months after Douglass returned from the valuation to Baltimore. Douglass now

---

[5] All quotations from Douglass 1845 are taken from the Gates edition.

back in St. Michael faces again hunger and severe whippings. In 1833 Douglass was hired out to Covey for one year to be broken in, because he refuses to obey his master's commands (Douglass 1845: 289).

Douglass had his first experiences as a field labourer under the authority of Covey, known to the slaves working on his farm as the 'snake'. Due to his lack of experience in dealing with animals and fieldwork Douglass was whipped almost weekly by Covey in the first six months. This weekly whipping ended when Douglass became sick on a very hot summer's day and was unable to work. He was kicked and hit over the head with a hickory stick by Covey. Douglass under the severe hot sun and pain in his head went to seek protection and justice from his master, but was told by his master to return to Covey or he would lose his earnings he was supposed to receive from Covey for his labour. Douglass was forced to return to Covey, but before his return he received a special root from a fellow slave, who told him that if he wore the root always on the right side of his person he would avoid being whipped by any White man. Even though Douglass did not place much value on the effectiveness of the root, he accepted it. After hiding out in the woods for two days Douglass is forced to return and face Covey. Covey tried to beat Douglass, but for the first time in his life Douglass fought back, this experience changed Douglass' life in slavery forever.

In 1834 Douglass was hired out to William Freeland and it was here that Douglass planned his first escape from slavery, but his plans were betrayed. Due to prejudices against Douglass in the district his master sent him back to his brother in Baltimore to learn calking. Here at Gardner shipyard Douglass was attacked, beaten and kicked in his eyeball by a group of White apprentices who did not wish to work with him, because of his status as slave and his color. Hugh enraged tried to seek justice, but because an African American person's testimony was insufficient against any White person's there was nothing to be done. Douglass then went to work in another shipyard where his master was foreman. After one year he was able to work as a calker. Douglass was soon able to hire himself out practicing his profession. He now had a bit more freedom, but he soon lost this freedom due to his failure to keep an appointment with master Hugh on a Saturday evening. After his master forced Douglass to give up the freedom of hiring himself out, Douglass finally decided to run away again. Douglass does not give any details as to the means which he used to escape, because as he explains such information would aid the master more than his fellow slaves.

The Narrative of the Life of Frederick Douglass Written by Himself, published in 1845 is referred to by one scholar as the crown jewel of all the slave narratives

(Chander in Nelson 2002: 102). The fugitive slave narrative describes from the point of view of the slave his or her experiences of slavery, and his escape into freedom. They were written with the objective to represent the horrors of slavery and their destructive impact upon the life and personalities of slaves and also aimed at ending slavery (Chander 2002: 101). Another scholar writes that the slave narratives were retrospective ventures to aid in creating new identities for the narrators as they seek to come to terms with their past experiences of slavery (Smith Foster 1979: 3). They are considered a sub-genre of the Black autobiographical mode (Chander 2002: 102). Slave narratives have three categories, one is the ghost written narrative, where the identity of the writer is unknown to the reader. The second type of slave narratives are those dictated by illiterate slaves to someone else; and finally the third category consists of those narratives written by the slaves themselves telling their experiences of slavery in their own words (Chander 2002: 101). These were considered more authentic and accepted by Anti-Slave societies as "the best testimony to the evil of slavery and the need for abolition of slavery" (Chander 2002: 101). Chander also refers to the political documentary quality of Douglass' *Narrative* (Chander 2002: 105). The slave narratives were very popular during the 19th century, maybe because of the combination of social and personal matters, which these texts delt with (Smith Foster 1979: 4). According to Henry Louis Gates Jr. the slave narratives represent "a countergenre, a mediation between the novel of sentiment and the picaresque, oscillating somewhere between the two in a bipolar moment, set in motion by the mode of confession" (Gates 1987: 81). When analyzing the slave narratives one however cannot overlook the significance of race, because "(R)ace was the most crucial factor in the development of the slave narratives because in the United States the slaves' experiences of bondage and freedom were a product of race" (Smith Foster 1979: 4).

In my analysis of how alienation and violence are thematized in African American and Jamaican cultures, I have chosen to examine Frederick Douglass' representations of alienation and violence that he observed and experienced as a slave. The goal of my analysis is to establish that from the inception of African American literary history, alienation and violence are two social themes that fugitive slaves and later their descents have exemplified in various cultural texts.

One of the first moments of alienation that the young child Douglass experiences is his lack of knowledge regarding his date of birth. Even though he points out that most slaves could not tell their age, Douglass compares himself with the White children who know their date of birth. "A want of information concerning my own was a source of unhappiness to me even during childhood.

The white children could tell their ages. I could not tell why I ought to be deprived of the same privilege" (Douglass 1845: 255). Douglass in comparing himself with White children exemplifies from the beginning the contrariety of status between White and Black people in the slave society. As I mentioned above one cannot overlook the significance of race in the slave narrative genre or in Douglass' text. The White children are aware of their date of birth; they are treated as human kind, while the Black child is treated as property. Gates points out that the "slave" who does not know his date of birth seems to have stood outside of time. He writes "(I)n antebellum America, it was the deprivation of time in the life of the slave that first signaled his or her status as a piece of property" (Gates 1987: 101). Douglass himself compares the slave's lack of knowledge regarding his date of birth with animals. "By far the larger part of the slaves knows as little of their ages as horses know of theirs, and it is the wish of most masters within my knowledge to keep their slaves ignorant" (Douglass 1845: 255). Douglass makes it clear in the first ten lines of his narrative that the condition of the slave is closer to that of animals than to other human beings. Huston Baker calls attention to the fact that Douglass uses animal motifs in his narrative to reinforce the "soul-killing" effects of slavery on the enslaved (Baker 1972: 75). Douglass continues the first stage of his narrative by pointing out that not only did he not know when he was born, he had no idea who his father was. Even though it was whispered that his master was his father, he was not able to confirm this with his mother (Douglass 1845: 256). From his mother he has been separated since he was an infant, so he did not have a chance to develop a normal relationship to her.

> My mother and I were separated when I was but an infant – before I knew her as my mother. It is a common custom, in the part of Maryland from which I ran away, to part children from their mothers at a very early age. (…) For what this separation is done, I do not know unless it hinder the development of the child's affection towards his mother, and to blunt and destroy the natural affection of the mother for the child. (Douglass 1845: 256)

Here, Douglass typifies one aspect of psychological alienation between family members under the system of slavery. Harish Chander contends that Douglass shows how slavery destroys the family beginning with his own (Chander 2002: 102), and Orlando Patterson in his study of global slavery also draws attention to the fact that a person who loses his connection with his ancestral community is confronted with alienation. The young Douglass and other slave children who are kept apart from their mothers, and lack of awareness as to the identity of their fathers, are estranged from their parents' love and affection. Gates refers to the ambiguity between father and son and master and slaves. He writes:

(...) if only because the two terms "father" and "master" are here embodied in one, with no mediation between them. It is this rather grotesque bond that links Douglass to his parent, a bond that embodies "the distorted and unnatural relationship endemic to slavery." (Gates 1987: 91)

Douglass' family relationships are displaced by the system of slavery. There are scholars who refer to the alternative family structures that developed during slavery. "Rawick maintains that the slaves created a family system that was more appropriate and consequently more beneficial than the nuclear family" (Smith Foster 1979: 139).

I am aware of the contemporary controversy as to the effects of slavery on the African American family, but when one focuses on Douglass' text one can read the negative effectives of slavery on his family relations. Due to the fact that his mother had to work from dust to dawn in the fields Douglass was able to see her only five times in his life, and only at night. Douglass states his reaction on receiving news that his mother was dead. "Never having enjoyed, to any considerable extent, her smoothing presence, her tender and watchful care, I received the tidings of her death with much the same emotions I should have probably felt at the death of a stranger" (Douglass 1845: 256). Douglass interprets his experiences of slavery as alienating to family relationships; he attributes his lack of emotion on receiving the information regarding his mother's death to the fact that either he or his mother was given the chance to cultivate a normal mother-child relationship. "Mothers were torn from their infants long before the period of lactation was over, in order to return full-time to the fields" (Patterson 1998: 39). For Douglass the customs of the slave system do not recognize his family relations.

In chapter one of his *Narrative* Douglass not only represents his personal alienation from his mother, he depicts his first observation and encounter with violence committed by the overseer and slave owner. He introduces us to Mr. Plummer "(...) a miserable drunkard, a profane swearer, and savage monster" (Douglass 1845: 258), who always carried a cowskin and a heavy cudgel. According to Douglass this overseer was so cruel that Captain Anthony threatened to whip him. Douglass refers to the daily whipping of one his aunts by Mr. Plummer. "I have often been awakened at the dawn of day by the most heart rendering shrieks of an aunt of mine, whom he used to tie up to a joist, and whip upon her naked back till she was literally covered with blood" (Douglass 1845: 258). Here Douglass presents the daily violence done to the slave by the overseer. Patterson points out that violence is not only used in the slave societies when new a person is introduced to the status of slavery, but also on a daily basis due to the low motivation of the slave regarding work (Patterson 1982).

Douglass also draws attention to the inhuman treatment of another aunt, Hester, by her master, on account of her being caught in the company of another slave named Ned, when her master wanted her.

> He made her get upon the stool, and tied her hands to the hook, she now stood fair for his infernal purpose. Her arms were stretched up at their full length, so that she stood upon the ends of her toes (…) he commenced to lay on the heavy cowskin, and soon the warm, red blood (amid heart-rendering shrieks from her, and horrid oaths from him) came dripping to the floor. (Douglass 1845: 259)

These two violent incidents are Douglass' initiation into the physical violence committed on the body of the slave. These scenes also forced Douglass to recognize the physical and mental hell of slavery (Smith 1987: 23). Katherine Fishburn in her study *The Problem of Embodiment*, refers to the fear of the child Douglass at the economic of violence that separates the master from the slave (Fishburn 1994: 59). The child Douglass is shocked at the physical force committed on his aunts. Patterson draws attention to the psychological trauma of children who were forced to witness the daily degradation of parents and other relatives (Patterson 1998: 40). Douglass here represents one aspect of violence that slave women have to endure when they refuse the possible advance of the male slave owner. Hester was beaten not only because she disobeyed her owner, but also because she prefers the company of another slave to the company of her master. The consequences of the slave woman denying the sexual advances of her master are well established in the slave narrative *Incident in the Life of A Slave Girl* by Harriet Brent Jacobs. Regarding Douglass' description of his aunt Hester's beating Huston Baker comments on the effects of Douglass' economy of literary style, which reinforce the poverty, and oppressiveness of the situations which he describes (Baker 1972: 72).

Another theme of alienation that Douglass represents in his narrative is the physical alienation suffered by the slaves. The slaves on Colonel Lloyd's plantation are given a monthly supply of eight pounds of pork or fish and four pecks of cornmeal. Their yearly allowances of clothing consisted of two course linen shirts and two pair of trousers, one jacket, one pair of stockings and one pair of shoes (Douglass 1845: 260). Douglass draws attention to the fact that the slaves who work from dust to dawn spend a large portion of their limited free time washing, mending and preparing their food for the evening meals and their meals for the next day in the field. When all of these tasks were accomplished the slaves of all ages and sex went to sleep on the damp floor. Douglass writes:

> (…) very many of their sleeping hours are consumed in preparing for the field the coming day; and when this is done, old and young, male and female, married and

single, drop down side by side, on one common bed, – the cold, damp floor, – each covering himself with their miserable blankets; and here they sleep till they are summoned to the field by the diver's horn. There must be no halting; every one must be at his or her post; and woe betides them who hear not this morning summon to the field; for if they are not awakened by the sense of hearing, they are by the sense of feeling: no age nor sex finds favor. Mr. Severe, the overseer, used to stand by the door of the quarter, armed with a large hickory stick and heavy cowskin, ready to whip any one who was so unfortunate as not to hear, or, from any other cause, was prevented from being ready to start for the field at the sound of the horn. (Douglass 1845: 261)

Fishburn argues that it is through these deprivations that the slaves learn in their bodies what it means to be the property of another person (Fishburn 1994: 60). Douglass' description of the physical alienation of the slave is also enforced by the physical violence that the slave encounters if he or she should attempt to end the physical deprivation of his or her body by sleeping late. Fishburn also refers to the centrality of the body in the American slave culture. She points out that slavery marks the body of the enslaved and finds it crucial that Douglass did not try to "white out" the body. She writes:

(…) but I find it significant that Douglass and other nineteenth century slaves narrators, in contrast to their immediate successors, did not choose to "white out" their bodies when they composed their narratives. In fact, the body is very much at the heart of these documents. Douglass records, more over, the process by which the body of the enslaved learns its debased status and how the body overcomes this status. (Fishburn 1994: 60)

I agree that one cannot overlook the importance of the body in the American slave culture, but one cannot ignore the psychological effects of slavery on the enslaved neither, which I will explain later.

Douglass in his narrative shows diverse aspects of physical displacements slave children undergo. In his account of his own experiences during childhood, Douglass refers to his discomfort caused by cold and hunger. He points out that the pen he is writing his narrative with could fit into the cracks of his feet caused by the frost.

In hottest summer and coldest winter, I was kept almost naked – no shoes, no stocking, no jacket, no trousers, nothing on but a coarse tow linen shirt, reaching only my knees. I had no bed. I must have perished with cold, but that, the coldest nights, I used to steal a bag which was used for carrying corn to the mill. I would crawl into this bag, and there sleep on the cold, damp, clay floor, with my head and in and feet out. (Douglass 1845: 271)

The physical discomfort of the slave children who are forced to endure the misery of cold and hunger represents the rupture of the slave children's lives from humane physical comfort.

Douglass also comments on the lack of food for slave children in his narrative. He writes:

> We were not regularly allowanced. Our food was coarse cornmeal boiled. This was called mash. It was put into a large wooden tray or trough, and set down upon the ground. The children were then called, like so many pigs, and like so many pigs they would come and devour the mash; some with oyster-shells, others with pieces of shingle, some with naked hands, and none with spoons. He that ate fastest got most; he that was strongest secured the best place; and few left the trough satisfied. (Douglass 1845: 271)

It is a moment of survival of the fittest for the slave children during the meals that Douglass represents in his narrative, this demonstrates certain elements of social and physical displacement. The slave children are treated as animals – little pigs. They are given their meals on the ground like the pigs, and like pigs they devoured their meals without spoons. The food is not enough, even for those children who are strongest. The pattern of inhuman treatment of the African descendent slaves in the American slave culture commences with the early separation of the mother from the child, as I mentioned above, and continues during early childhood of the slave child. The children are denied most normal social treatments. The slave children are not allowed to sit on chairs or at tables to partake of their meals. No mother stands around to see that every child has a proper portion of the meal or to look that there is enough for everyone. Patterson draws attention to the fact that slave children were sometimes horribly malnourished. "(O)wners hedged their bets, not wanting to invest resources in the offspring of their slaves until they were certain that they would become productive adults" (Patterson 1998: 39). The children are not yet productive; they are not given shoes or socks to cover their feet. They must suffer cold and hunger, and as illustrated in the killing of the old man fishing for oyster, might even be killed if they try to remedy their natural human needs for nourishment.

Another aspect of violence is the arbitrariness of reasons for the violence committed on the slaves by their masters and other Whites. Douglass in his depiction of the plight of young and old Barney exemplifies one characteristic of the arbitrary infliction of violence on the slave. The father and son Barney, responsible for the care of Colonel Lloyd's stable and carriage house, were never safe from punishment. They might be whipped for feeding the horses too much or too little, or if a horse refuses to hold its head high enough. Douglass claims that the complains that both father and son had to endure were numerous and capricious.

> It was painful to stand near the stable-door, and hear the various complaints against the keepers when a horse was taken for use. "This horse has not had proper attention. He has not been sufficiently rubbed and curried, or he has not been properly fed; his food was too wet or too dry; he got it too soon or too late; he was too hot or too cold; he had too much hay, and not enough grain; or he had too much grain, and not enough hay; instead of old Barney's attending to the horse, he had very improperly left it on his son." (Douglass 1845: 265)

Patterson points to how the life conditions of slaves differ from other people.

> Slaves differed from other human beings in that they were not allowed freely to integrate the experiences of their ancestors into their lives, to inform their understanding of social reality with the inherited meaning of their natural forebears, or to anchor the living present in any conscious community of memory. (Patterson 1982: 5).

The particular circumstances of father and son working together and the experiences of old Barney in dealing with horses does not reduce the chances of young Barney being punished. The father's knowledge of horses cannot be passed on to his son to prevent him from being abused. Old Barney himself even after years of experiences in taking care of Colonel Lloyd's horses still faces punishment. "I have seen Colonel Lloyd make old Barney, a man between fifty and sixty years of age, uncover his bald head, kneel down upon the cold, damp ground, and receive upon his naked and toil-worn shoulders more than thirty lashes at the time" (Douglass 1845: 265). Barney the old slave is not only unable to pass on vital information that would prevent his son from being punished, but also he himself is not able to use his knowledge and experiences in preventing his own maltreatment. The arbitrariness of violence that is inflicted upon the slave is further demonstrated in Douglass' tale regarding Colonel Lloyd's fruit garden. The spectacular character of the garden attracts not only people from far and near, but also the slaves on the plantation, but the slave who is tempted to try the fruits of the garden must pay dearly. Douglass mentions that after diverse methods failed to prevent the slaves from entering the garden, the fence all around the garden was tarred and any slave found with tar on their person was punished.

> The last and most successful one was that of tarring his fence all around; after which, if a slave was caught with any tar upon his person it was deemed sufficient proof that he had either been into the garden, or had tried to get in. In either case, he was severely whipped by the chief gardener. (Douglass 1845: 264)

One might read Colonel Lloyd's garden as the garden of Eden, and people of African descent are barred from entering according to the American racial policies. One could also connect the defilement of tar to the Black skin color of the slave and the one drop of African blood, which was enough in the American racial ideology to make one a slave.

The fact that any slave found with tar on his person was whipped demonstrates the whimsicality of violence that was inflicted upon the slave by the master. It was not deemed necessary to prove where the tar came from, it was enough to assume that if one is found with tar on their person that it came from the garden.

Douglass in his representation of Rev. Daniel Weeden and Rev. Rigby Hopkins continues his description of the capricious reasons given by the slave masters for inflicting physical violence upon their slaves. Douglass relates that the Rev. Weeden kept the back of his woman slaves literally raw for weeks. He states that the dictum of this religious slave master was to whip to demonstrate his power over his slaves. "His maxim was, behave well or ill, it is the duty of a master occasionally to whip a slave, to remind him of his master's authority" (Douglass 1845: 302). Patterson refers to the social facet of power, which involves the use, or threat of violence by the master to control his slave (Patterson 1982: 1). Douglass also draws attention to Mr. Hopkins' peculiar feature of governing his slaves by whipping them in advance of any offences. His Monday morning practice of lashing one or two of his slaves just to strike terror in other slaves again signals the capricious character of violence by the slave holding class. Douglass writes:

(A) mere look, word, or motion, – a mistake, accident, or want of power, – are all matters for which a slave may be whipped at any time. Does a slave look dissatisfied? It is said, he has the devil in him, and it must be whipped out. Does he speak loudly when spoken by his master? Then he is getting high-minded, and should be taken down a button-hole lower. Does he forget to pull off his hat at the approach of a white person? Then he is wanting in reverence, and should be whipped for it. Does he ever venture to vindicate his conduct, when censured for it? Then he is guilty of impudance, – one of the greatest crimes of which a slave can be guilty. Does he ever venture to suggest a different mode of doing things from that pointed out by his master? He is indeed presumptuous, and getting above himself, and nothing less than a flogging will do for him. Does he, while ploughing, break a plough, – or, while hoeing, break a hoe? It is owing to his carelessness, and for it a slave must always be whipped. Mr. Hopkins could always find something of this sort to justify the use of the lash, and he seldom failed to embrace such opportunities. (Douglass 1845: 302–303)

The whimsical reasons given for inflicting force upon the slave can be explained by the absolute power and control that the slave masters have over their slaves. Patterson refers to the powerlessness of the slave compared with the master (Patterson 1982), which allows the master to beat his slave whenever and for what ever reason he personally sees fit.

Another aspect of violence that Douglass shows in his narrative is the deadly violence perpetrated against slaves. In his account of the killing of the slave Demby by the overseer Mr. Gore, Douglass demonstrates the barbarity committed upon the slave. Mr. Gore wanted to whip Demby, but then Demby ran and plunged himself into the creek and refused to come out. Mr. Gore informed Demby that he would call him three times and if he did not come out he would shoot him. After calling Demby three times with no response Mr. Gore shot him, killing him. When questioned by the head overseer Mr. Gore replied that Demby had become unmanageable and was setting a bad example for other slaves. Mr. Gore

(…) argued that if one slave refused to be corrected, and escaped with his life, the other slaves would soon copy the example; the result of which would be, the freedom of the slaves, and enslavement of the whites. Mr. Gore's defence was satisfactory. He was continued in his station as overseer upon the home plantation. His fame as an overseer went abroad. His horrid crime was not even submitted to judicial investigation. (Douglass 1845: 269)

The physical violence, which Douglass demonstrates in his account of Demby's murder, can only be explained due to the absolute power which slave owners and their overseers have over the lives of the slaves. In Douglass' narrative "humans are whipped and slaughtered like animals; men and women are changed into maniacal and sadistic creatures by power; the strength of mind and body is destroyed by an avaricious and degrading system" (Baker 1972: 76). Demby is seen as a threat to the control and social order of slavery, and must pay with his life for attempting to undermine this social order. It is also the fear of the Whites that the Blacks want to take their social positions.

Douglass shows that it was not only White males that committed violence upon the slaves in his tale of the young girl that fell asleep when she should be taking care of her mistress's baby.

The offence for which this girl was thus murdered was this: She had been set that night to mind Mrs. Hicks's baby, and during the night she fell asleep, and the baby cried. She, having lost her rest for several nights previous, did not hear the crying. They were both in the room with Mrs. Hicks. Mrs. Hicks, finding the girl slow to move, jumped from her bed, seized an oak stick of wood by the fireplace, and with it broke the girl's nose and breastbones, and thus ended her life. (Douglass 1845: 269)

The brutal act by Mrs. Hicks upon the slave girl indicates the inhuman treatment of the slave by their owners. The young girl's only crime was her bodily fatigue, and for her very human reaction to her fatigue, she was murdered. One would consider it as normal that Mrs. Hicks, the mother, should hear her child crying before the young girl, and that the young girl should sleep when she is tired. The denial of humane actions or agency on the part of the slaves by the slaveholder is represented in Douglass' narrative of the above atrocity.

Another aspect of social displacement that Douglass represents is his familial alienation in his account of his lack of pain in leaving Colonel Lloyd's plantation for the one of Baltimore. He points out that he did not feel at home there, even though his brother and two sisters were there.

> My home was charmless; it was not home to me; on parting from it, I could not feel that I was leaving any thing which I could have enjoyed by staying. My mother was dead; my grandmother lived far off, so that I seldom saw her. I had two sisters and one brother that lived in the same house with me; but the early separation of us from our mother had well nigh blotted the fact of our relationship from our memories. I looked for home else-where, and was confident of finding none which I should relish less than the one I was leaving. If, however I found in my new home hardship, hunger, whipping, and nakedness, I had the consolation that I should not have escaped anyone of them in the house of my old master, and having endured them there, I very naturally inferred my ability to endure them elsewhere (…). (Douglass 1845: 272)

Douglass here in his representation of his relationship to his siblings shows the displacement of family members. This is a displacement perpetuated by the system of slavery. The seven year old child Douglass is leaving the slave plantation for the possibility of a better life, but even if his life in Baltimore does not turn out right he thinks that it cannot be harder than what he has already endured. Patterson in his analysis of African American gender relations points out that the 'family' did not exist and could not exist during slavery. Here, Douglass also demonstrates his lack of emotions regarding his feelings and attachment to his family.

In Baltimore Douglass came to understand how lack of knowledge or being forbidden to acquire literacy contributes to the perpetual social displacement that he and other slaves have to undergo. As I indicated above Mrs. Auld who had never owned a slave before Douglass went to live with her family commenced to teach him how to read. Mr. Auld found out about his wife teaching the young Douglass to read and write and immediately forbade her to instruct him further, telling her, among other things that it was unlawful, as well as unsafe, to teach a slave to read. According to Douglass he said,

"If you give a nigger an inch, he will take an ell. A nigger should know nothing but
to obey his master – to do as he is told to do. Learning would spoil the best nigger in
the world. Now" said he, "if you teach that nigger (speaking of myself) how to read,
there would be no keeping him. It would forever unfit him to be a slave. He would at
once become unmanageable, and of no value to his master (…)." (Douglass 1845: 274)

With Mr. Auld comments Douglass finally realizes the social injustices committed against the slaves by their masters.

It was a new and special revelation, explaining dark and mysterious things, with
which my youthful understanding had struggled but struggled in vain. I now understood what had been to me a most perplexing difficulty – to wit, the white man's
power to enslave the black man. It was a grand achievement, and I prized it highly.
(Douglass 1845: 275)

Even though he is losing the kind aid of his mistress in learning to read,
Douglass the child realizes that Mr. Auld has given him vital information for
life. "It was a grand achievement and I prized it highly. From that moment, I
understood the pathway from slavery to freedom" (Douglass 1845: 275).
Douglass finally understands one of the main consequences of being denied the
chance to acquire literacy. The slaves that were forbidden to learn to read and
write are locked in a world of darkness about their conditions, and maybe more
willing to accept the master's reasons for their status as slaves. Valerie Smith
points to the importance of the theme of literacy in Douglass' text and for future
African American writers. She writes that "(I)n this episode he creates what has
become a prototypical situation for later Afro-American writers by linking the
acquisition of literacy to both the act of rebellion and the achievement of freedom" (Smith 1987: 23). Later in my analysis I will demonstrate the significance
of literacy in the Jamaican culture pointing to similarities and differences between African American and Jamaican cultural representations.

Douglass in his narrative compares the conditions of the slaves on the plantation with that of the slaves in the city. This comparison is important for my
analysis, because later in my text I will examine the social conditions of African
Americans in the urban landscape. He indicates that slaves in the city enjoy
privileges unknown to the slaves on the plantation. Nevertheless he represents
one of the painful exceptions of brutality committed on the city slaves in his
depiction of Mrs. Hamilton treatment of her two female slaves. He writes:

(T)heir names were Henrietta and Mary. Henrietta was about twenty-two years of
age, Mary was about fourteen, and of all the mangled and emaciated creatures I ever
looked upon, these two were the most so. (…) The head, neck and shoulders of Mary
were literally cut to pieces. I have frequently felt her head, and found its nearly

covered with festering sores, caused by the lashes of her cruel mistress. (Douglass 1845: 276)

The naked violence committed on these two female slaves in the city of Baltimore demonstrates that slaves in the city as well as on the plantation were never safe from violence. Mrs. Hamilton not only brutalizes her slaves physically, but she also half starves them. "They seldom knew what it was to eat a full meal. I have seen Mary contending with the pigs for the offal thrown into the streets. So much was Mary kicked and cut to pieces, that she was oftener called 'pecked' than by her name" (Douglass 1845: 276). Here, Douglass again compares the condition of the slave with animals. The inhuman behaviour of the slaves' masters forces the slaves to compete with the animals for food. Huston Baker points out that "Douglass is aware of American slavery's chattel principle, which equated slaves with livestock, and he is not reluctant to employ animal metaphors to capture the general inhumanity of the system" (Baker 1972: 76).

Douglass in his text does not only refer to the dehumanizing effect of slavery on Blacks, but he also shows its effect on Whites. He draws attention to Mrs. Auld's pious and warm character when he first went to live with her family. After the influence of slavery Mrs. Auld was divested of her warm characteristics.

Under its influence, the tender heart became stone, and the lamblike disposition gave way to tiger-like fierceness. The first step in her downward course was in her ceasing to instruct me. She now commenced to practice her husband's precepts. She finally became even more violent in her opposition than her husband himself. (Douglass 1845: 277).

Douglass indicates clearly that the system of slavery is as harmful to the slave as well as the slave holder, and Baker comments that "practically every character we encounter in the *Narrative* is rendered less human by the effects of slavery" (Baker 1972: 76).

Douglass exemplifies how his capacity to read aids in his feelings of displacement, even though it helps him to become better aware of how Whites are able to enforce their power over Blacks.

As I read and contemplated the subject, behold! That very discontentment which master Hugh had predicted would follow my learning to read had already come, to torment and sting my soul to unutterable anguish. As I writhed under it, I would at times feel that learning to read had been a curse rather than a blessing. It had given me a view of my wretched condition, without the remedy. (Douglass 1845: 279)

Douglass at times even envies his fellow slaves who were unable to read and write, he is aware of his social condition but is unable to change it at the moment. He is displaced in the society he is forced to live in.

Douglass expresses how violence and overwork can turn the most sensitive and intelligent person into a brute in his characterization of his mental state the first six months that he stayed at Covey's farm. The brutal treatment that Douglass experiences under Coveys governance forced him to defend himself, and maybe even come to recognize the liberating factor of force.

> He only can understand the deep satisfaction which I experienced, who has himself repelled by force the bloody arm of slavery. I felt as I never felt before. It was a glorious resurrection, from the tomb of slavery, to the heaven of freedom. My long crushed spirit rose, cowardice departed, bold defiance took its place; and I now re-solved that, however long I might remain a slave in form, the day had passed forever when I could be a slave in fact. I did not hesitate to let it be known of me, that the white man who expected to succeed in whipping me must also succeed in killing me. (Douglass 1845: 299)

Douglass indicates his unwillingness to accept the dehumanizing violence that is perpetuated on the body of the slave. He is willing to fight for his human dignity. He would rather die than suffer the affront of being whipped. Douglass in defending himself understands as Franz Fanon, almost a century later, that the oppressor understands nothing but violence. Katherine Fishburn states that Douglass "(…) in successfully resisting one who literally embodied the slavo-cracy, brought to light what his body-self had forgotten how to say but knew that, in *fact*, he was no slave" (Fishburn 1994: 64).

Douglass' decision to defend himself against violence from Whites is put to a test when he is beaten by four apprentices in the shipyard in Baltimore. Douglass in keeping his vow struck back at the Whites who want to beat him.

> They, however, at length combined, and came upon me, armed with sticks, stones, and heavy handspikes. One came in front with a half brick. There was one at each side of me and behind me, while I was attending to these in front, and on either side, the one behind run up with the handspike, and struck me a heavy blow upon the head. It stunned me. I fell, and with this they all run upon me, and fell to beating me with their fists. In an instance, I gave a sudden surge, and rose to my hands and knees. Just as I did that, one of their members gave me, with his heavy boot, a powerful kick in the left eye. My eyeball seemed to have burst. When they saw my eye closed, and badly swollen, they left me. (…) All this took place in sight of not less than fifty white ship-carpenters, and not one interposed a friendly word; but some cried, "kill the dammed nigger! Kill him! Kill him! He struck a white person." (Douglass 1845: 313)

Douglass demonstrates the minority position of the slave. Fighting against one White person Douglass is able to defend himself, but against the combined strength of four he has to admit his defeat. Here one recognizes another element of power in the American slave holding society: The Whites are in the majority compared with the Blacks that are a minority. This is relevant for my analysis and comparison between the African American and Jamaican cultures because in Jamaica the people of African descent are in a majority position.

Summary

In the *Narrative* Douglass and other young slave children of African descent experience diverse forms of emotional alienation due to their lack of knowledge regarding their date of birth and the displacement of their family relationships. The deprivation of time in the slave child's life is one of the first signals of his or her status as property. The lack of knowledge regarding his or her father's identity and the lack of connection with their ancestral community lead to alienation and are conditioned by the system of slavery. The slaves of African descent in the American slave society suffer physical displacement because of insufficient food and clothing. It is through this physical deprivation that the slaves further learn what it means to be the property of another person and the dehumanizing consequences of such an identity. The enslaved person is alienated because he does not own himself and is unable to control his or her life. In Douglass' *Narrative* physical violence is committed on the slaves almost daily. The reasons for the use of violence on the slaves by their masters and overseers are to demonstrate their power and authority over the slaves, and to control the social order of slavery. The majority position of the European descendants over African descendants in America enable the dominant European Americans to brutalize and violate the African slaves without any consequences whatsoever. In the American slave system violence was used to control and force the African descendants to accept their role as property of European Americans.

4.2. Richard Wright's *Black Boy*

In 1945, one hundred years after Fredrick Douglass published his first auto-biographical text, the *Narrative of the Life of Fredrick Douglass an American Slave Written by Himself*, Richard Wright published the first part of his autobiographical manuscript *Black Boy*.[6] Both texts pay close attention to the effects of American White supremacist racial policy on the African American individual and his community. Even though one might indicate the difference in time, legal status, and circumstances, under which both authors wrote their biographies, there are certain oppressive forces from the ruling European American society that encourage closer examination and comparisons. I will refer again to this point later in my analysis.

Richard Nathaniel Wright was born on September 4, 1908 near Roxie, Mississippi. His father Nathan Wright was an illiterate sharecropper and his mother Ella Wilson was a schoolteacher. Richard's brother Leon Alan was born two years later. In 1912/13 the family moved to Memphis, the father soon left his wife for another woman. Three years later Ella Wilson took her sons to live with her sister Maggie and her husband Hoskins in West Helena, Arkansas. In 1917/18 Hoskins was murdered by Whites who wanted to have control of his thriving alcohol store. Ella and her sister were forced to flee West Helena and went back to live with their family in Jackson, Mississippi. A few months later the sisters returned to West Helena, but Wright's mother soon suffered a paralyzing stroke, and was brought back home to Jackson, it is here where Wright will spend the rest of childhood.

Part one of *Black Boy* is entitled *Southern Nights* and starts with two quotations from the book of Job: "They meet with darkness in the daytime and they grope at noondays as in the night (…)" and "His strength shall be hunger-bitten, and destruction shall be ready at his side."

According to *The Original African Heritage Study Bible*, Job is described in Hebrew as "one who endures great sorrow and suffering." Job is also referred to in the same text as the epitome of patience, tolerance, and faith through suffering, maintaining his integrity throughout the critical reproaches brought against him by his so-called friends (*African Heritage Study Bible*, 1998). It could be seen as ironic that Wright chooses to start his autobiographical text with quotations from the Bible, even though he demonstrates in different contexts his alienation from his family expressive daily religious life and the 'Negro Church' culture as a whole. By using a citation from the book of Job Wright accomplishes various things. First he allies himself with the African American

---

[6] All biographical notes are taken from the text *Black Boy* 1991.

culture, a culture, which he points out in his text, *Blueprint for Negro Writing*, stems from the 'Negro Church' and the 'Negro Folklore'; the second part of his autobiography, *The Horror and the Glory – American Hunger*, starts with a quotation from a 'Negro Folk Song'. The citations from the book of Job could also be read as symbolizing Wright's own individual integrity in the face of opposition in his family, and also refers to the wider African American community's patience to endure tyranny from the prevailing White supremacist Southern American society. Later when he moves to the North, Wright examines the position of African Americans in the wider American society, and subsequently the place of oppressed people in the Western capitalist world order. The two quotations mentioned above may also be read as a metaphor for how Wright sees the conditions of African Americans in the United States, and in Western civilization, after three hundred years of subjection, where the personalities of Black folks are still numb from the shocks of slavery and the regulating limits set on the contour of their lives (Wright, 1941). Dan McCall in reference to the citation also connects Wright's text to the social history of African Americans in the United States, when he states that "(T)he burden of *Black Boy* is to show how the blindness of the communities, black and white came about" (McCall 1969: 121).

As a writer Wright concentrates on the personal, regional, national, and later on in his life and works on the global positions of subjugated people in general. In this sense one could read Wright's life and works as expressive of the African diasporic identity. For my analysis I will only focus on his works in the context of his representation of the personal, regional, and national condition of African American people living in America. The African diasporian scholar Paul Gilroy has already focused on the wider diasporic quality of Wright's life and works (Gilroy, 1993). In the narrative *Black Boy: American Hunger*, Richard Wright recounts his experiences of coming of age in the South under the political policy of Jim Crow laws. Even though the text is based on autobiographical facts one senses that the text also strives to depict a general cultural background of what it means to come of age for an African American male in the racially oppressive conditions of the South. Selwyn R. Cudjoe in his essay on the specific public gesture points to the *Autobiographical Statement* in Maya Angelou's works, which I am postulating can be used to analyze Wright's work, and draws attention to the general meaning of the autobiographical statement for African American cultures. He states that "(…) the Afro-American autobiographical statement emerges as a *public* rather than a *private* gesture, *me-ism* gives way to *our-ism* and superficial concerns about *individual subject* usually give away to the *collective subjection* of the group" (Cudjoe in Evans 1984: 10). In the *The African* review of 1945 one critic called *Black Boy* a pseudo-autobiography, because the text recounts not just Wright's personal experiences, but experiences of thousands of African Americans (Reilly 1978: 158). Another reviewer for the *The Call* in 1945 also points out that *Black Boy* tells the story of millions of 'Negro' children (Reilly 1978: 156). This 'cultural biographical'[7] aspects of Wright's work is one of the reasons why I choose to focus on the text. Other reasons for concentrating on the text are the various aspects of power and displacement that Wright addresses in his text. His depictions of the social conditions for African Americans in the South in the early part of the twentieth century, his experience of migration to the North at a time when the demographics of American society were shifting from the rural to the urban, are all elements which contribute to my interest and the reasons for choosing Wright's text.

One of the first episodes of his childhood that Wright mentions in his autobiographical text is the beating he endures from his mother as a four year old child after he almost burned down his grandparent's home and hid himself under the burning house. The force of his mother's beating left a lasting impression on the young Wright, who indicates his restraint whenever he remembered how close his mother had come to kill him (Wright 1991: 8). The mother's violent reaction caused by her fear for her child's life is a recurring motif in the text. We witness again his mother's violent reaction due to her despair and helplessness after he starts drinking as a young child of six years (Wright 1991: 25). According to Orlando Patterson the violent mode of disciplining children in the African American and Jamaican cultures is a legacy from the slave cultures (Patterson 1998: 136). I will refer to this point again in my analysis of Jamaican cultural texts.

Another significant theme throughout the text is physical hunger and emotional deprivation that the young Wright undergoes. The author first connects his physical hunger with the abandonment of the family by his father. He writes that "(A)s the days slid past the image of my father became associated with my pangs of hunger, and whenever I felt hunger I thought of him with a deep biological bitterness" (Wright 1991: 18). As a young child Wright associated his father's desertion of the family with his hunger. The psychical deprivation that the author endures can be tied to his displaced family structure. The author continues his narrative referring further to the effects of his father's abandonment on the family. He shows how his mother tries to explain the consequences of their father's absences on their lives. He writes that

---

[7] I will use the concept 'cultural biography' to refer to elements of the text that appear to affect not only the author personally but also the wider African American community.

she would call us to her and talk to us for hours, telling us that we now had no father, that our lives would be different from those of other children, that we must learn as soon as possible to take care of ourselves, to dress ourselves, to prepare our own food; that we must take upon ourselves the responsibility of the flat while she worked. Half frightened, we would promise solemnly. We did not understand what had happened between our father and our mother and the most that these long talks did to us was make us feel a vague dread. (Wright 1991: 18)

These two young children are confronted with information and responsibilities more complex than they are able to cope with. The young child is alienated from the normal carefree existence of most children. The lack of supervision caused by circumstances of a single-mother reality allows the young child to roam the street with "a crowd of black children abandoned for the day by their working parents" (Wright 1991: 21). The displaced quality of the child's existence appears to be shared by other African American children whose parents are forced to leave their children unattended in order to earn money to make a living. A quarter of a century later when Wright saw his father again, he reflects on the effects of slavery and sharecropping cultural history on his father's life and on the lives of other African American peasants who have gone to the city to seek a new way of life. He draws attention to how his father's memories were tied to a crude and raw past, and states that his father had not had the chance to learn the meaning of loyalty, of sentiment, or tradition from the White landowner above him (Wright 1991: 40). Here, Wright represents and connects important elements of alienation in the African American family structure with the socio-economic history of African Americans in the United States. Orlando Patterson also ties the sometimes displaced role of the father in certain sections of the African American society to the history of slavery and its aftermath, the neo-slavery of Jim Crow laws (Patterson 1998: XII).

In his book of African American folk history, *12 Million Black Voices* (1941), with text and pictures, Wright mentions the un-preparedness of African American folks for living in the city. He states

we, who had barely managed to live in family groups; we, who needed the ritual and guidance of institutions to hold our atomized lives together in lines of purpose (…) were such a folk as this when we moved into a world that was destined to test all we were (…). (Wright 2002: 93)

Wright's father, the illiterate peasant, was not able to cope with life in the urban landscape and the pressures of raising a family. Robert Stepto points out that Wright's persona rejects all that his father represents and saw his father as one of the first elder kinsmen that were "warnings" instead of "examples" (Stepto in Bloom 1987: 83). The author's mother too was unable to cope with the demands of raising two children alone in the urban surroundings, and was forced to return to her family due to her illness. One could speculate that his mother's illness was caused by the stress of working too long hours and too hard in trying to raise a family on her own. The illness of Wright's mother caused the young child to cease to feel and react as a child (Wright 1991: 100). He writes that her continued suffering

> grew into a symbol in my mind, gathering to itself all the poverty, ignorance, the helplessness; the painful, baffling, hunger-ridden days and hours; the restless moving, the futile seeking, the uncertainty, the fear, the dread; the meaningless pain and the endless suffering. (Wright 1991: 117)

Dan McCall indicates that Wright's mother is the representative figure for the African American community in the novel "(…) embodying its pain and making its quick, crippling gestures toward release" (McCall 1969: 127). Wright's mother tried to overcome her suffering caused by psychical illness just as the African American community tries to overcome the oppressive forces in their lives, caused by the Jim Crow laws of the South, and the unofficial oppressive racial policies of the North. His mother never fully recovered from her illness, and one might draw attention to the fact that even today certain sections of the African American society are still confronted with racism. Here I am referring to the use of negative stereotype images of African American males in American media. (I will demonstrate this when I turn my attention to Spike Lee's film *Bamboozled*.)

Wright's mother reacts forcefully when he questioned her on the subject of race. The young child, Wright, while visiting his grandparents in Jackson became strongly aware of the two races. On his way by train to Arkansas he tries to question his mother about "these two sets of people who lived side by side and never touched, it seemed, expect in violence" (Wright 1991: 54). The mother, unwilling and maybe unable to explain to the young child the complexity of American racial constitution (Wright's own grandmother looks white), slapped the child when asked why she does not wish to explain the situation to him. Here, the mother uses force when confronted with difficult questions. George E. Kent in his essay *Blackness and the Adventure of Western Culture* refers to the suppression of the African American individual in order to protect the group.

> The self is battered by the white racist culture, and, for, the most part, by a survival-oriented black culture, that counters the impulse to rebelliousness and individuality by puritanical repressiveness, escapism, and base submission. That is, black culture suppressed the individual, in order to protect the group from white assault. (Kent in Bloom 1987: 21)

Wright's mother is afraid, because she is aware of the dangers that confront African American lives in the South, so she tries to school her child into not questioning too closely the racial circumstances that govern their lives.

In Arkansas the young child has one of his first close experiences with European Americans using deadly force against African Americans. European Americans desiring the flourishing alcohol business of his aunt's husband Hoskins murdered him (Wright 1991: 63). The young child is naturally shocked at the scope of racial terror. Wright writes:

> There was no funeral. There was no music. There was no period of mourning. There were no flowers. There was only silence, quiet weeping, whispers, and fear (…) this was as close as white terror had ever come to me and my mind reeled. Why had we not fought back, I asked my mother, and the fear that was in her made her slap me into silence. (Wright 1991: 64)

The young child is not yet able to understand why his family does not defend itself against the violence of the European Americans that murdered his uncle. It is a question that we see the young child asking over and over again. Here Wright also connects racial violence with economics: European Americans killed his uncle because they wanted to have his liquor business. A few months later when he saw the chain gang and his mother explains that the authorities are harder on Black people than Whites, again he asks why the majority of Black prisoners do not fight against the few Whites guards. As his mother points out "'(…) the white men have guns and the black men don't'" (Wright 1991: 68). The young child is learning to see the relation of power that governs the lives of African Americans in the South. As Wright quotes from a friend in his essay, *The Ethic of Living Jim Crow*, "'Lawd, man! Ef it wuzn't fer them polices 'n' them ol' lynch-mobs, there wouldn't be nothin' but uproar down here!'" (Emanuel and Gross 1968: 248). The young child has not yet learned the *'Ethics of Living Jim Crow,'* but as we see he will be consorted in the social principles of living in an oppressive society that is controlled by violence.

Wright continues to represent his socialization into the racial power relations that govern the lives of African Americans with diverse stories of racial violence that he heard. He states that nothing challenged his personality as much as the pressure of hate and threat that he felt stemmed from the invisible European Americans. For the young Wright the numerous stories of a White woman slapping Black woman, or a White man killing a Black man were all stories that he would stand for hours listening to (Wright 1991: 85). He renarrates the story of a young Black being beaten by a White man, which he assumed was the boy's father, but his mother explanation that there was no kinship between the White man and the Black boy leaves the young child naturally puzzled and with more questions than his mother is willing to answer (Wright 1991: 28). Then there is the story of the Black woman whose husband was murdered by the White mob: The Black woman carries a white sheet with a gun, then pretends to be humble and pleads for the body of her dead husband; when given permission, she opens fire and kills four Whites before she is killed. Wright writes:

> I did not know if the story was factually true or not, but it was emotionally true because I had already grown to feel that there existed men against whom I was powerless, men who could violate my life at will. I resolved that I would emulate the black woman if I were ever faced with a white mob. (Wright 1991: 86)

This story made a lasting impression on Wright, because he used this narrative again later in one of his early short stories, *Bright and Morning Star.* This is the story of a mother avenging her son's death after an informer in the communist party betrayed him; the story appears in the collection *Uncle Tom's Children.* The young child is already socialized into the violence that affects the African American communities. He feels completely helpless against the threat of force by the White mob that confronts him. He indicates that his fantasies were a moral bastion that enabled him to keep his emotional integrity. He writes "(T)hese fantasies were no longer a reflection of my reaction to the White people, they were a part of my living, of my emotional life; they were a culture, a creed, a religion" (Wright 1991: 87). The sociologist Ron Eyerman in his analysis of trauma in the African American culture points out that trauma is articulated in intellectual discourse. Wright, the author, is able to articulate his experiences of racial violence as well as the African American community's ordeal with racial violence. Selwyn R. Cudjoe comments on the importance of speech for Maya Angelou and the African American community in general. He states that

> (O)ur speech is most directly personal, and every black person assumes that every other black person has a right to a personal opinion. In speaking of great matters, *your personal experience is considered evidence.* With us, distanced statistics are certainly not as important as the actual experience of a sober person. (Cudjoe in Evans 1984: 9)

In writing about the stories of racial force that he experienced and heard of in the South, Wright represents the traumatic effects of racial violence for African Americans living under the legal system of Jim Crow. As Eyerman points out the discourse of trauma 'speaks' for the speechless (Eyerman 2001: 29).

Years later as a teenager, Wright is confronted with the death of a classmate's brother who was killed by the 'White mob' because of his possible sexual relationship with a White prostitute. The effect of the news of his classmate's brother being caught by the 'white death' caused the author temporary paralysis of will and impulse for the day. Before he was on his way to town to search for a job, but after hearing what had happened to the brother of his classmate, he sits on his grandmother's porch and contemplates his place in the society in which he lives. As he reflects on "the white brutality", he draws attention to how such incidents control his behaviour, and the behaviour of other African Americans living in the South. He writes:

> (T)he penalty of death awaited me if I made a false move and I wondered if it was worth-while to make a move at all (…) The actual experience would have let me see the realistic outlines of what was really happening, but as long as it remained some-thing terrible and yet remote, something whose horror and blood might descend upon me at any moment, I was compelled to give my entire imagination over to it, an act which blocked the springs of thought and feeling in me, creating a sense of distance between me and the world in which I lived. (Wright 1991: 202)

The violence that is committed against his classmate's brother caused an ele-ment of alienation between the author and the society he is forced to live in. Farah Jasmine Griffin in her work on migration in African American narratives indicates that lynching was used in maintaining social order in the South. She writes that "(I)nitially the sign of lynching was used by the dominant White culture of the South to evoke fear in the hearts of African Americans in so doing maintain the social order" (Griffin 1995: 47). The effective use of force by certain sections of the White Southern society in controlling the African American com-munity is very well represented here. Wright will demonstrate his false move when he is offered a ride and a drink by some young European American men.

> The words were barely out of my mouth before I felt something hard and cold smash me between the eyes (…) I saw stars, and fell back-wards from the speeding car into the dust of the road (…) "Nigger, ain't you learned no better sense'n that yet?" asked the man who hit me. "Ain't you learned to say *sir* to a white man yet?" (Wright 1991: 214)

Wright in forgetting to call the young European American men *sir*, as was demanded of every African American in the South regardless of age, was con-fronted with brute force. As the young White man said

> "Nigger, you sure ought to be glad it was us you talked to that way. You're a lucky bastard, 'cause if you'd said that to some other white man, you might've been a dead nigger now." (Wright 1991: 214)

Here Wright represents the whimsical reasons given for the use of force by the European American Southern society against the African American community.

When one examines Patterson's arguments concerning power it is clear that these young White men are in a position to demand respect through the use of violence and their dominant position in the society. They are able to "transform force into right, and obedience into duty" (Patterson 1982: 1). Wright exemplifies the vague reasons used in displacing the African American community by the European American society in the South. He refers to his inability to accept the brutality of what he sees going on around him everyday. He could not play the role of the 'smiling nigger'. One day one of his bosses asked why he did not laugh and talk like other 'niggers'? After he explains to his boss that there was not much to laugh and talk about, he was tossed a few dollar bills and told "'I don't like your looks, nigger. Now, get!'" (Wright 1991: 215). Working in another store he drops a bottle of syrup and his boss tells him that he is going to deduct it from his pay. Wright explains that he said yes, it was his fault, this just whipped his boss into a frenzy, when Saturday night came his boss gave him his money and told him "'Don't come back. You won't do'" (Wright 1991: 231). Wright does not play the role of the 'laughing nigger' or the 'foolish nigger' so he is not welcomed in Southern society. The obscure reasons that Wright represents for his mistreatment by the society could be connected to the vague reasons that Douglass exemplifies in his *Narrative* (see above analysis) for the slave master's use of force against his slaves.

Wright also draws attention to the difference in the way White and Black Americans live in the South. He points to the two meals a day that his family is able to afford, he eats 'mash' at eight in the morning and greens at seven at night (Wright 1991: 148). In the White family home that he goes to work in the dining table for breakfast contains eggs, bacon, toast, jam, butter, milk, and apples (Wright 1991: 175). The difference in the abundance of food that Wright represents can be compared with Douglass' exemplification of Colonel Lloyd's family table and the 'mash' that the slave children get everyday. Wright also tells of the thick plate of molasses with green and white bits floating on the surface with a hard hunk of bread that he received from one White family, while the family had eggs, bacon, and coffee (Wright 1991: 172). Further I collate the White family breakfast with Frantz Fanon's concept of the Manichean division of the colonized world. "The settler's town is a well-fed town, (...) its belly is always full of good things" (Fanon 1962: 39). The European American families are well fed with good things, while Wright and his family are almost starving.

Wright also writes of his experiences of going to work with his mother and having to stand by and watch her serving hot dishes of food to White Americans while he and his brother are waiting in the kitchen. He and his brother were only able to eat well if there was something left over from the European Americans, otherwise they would eat bread and drink tea. He writes:

(W)atching the white people eat would make my stomach churn and I would grow vaguely angry. Why did I always have to wait until others were through? I could not understand why some people had enough food and others did not. (Wright 1991: 22)

The young child cannot understand the inequality of the society around him. He also comments on the difference in the quality of housing that he and his family and other African Americans were forced to live in.

The neighbourhood swarmed with rats, cats, dogs, fortune-tellers, cripples, blind men, whores, sales, rent collectors, and children. In front of our flat was a huge roundhouse where locomotives were cleaned and repaired. There was an eternal hissing of stem, the grunting of steel engines, and the tolling of bells. Smoke obscured the vision and cinders drifted into the house, into our beds, into our kitchen, into our food; and a tar like smell was always in the air. (Wright 1991: 69).

Wright is impressed with the quietness of the White world. He writes:

(...) marvelling at the cleanliness, the quietness of the white world. How orderly everything was! Yet I felt out of place. I had no desire to live here. Then I remembered that these houses were the homes in which lived those white people who made Negroes leave their homes and flee in the night. I grew tense. (Wright 1991: 81)

The young child is impressed by the quietness of his surrounding, but he is also alienated and aware that European Americans who brutalize African Americans also live in these quiet surroundings. When one examines the surroundings in which African Americans live there is a close parallel to Fanon's description of the colonized world. He writes that

(T)he town belonging to the colonized people, or at least the native town, the Negro village, the medina, the reservation, is a place of ill fame, peopled by men of evil repute. They are born there, it matters little where or how; they die there, it matters not where, nor how. It is a world without spaciousness; men live there on top of each other (...). (Fanon 1962: 39)

In his famous novel *Native Son*, Wright demonstrates the negative effects of the unofficial racial segregation on social, political, economical and historical policies for the African American protagonist Bigger Thomas.

Another aspect which Wright describes in his *Black Boy*, is how European Americans contribute to the mistrust and violence among African Americans. He relates the incident of how White bosses sometimes lie to young Black boys, telling them stories about each other in the hope of getting them to fight against each other. Wright's boss Mr. Olin told him that another young Black man,

Harrison wanted to stab him because he insulted him. When Wright confronted
Harrison, Harrison claims that the same man, Mr. Olin told him the same story.

> "Shucks, I thought *you* was looking for me to cut me," Harrison explains. "Mr. Olin,
> he came over here this morning and said you was going to kill me with a knife the
> moment you saw me. He said you was mad at me because I had insulted you. But I
> ain't said nothing about you." (Wright 1991: 279)

The European American boss wanting to see these two poor Black boys fighting
against each other and tries to poison their minds against each other. Mr. Olin
later asks Wright whether he has a knife and when told "no", he offers to lend
him his. When he refuses his boss states, "'Nigger, you're a fool,' he spluttered.
'I thought you had some sense! Are you going to just let that nigger cut your
heart out? His boss gave *him* a knife to use against *you*! Take this knife, nigger,
and stop acting crazy!'" (Wright 1991: 281). Even though Harrison and Wright
wish to trust each other, they are insecure about each other. Wright writes:

> (W)e were toying with the idea of death for no reason that stemmed from our own
> lives, but because the men who ruled us had thrust the idea into our minds. Each of
> us depended upon the whites for the bread we ate, and we actually trusted the
> whites more than we did each other. Yet there existed in us a longing to trust men of
> our own color. (Wright 1991: 282)

Even though they doubt each other Harrison and Wright did not use their
knives to kill each other. When the European American bosses realized that
these two African American youths were not going to use their knives on each
other, they offer them five dollars each to box in a ring. Wright points out that
he did not want to, but Harrison stressed that five dollars was almost a week's
wage. After being begged to fight by the White men from both firms the Black
youths decided to fight each other in a boxing ring. Even though, they promised to fool the Whites and not really fight each in the ring, the two African
American youths were not knowledgeable enough about boxing to accomplish
this. In the end they brutalized each other.

> I lashed out with a timid left. Harrison landed high on my head and, before I knew it,
> I had landed a hard right on Harrison's mouth and blood came. Harrison shot a blow
> to my nose. The fight was on (…) I felt trapped and ashamed (…) We fought four
> hard rounds, stabbing, slugging, grunting, spitting, cursing, crying, bleeding. The
> shame and anger we felt for having allowed ourselves to be duped crept into our
> blows and blood ran into our eyes half blinding us. (Wright 1991: 286)

These two African American youths are powerless against their European American aggressors, so they take their anger out at each other. One could use Fanon's specific argument on colonized subjects to analyze the incident of force that Wright exemplifies here. Being aware that African American society is not a colony, but there are certain features of African American society (see above) in relation to the wider American Society that encourages the comparison with the colonized world order. Fanon points out that colonized people who are unable to take out their anger on the oppressors will use violence against each other instead. Even though Wright and Harrison are aware that the European Americans are only using them as objects for their own sport, they don't think that they have much to lose. When Wright indicates that he does not want to fight for White men, because he is not a dog or rooster, Harrison only replies that he needs the money. Then he calls attention to the fact that European American men will look at them and laugh, Harrison points out that "'They look at you and laugh at you every day nigger'" (Wright 1991: 284). Wright tells of his uneasy feeling he had when heard of similar fights being staged between other Black boys. "I felt that I had done something unclean, something for which I could never properly atone" (Wright 1991: 287). Griffin states that according to Michael Foucault, "Nothing is more material, physical, corporal, than the exercise of power" (Griffin 1995: 16). These two African American boys, even though they are aware that the European American men just want to see them hurt each other, are still caught in the economic bind of needing the money, so they are willing to physically violate each other and themselves.

Wright further exemplifies in the character of Shorty the willingness of individual African Americans to let themselves be debased by European Americans for monetary gain. Even though he indicates that Shorty was proud of his "race," and "indignant about it wrongs," Shorty let a European American man kick him in the ass for a quarter. When Wright questions him as to how he could do that, Shorty replies that "'I needed a quarter and I got it,' he said soberly, and proudly. 'But a quarter can't pay you for what he did to you,' I said. 'Listen, nigger,' he said to me, 'my ass is tough and quarters is scarce'" (Wright 1991: 269). Wright represents here how economic dependence of Black Americans on White Americans in the South helped to contribute to the self-displacement of many African Americans.

At the age of nineteen Wright moved to Chicago with his aunt Maggie to prepare a place for his brother and mother who would join them later. He doubted if he should have gone there, but as he writes, "I had fled a known terror, and perhaps I could cope with this unknown terror that lay ahead" (Wright 1991: 308). In Chicago he worked in different jobs as porter, dishwasher, post office clerk, insurance salesman and as an orderly in a hospital.

Wright draws attention to the fact that even though there was no sign on the wall there were still racial lines drawn. He refers to the underworld position occupied by the four African American men working in the Chicago Research Institute, cleaning the operating rooms and feeding the animals. When they were not working at their task they were restricted to the basement. He also indicates the sharp line of racial division drawn by the hospital in the two lines of White nurses and Black cleaning women.

> A line of white girls marched past, clad in starched uniforms that gleamed white; their faces were alert, their steps quick, their bodies lean and shapely, their shoulders erect, their faces lit with light and purpose. And after them came a line of black girls, old, fat, dressed in ragged gingham, walking loosely, carrying tin cans of soap power, rags, mops, brooms (…) I wonder what law of the universe keep them from being mixed? The sun would not have stop shining had there been a few black girls in the first line, and the earth would not have stopped whirling on its axis had there been a few white girls in the second line. But the two lines graded status in purely racial terms. (Wright 1991: 356)

In the North Wright is again confronted with the racial division that governs American society; here it is in-official, but nevertheless there. Both Douglass and Wright went to the North to seek freedom, while one might argue that the Northern society was not as repressive as the South, they both came to the conclusion that the North was racist as well, and took its toll on the African American lives.

Here in the city Wright contemplates the effects of racial oppression on the psyche of African Americans. He deliberates on the psychic pain of African American existence in America caused by limitation of possibilities that come from living in an oppressive and racial society.

> Slowly I began to forge in the depths of my mind a mechanism that repressed all the dreams and desires that the Chicago streets, the newspapers, the movies were evoking in me. I was going through a second childhood; a new sense of the limit of the possible was being born in me. What could I dream of that had the barest possibility of coming through? I could think of nothing. And, slowly, it was upon exactly that nothingness that my mind began to dwell, that constant sense of wanting without having, of being hated without reason. A dim notion of what life meant to a Negro in America was coming to consciousness in me, not in term of external events, lynching, Jim Crowism, and the endless brutalities, but in terms of crossed-up feelings, of psyche pain. I sensed that Negro life was a sprawling land of unconscious suffering, and there were but few Negroes who knew the meaning of their lives, who could tell their story. (Wright 1991: 314)

Wright represents the alienation that confronts him and other African Americans in the urban landscape. The threat of physical violence is removed, but the displaced quality of life set by the limited possibilities for the people of African descent remains, even in the North. The author exemplifies the cultural trauma that most African Americans face in the realization that there was really no 'safe space' in the American society where African Americans have the chance to develop to their full human potential. The traumatic effect of knowing that one will always be judged first by one's color and not by one's human capability leaves African Americans in a displaced position, living in a society but not fully part of the society. Wright states in the introduction to *Black Metropolis*, a scientific study of African American life in the urban landscape, how science helps him to discover some of the meanings of the environment that battered and taunted him. The influence of the Chicago School of science on Wright's writing is clear. Wright himself states that

> (I)t was from the scientific findings of men like the late Robert E. Park, Robert Redfield, and Louis Wirth that I drew the meanings for my documentary book, *12,000,000 Black Voices*; for my novel, *Native Son*; it was from their scientific facts that I absorbed some of that quota of inspiration necessary for me to write *Uncle Tom's Children* and *Black Boy*. (Wright in Clayton and Drake 1945: xvii)

With the aid of scientific facts Wright tries to represent the effects of American racial policies on African American lives in the United States in the early twentieth century.

> Color hate defined the place of black life as below that of white life; and the black man, responding to the same dreams as the white man, stove to bury within his heart his awareness of this difference because it made him lonely and afraid. Hated by whites and being an organic part of the culture that hated him, the black man grew in turn to hate in himself that which others hated in him. (Wright 1991: 312)

Richard Wright tries to represent in his fiction and non-fiction how the oppressive racial condition of American society influences the African Americans' personality, their culture, and their entire lives. The economic and social dislocation inflicted on African American communities contributes to the themes of violence and alienation as exemplified in the cultural text *Black Boy*. In my analysis of Jamaican cultural texts I will point to the similar theme of race and its contribution to self-hate that is represented in the novel *The Children of Sisyphus*.

Summary

Wright represents in his text the force used against him by his mother. The violent mode of disciplining children in African American and Jamaican cultures is
a legacy of the slavery that both societies underwent. The subject of race
contributes to the violence used by Wright's mother when the child questions
too closely the complexity of the American racial constitution. The physical and
emotional alienations suffered by Wright as a child can be tied to the displaced
role of his father; a role conditioned by the legacy of slavery and the socio-
economic history of African Americans in the United States. Violence is used by
European Americans in the text for economic gains as well as maintaining the
Jim Crow social order in the South. As with the slave system European
Americans use violence against African Americans to control and force them to
accept the political order of the dominant European American society. Wright is
emotionally alienated from the society he is forced to live in due to racial
violence and oppressive racial conditions. Diverse stories of racial violence that
Wright heard as a child lead to a trauma for Wright who articulates the
traumatic effects of racial violence for African Americas living under the legal
system of Jim Crow in his novel.

   The Manichean division of the South with its inequalities in living standards
is also a contributing factor for the physical and emotional alienations that
Wright and other African Americans undergo. The oppressive racial conditions
in the North lead to emotional alienations for Wright and other African
Americans who are forced to live with the limitation of possibilities placed on
their lives by a racial oppressive society.

4.3. Toni Morrison's *Song of Solomon*

The African American author Toni Morrison was born Chloe Anthony Wofford on February 18, 1931, in Lorain, Ohio, a multiracial steel town. At the age of eighteen she attended Howard University, and in 1953 she graduated with a BA in English and a minor in Classics. After leaving Howard Morrison studied at Cornell University for two years where she graduated in 1955 with a MA in English.[8] Morrison then went back to Howard University to teach for several years and later worked as an editor for Random House Publishing; she published her first novel *The Bluest Eye* in 1970. To date Toni Morrison has published nine novels, three non-fictional works and edited a number of texts. Considered one of the most successful American authors, Toni Morrison has won a number of literary awards including the Nobel Prize in 1993; she is also a prominent professor holding the Robert F. Goheen chair for humanities at Princeton University.

In my analysis of *Alienation and Violence in African Diaspora Cultural Texts* I have chosen to examine Toni Morrison's third novel *Song of Solomon* (1977). The novel was the first by an African American to appear in the Book-of-the-Month Club selection since Richard Wright's *Native Son* in 1940. The novel stayed on the bestseller list for four months and sold 570,000 copies in the first year (Furman 1996). Over the years the novel has been read from multiple perspectives. Jill Matus points out that *Song of Solomon* is a novel about fathers and lost fathers and the history and future of African American men (Matus 1998: 72). Barbara Christian refers to the myth of the flying African, a myth she claims that is found wherever Africans were enslaved (Christian 1985: 60). Farah Jasmine Griffin places the novel in the tradition of the urban male narrative (Griffin 1995: 171). In my analysis of *Song of Solomon* I will focus on a scope themes of alienation and violence that Morrison represents in her novel.

The novel is structured into two parts and contains fifteen chapters. The novel tells the story of the Dead family history with the main focus on Macon Dead III, also named Milkman, from childhood to adulthood and his quest for gold. Milkman is a spoiled middle-class African American young man with a lack of focus in his life. He finally finds his center when instead of gold he discovers his true family history in his journey from home in Michigan to Pennsylvania and eventually to Virginia. The tale is told in a non-linear fashion, with flashbacks and multiple perspectives from different characters. It is not only the story of the Dead family that is told, but also the stories of these various characters with whom Milkman interacts. The novel covers over eighty

---

[8] See Jill Matus' *Toni Morrison* for a more detailed biography of the author.

years of the Dead family history, but it also makes reference to significant violent dates in the African American history in the United States.

The opening scene of the novel takes place on February 18, 1931, the author's own birthday; moreover 1931 was the same year that nine young African American men were arrested and convicted of the alleged rape of a White woman of uncertain reputation (Bennett 1982: 364) in Scottsboro, Alabama. The Scottsboro case lead to public outcries in America and internationally. The dates Morrison mentions throughout her text are significant in calling attention to different elements of racism against African Americans in the United States. The Dead's story starts with Macon Dead I Jake who went to register at the Freemen Bureau in 1869. Then in 1896 the only colored doctor (Milkman's grandfather) moved to Main Avenue, which became known to African Americans as Doctor Street (Morrison 1977: 4), it is the year of the US Supreme Court ruling in the case of *Plessy vs. Ferguson*, which lead to official segregation and Jim Crow laws in the South. The text further draws attention to the year 1918 as the year that Doctor Street acquired a quasi-official status (Morrison 1977: 4). It was also the year that approximately 300,000 African Americans were drafted into the armed forces. Also in 1918 one of the most barbaric lynchings took place in Valdosta, Georgia, the pregnant Black woman Mary Turner was hanged to a tree then gasoline and motor oil was poured on her. She was burned then her stomach was cut open with a pocket knife. The premature baby was crushed by the heel of a stalwart man (Bennett 1981: 352). In 1916 the same year that Macon Dead II, a colored man of property (Morrison 1977: 23), approaches Doctor Foster to ask to marry Ruth was the same year that Marcus Garvey founded *The Universal Negro Improvement Association*, the first mass movement of African diasporians in the so-called New World. Macon Dead II married Ruth Foster in 1917, the year America entered World War I, it was also a year marked by extended racial violence in the United States: Ten thousand African Americans marched down Fifth Avenue, New York City in a silent parade protesting lynching and racial indignities. In Houston a race riot took place between the Twenty-fourth Infantry Regiment made up of Black soldiers and White citizens. In 1919, the year that Corinthians Dead was born, America witnessed the lynching of over seventy-six African Americans and twenty-six race riots in what is sometimes referred to as the Red Summer of 1919. In the year 1920 the formation of the Seven Days was triggered by the castration of a soldier from Georgia and a veteran being blinded after he returned from France (Morrison 1977: 155). In 1942, the year Pilate's daughter Reba won her diamond ring for being the five hundred thousandth customer in Sears, but was denied the publicity because of her African American heritage (Morrison 1977: 43), is the same year that CORE *The Congress of Racial Equality* was founded. The year 1955 when Milkman hit his father after his father hit his mother is also the same year that Emmett Till was lynched in Alabama; his murder lead to riots in many urban centers. In 1963 the bombing of four little Black girls in a church in Alabama became one of the reasons why the character Guitar needs the gold to revenge their death. The year 1963 also represents one hundred years of Emancipation, and is also the year of the Civil Rights March in Washington.

In her representation of Macon Dead I who was shot dead by greedy Whites that wanted his prosperous farm, Morrison focuses on one of the major motifs for racial violence against African Americans in the United States after Emancipation. Macon Dead I, a former slave with nothing but free papers managed to build a successful farm.

> He had come out of nowhere, as ignorant as a hammer and broke as a convict, with nothing but free papers, a Bible, and a pretty black-haired wife, and in one year he'd leased ten acres, the next ten more. Sixteen years later he had one of the best farms in Montour County. (Morrison 1977: 235)

Macon Dead I, an 'ignorant' former slave without any education or formal qualification, managed to accomplish economic success and independence, but he or his children were not allowed to enjoy the fruits of his hard labour. Macon Dead I was killed because he had accomplished what was thought to be impossible for the former slaves, carving out of wild woods one of the best farms in Montour County. An accomplishment that sparks inspiration to African Americans and

> (…) colored their lives like paintbrush and spoke to them like a sermon. "You see?" the farm said to them. "See? See what you can do? Never mind you can't tell one letter from other, never mind you born a slave, never mind you lose your name, never mind your daddy dead, never mind nothing. Here, this here, is what a man can do if he puts his mind and his back in it (…)." (Morrison 1977: 235)

Even though Macon Dead I Jake is denied his true name by a drunken Union soldier who confused his point of departure and his father's condition with his name, he managed against all odds to carve out of the woods a prosperous farm. "'They had a fine place. Mighty fine. Some white folks own it now. Course that's what they wanted. That's why they shot him. Upset a lot of people here, a whole lot of people. Scared 'em too'" (Morrison 1977: 230). The diverse usage of force by European Americans for economic gain as well as control over the African American communities is represented here. Griffin points out that Morrison is taking the lead of Ida B. Wells in connecting lynching with economic threat instead of sexual threat. She writes, "(I)n stressing the link between black economic self-sufficiency and lynching, Morrison is following

Ida B. Wells, who at the turn of the century argued that lynching was 'an excuse to get rid of Negroes who were acquiring wealth and property'" (Griffin 1995: 42). Richard Wright also connects racial violence against African Americans with economic self-sufficiency in his representation of his uncle being murdered because Whites wanted to own his thriving liquor store. The effect of Macon Dead I's death on the African American community in Denville, Montour County is traumatic. The narrator tells us that "(…) even as boys these men began to die and were dying still. Looking at Milkman in those nighttime talks, they yearned for something. Some word from him that would rekindle the dream and stop the death they were dying" (Morrison 1977: 235). According to Margaret I. Jordan, Macon Dead I or Jake's death left his community with another example at how a Black man can make every effort to have a certain kind of life, and in the end have it all taken away by avaricious White people (Jordan 2004: 219). The violent death of Macon I not only traumatized his community but also his children. Macon II reflects on the effect of seeing his father shot to death.

> The numbness that has settled on him when he saw the man he loved and admired fall off the fence; something wild ran through him when he watched the body twitching in the dirt. His father had sat for five nights on a split-rail cradling a shotgun and in the end died protecting his property. (Morrison 1977: 50)

His two children Macon Dead II and his sister Pilate Dead witnessed their father's murder and fearing for their own lives, were forced to leave Denville, Pennsylvania after hiding and living in the wilderness for a few weeks. The siblings separated after Macon II wounded a White man they found in a cave used by hunters; they also found gold in the cave which Macon II wanted to take along, but his sister refused, which lead to a fight and separation. The two young children forced to survive on their own after their father's death are displaced and traumatized by the effect of their father's brutal murder.

Pilate is a young woman who was born without a navel lacked the guidance of a community that knows "her people". She travels the country from one end to the other in the hope of finding her "people". Pilate is an outsider because of her lack of a navel. Pilate's lack of a navel is her "missing link" to "her people". After finding and travelling with pickers Pilate is asked to leave and abandoned after it is known that she does not possess a navel.

> It isolated her. Already without family, she was further isolated from her people, for, except for the relative bliss on the island, every other resource was denied her: partnership in marriage, confessional friendship, and communal religion. Men frowned, women whispered and shoved their children behind them. Even a travelling side show would have rejected her, since her freak quality lacked that important

ingredient – the grotesque. There was really nothing to see. Her defect, frightening and exotic as it was, was also a theatrical failure. It needed intimacy, gossip, and the time it took for curiosity to become drama. (Morrison 1977: 148)

After her realization that other people could not accept her difference Pilate is compelled to "throw away every assumption she had learned and began at zero" (Morrison 1977: 149). Pilate is able to accept her outside status by searching for new ways to live her life. She is not afraid of the dead, because she is used to have conversation with her dead father.

That plus her alien's compassion for troubled people ripened her and – the consequence of the knowledge she had made up or acquired – kept her just barely within the boundaries of the elaborately socialized world of black people. Her dress might be outrageous to them, but her respect for other people's privacy – which they were all very intense about – was balancing. She stared at people, and in those days looking straight into another person's eyes was considered among black people the height of rudeness, an act acceptable only with and among children and certain kinds of outlaws – but she never made an impolite observation. And true to the palm oil that flowed in her veins, she never had a visitor to whom she did not offer food before one word of conversation – business or social – began. (Morrison 1977: 149)

Valerie Smith points to Pilate's abilities to affirm spiritual values, she writes "Pilate's sheer disregard for status, occupation, hygiene, and manners is accompanied by an ability to affirm spiritual values such as compassion, respect, loyalty, and generosity" (Smith 1995: 12). Even though Pilate is displaced from the African American community she is able to make and find her own space in that community. Jan Furman states that

Pilate, of course, is one of Morrison's ancestors, one of the timeless people who dispatch their wisdom to others, who consciously or unconsciously initiate others to the ways of African American culture that give life continuity and intent. (Furman 1996: 45)

Due to her curious physiognomical defect Pilate is accepted in the African American community as a "certain kind of outlaw". Some people believe that she had "(…) the power to step out of her skin, set a bush afire from fifty yards, and turn a man into a ripe rutabaga – all on account of the fact that she had no navel" (Morrison 1977: 96). Even though Pilate is alienated from certain human relationships she is able to gain respect due to her capacity for self-creation (Smith 1987 and Furman 1996). Pilate according to Barbara Christian represents the tradition that identifies with nature, and she has no wish for material wealth. She writes, "Pilate is presented in the novel as the healer of spirit, the guide to essences beyond outward appearance or material things" (Christian

1985: 55). Even though Pilate is able to guide her nephew Milkman beyond material things, she is not as successful in guiding her granddaughter Hagar away from the danger of commercial beauty standards of the main stream American culture.

Milkman, after having a love affair with his older cousin Hagar for over fourteen years, rejects her callously with a "thank you" note one Christmas after she began to make demands on him. Hagar, Pilate's granddaughter believes that Milkman rejects her because she does not have limey skin color and silky hair.

> The "thank you" cut her to the quick, but it was not the reason she ran scurrying into cupboards looking for weapons. That had been accomplished by the sight of Milkman's arms around the shoulders of a girl whose silky copper-colored hair cascaded over the sleeves of his coat (…) when she turned, laughing, towards Milkman, and Hagar saw her grey eyes, the fist that had been just sitting in her chest since Christmas released its forefinger like the blade of a skinning knife. (Morrison 1977: 127)

Hagar believes in the dominant American cultural images of beauty, she is not as strong as her grandmother or simple like her mother to cope with the demand of the world she lives in.

> Neither Pilate nor Reba knew that Hagar was not like them. Not strong enough, like Pilate, nor simple enough, like Reba, to make up her life as they had. She needed what most colored girls needed: a chorus of mamas, grandmamas, aunts, cousins, sisters, neighbors, Sunday school teachers, best girl friends, and what all to give her the strength life demand of her – and the humor with which to live it. (Morrison 1977: 307)

Even though Hagar is spoiled and given everything that she wishes for from Pilate and Reba it is not enough, the extend chorus of family is not there. Morrison draws attention in her essay, *Rootedness: The Ancestor as Foundation,* that Hagar's problems stem from her distance to her ancestors. She writes, "(T)he difficulty of Hagar (youngest of the trio of women in that household) has to do with how far removed she is from the experience of the ancestor" (Morrison in Evans 1984: 344). Pilate due to her own special displacement from her brother and the African American community cannot offer her granddaughter the relationships that she needs to survive. In the end Hagar goes shopping in the hope of making herself acceptable to Milkman.

> The cosmetics department enfolded her in perfume, and she read hungrily the labels and the promise. Myrurgia for primeval woman who creates for him a world of

tender privacy where the only occupant is you mixed with Nina Ricci's L'Air du Temps. Yardley's Flair with Tuvache's Nectaroma and D'Orsay's Intoxication. (Morrison 1977: 311)

Hagar attempts to remake herself cosmetically is ruined and washed away in the pouring rain after she leaves the department store. Hagar believes in the dominant American standard of beauty, because of her skin color, she cannot accomplish this standard, so in the end she fails to see her own beauty.

> She lay in her little Goldilocks-choice bed, her eyes sand dry and as quiet as glass. Pilate and Reba, seated beside the bed, bent over her like two divi-divi trees beaten forward by a wind always blowing from the same direction. Like the trees, they offered her all they had: love murmurs and protective shade. "Mama." Hagar floated up into an even higher fever. "Hmmm." "Why don't he like my hair?" "Who, baby? Who don't like your hair?" "Milkman." "Milkman does too like your hair," said Reba. "No. He doesn't. But I can't figure out why. Why he never liked my hair." (Morrison 1977: 314)

Orlando Patterson points out in his comparative study of slavery that one of the major characteristics used to distinguish slave and non-slave population in the United States was hair texture. He writes:

> (V)ariations in hair were another matter. Difference between whites and blacks were sharper in this quality than in color and persisted for much longer with miscegenation. Hair type rapidly became the real symbolic badge of slavery, although like many powerful symbols it was disguised, in this case by the linguistic device of using the term "black," which normally threw the emphasis to color. No one who has grown up in a multiracial society, however, is unaware of the fact that hair difference is what carries the real symbolic potency. (Patterson 1982: 61)

Even though Hagar is not living in a slave culture she is still affected by oppressive symbols of the slave culture. Hagar is traumatized by her inability to fulfil the dominant White standard image of beauty, which is silky long hair. Jill Matus draws attention to the concept of 'insidious trauma' articulated by feminist psychologists and therapists, she defines the concept as "traumatogenic effects of oppression that are not necessarily overtly violent or threatening to bodily well-being at the given moment but that do violence to the soul and spirit" (Matus 1998: 28). Hagar's inability to save her own life after Milkman rejects her shows the 'traumatogenic effect' of the image of long silky hair texture and "lemon-colored skin, gray-blue eyes, and thin nose" as major symbols of beauty in America; these images affect Hagar's soul and spirit violently. She is traumatized by her inability to fulfil these beauty requirements. Jan Furman in his essay *Male Consciousness in Song of Solomon* writes that

"(M)orrison's work is a warning shot for those who would be victim to a false standard of beauty like Hagar and Pauline Breedlove before her" (Furman 1996: 44). Both characters Pauline Breedlove (from *The Bluest Eye*) and Hagar are strongly influenced by Eurocentric expressions of beauty. They are alienated from themselves, because they too readily accept the dominant White American standard of beauty and thereby reject their own beauty. Denis Heinze points out that Milkman's boredom with Hagar is a function of his own desire for growth, which is not shared by Hagar who has divorced herself from her African American heritage (Heinze 1993: 32).

Corinthians, the middle-class, middle-aged daughter of Macon Dead II is another displaced woman that Morrison confronts us with in her novel. Corinthians was

> (U)nfit for any work other than the making of red velvet roses, she had a hard time finding employment befitting her degree. The three years that she spent in college, a junior year in France, and being the granddaughter of the eminent Dr. Foster should have culminated in something more elegant than the two uniforms that hung on Miss Graham's basement door. (Morrison 1977: 187–8)

Margaret I. Jordan states that Corinthians' elite class status protected her from the full impact of Jim Crow laws. She writes:

> Corinthians belongs to a class of elite black people in a position to often avoid the full impact, "the insult, the substandard treatment, and the poor facilities that the Jim Crow laws had left for blacks" by virtue of their wealth and social isolation. (Jordan 2004: 214)

Even if Corinthians is from a very prosperous middle-class background and is well educated, she is only able to find work as a maid. Corinthians, who woke one day at the age of forty-two a maker of rose petal, suffered from severe depression, she decided to get out of her house and find a job. "High toned and yellow, she believed what her mother was also convinced of: that she was prized for a professional man of color" (Morrison 1977: 188). Even though she was pretty, pleasant, and her father had enough money, she was too comfortable in her middle-class status for most professional Black men. Corinthians believes in her own social position.

> She avoided the other maids on the street, and those whom she saw regularly on the bus assumed that she had some higher household position than theirs since she came to work in high-heeled shoes and only a woman who didn't have to be on her feet all day could stand the pressure of heels on the long ride home. (Morrison 1977: 190)

Corinthians denies herself the company and comfort of the other working class African American women because she believes that her middle-class social status qualifies her as better than the other Black maids on the bus. "In *Song of Solomon*, servitude is one factor that divides classes in the Black community. But servitude is also, ultimately, the great equalizer" (Jordan 2004: 212). Due to racism against African Americans, Corinthians' middle-class status does not protect her from the reality, that for most Black women in the early 1960s the only available work was domestic work. Corinthians may be able to enjoy the benefits of her class status only in a limited space. When Porter, a man that does garden work, courts her and they start having a relationship, Corinthians is ashamed to be seen with him fearing her father's reaction. When Porter points out to her that he does not want a doll baby, but a woman that is not afraid of her father, Corinthians demonstrates her prejudice against poor working class African American women.

> "You mean like those women on the bus? You can have one of *them*, you know. Why don't you drop a greeting card in one of *their* laps?" His word hit home; she had been compared – unfavourably, she believed – with the only people she knew for certain she was superior to. "They'd love to have a greeting card dropped in their lap. Just love it. But oh, I forgot. You couldn't do that, could you, because they wouldn't be able to read it. They'd have to take it home and wait till Sunday and give it to the preacher to read it to them. Of course when they heard it they might not know what is meant. But it wouldn't matter – they'd see the flowers and the curlicues all over the words and they'd be happy." (Morrison 1977: 196)

Corinthians feels superior to the other Black women on the bus, because she can read, and they might not be able to. Joyce Irene Middleton in her essay, *From Orality to Literacy: Oral Memory in Toni Morrison's Song of Solomon*, draws attention to how much Corinthians' background in schooling and her highly literate training contribute to her belief in her superior self-image (Middleton in Smith 1995: 30). Instead of finding companionship with other working women Corinthians isolates herself, because of her conviction that she who can read, granddaughter of the eminent Dr. Foster, and daughter of the prosperous businessman Macon Dead II, is better than other Blacks. To her it does not matter that with all her class accomplishment she is still only able to work as a maid. According to Middleton Corinthians fictionalizes other Black women, she writes:

> She fictionalises them (…) and uses clichés and stereotyped images (…) in order to invent the arguments that support her views of superiority. It is from this hierarchical and distanced position that she too easily critiques their inabilities. (Middleton in Smith 1995: 319)

Corinthians and her family have been assimilating into the European American values, even as a child. When on their weekly drive in their 'hearse', the name given to the Packard car by other African Americans, it is Corinthians who wants to know if her father would rent a beach house in the future to a barmaid even if she owns her own bar. She is from the beginning very conscious of her social position.

> "You really think there'll be enough colored people – I mean nice colored people – in this city to live there?" "They don't have to be from the city, Corinthians. People will drive to a summer house. White people do it all the time." (…) "Negroes don't like water." Corinthians giggled. (Morrison 1977: 35)

Corinthians accepts the European American stereotype and cliché images of African Americans. According to *The Original African Heritage Study Bible* the importance of I Corinthians is the attention the text calls to the split between congregations calling themselves Christians. In II Corinthians the apostle Paul addresses the internal problem of the church and defends himself and his ministry. By naming Macon Dead II's daughter Corinthians with 's' Morrison might be referring to the class 'split' in the African American community that Corinthians voices and represents; she is middle-class, but also a servant; plus Corinthians' passionate defence of herself when Porter points out to her that he would like a woman, not a doll-baby that is afraid of her father. These are elements which connects Morrison's representation with the biblical figure of Job.

Macon Dead III called Milkman is one of the main characters in the novel. He is a young man who abandons Hagar after fourteen years of relationship; he is over thirty years old and still living at home and working for his father. Milkman is a selfish young man who is interested only in his own pleasure. When the young Emmett Till is killed, and everyone who is listening to the radio becomes upset, Milkman only thinks of his own family problems, he had just hit his father after his father hit his mother. Milkman wants to talk to his friend Guitar, but Guitar and everyone else at the barbershop can only talk about the racial violence and humiliation that they themselves have experienced. "The men began to trade tales of atrocities, first stories they had heard, then those they'd witnessed, and finally the things that had happened to themselves. A litany of personal humiliation, outrage, and anger turned sicklelike back to themselves as humor. They laughed then, uproariously, about the speed with which they had run, the pose they had assumed, the ruse they had invented to escape or decrease some threat to their manliness, their humanness" (Morrison 1977: 82). Milkman does not contribute to the tales, because like his sister Corinthians, he is spared such humiliations, due to his social class background.

Guitar who lives on the Southside is 'consumed' with racial love; he becomes a member of the Seven Days, a secret organization that revenges the racial killings of African Americans. Guitar, who later comes to believe that his friend Milkman has cheated him and the Seven Days by finding the gold and keeping it for himself, tries to kill Milkman. Guitar needs money to finance his revenge of the four little girls killed in the bombing of the African American church in Alabama. Here Morrison takes up a factual event that demonstrates the brutal racial violence of some European Americans against African Americans in the South. The tragic killing of the four little girls in the Alabama church represents a traumatic experience for many African Americans. Over thirty years later Spike Lee also returns to this story in his film *4 Little Girls*. Guitar has past experience of the inequality of American racial policies. He witnessed how little worth is placed on the life of a Black man, when his father was sawed in two while working in the sawmill. After his father's death the owner gave him and his siblings candy and his mother forty dollar instead of money from a work insurance. According to Marianne Hirsch in her essay *Knowing Their Names: Toni Morrison's Song of Solomon*, Guitar is permanently shaped not so much by his father's death, but by the unfitness of the owner's offerings. She writes that:

> What is wrong here, what Guitar literally cannot swallow when he rejects the candy, is the father's unnatural death in the service of white capitalist patriarchal production and consumption and the intervention of the white industrialist who equates the black male with cash and candy. (Hirsch in Smith 1995: 81)

Guitar hates Whites and any Blacks that he thinks might be willing to love Whites. Guitar hates Pilate even though she willingly "clowned and crawled" to get him and Milkman out of jail, because she reminds him of his mother, who he thought was willing to love Whites. "And he remembered anew how his mother smiled when the white man handed her the four ten-dollar bills. More than gratitude was showing in her eyes. More than that. Not love, but a willingness to love" (Morrison 1977: 225). Guitar is unable to appreciate Pilate or his mother's performance. According to Jordan, Guitar does not recognize that his mother's attitude towards White is a product of the society in which they live in. She writes:

> Guitar does not consider that his mother has limited alternatives for response. To Guitar, she is flawed and weak. He is incapable of considering that she is emotionally disabled by shock and grief, habituated to receiving less than she deserves, but with

what grace and dignity she can muster (…) His easy assessment and hate-filled mindset will also not allow him to consider, with empathy and love, that she is conditioned to acquiesce out of fear – she is a product of the world in which she lives. She is not to be blamed, rather the society in which she lives that makes such behaviour necessary. (Jordan 2004: 226)

Guitar shoots Pilate in his attempt to kill Milkman. In the end Guitar kills an old Black woman even though at the beginning he is convinced that what he is doing is about love. "'Didn't you hear me? What I'm doing ain't about hating white people. It's about loving us. About loving you. My whole life is love.' 'Man, you're confused'" (Morrison 1977: 159). Even though one recognizes Guitar's anger at Whites for the racial violence committed against African Americans, he is according to Milkman confused, when he is unable to see and accept his friend's innocence. Guitar not only hates Blacks who he believes show a willingness to love Whites, but also African Americans that he thinks have assimilated too much into the White culture. When he critizes Milkman about his high tone friends on Honoré Island, Milkman tells his friend that he is welcomed to go wherever he goes. "'You're welcome everywhere I go. I tried to get you to come to Honoré' – 'Fuck Honoré! You hear me? The only way I'll go to that nigger heaven is with a case of dynamite and a book of matches'" (Morrison 1977: 103). Here Guitar demonstrates his willingness to use violence not only on Whites but also on the economic elite class of African Americans who are able to afford beach houses on Honoré Island. He seems to feel that they have forgotten the plight of other African Americans who are barely able to survive, much less afford a summer house. Guitar is convinced that he and the Seven Days are only performing justice that the legal court of laws denied African Americans.

> There are places right now where a jury, the court, are legally bound to ignore any-
> thing a Negro has to say. What that means is that a black man is a victim of a crime
> only when a white man says he is. Only then. If there was anything like or near
> justice or courts when a cracker kills a Negro, there wouldn't have to be no Seven
> Days. (Morrison 1977: 160)

The determination of a certain sector of the African American community in the 1960s to defend their person against White aggression and to demand their civil rights becomes confused in Guitar's mind. Even though Guitar is confused it becomes clear that he is more interested in justice than his friend Milkman. Margaret I. Jordan points out that "(I)t is the poor, powerless and downtrodden who truly and desperately dream of equality and justice" (Jordan 2004: 207).

Another element of violence that Morrison represents in her novel is the domestic violence committed by Macon II against his wife Ruth. Macon hates

Ruth because he believes that a certain incestuous love existed between her and her father. Ruth loves her father dearly because as she claims he was the only person to ever really care if she lives or dies (Morrison 1977: 124). Barbara Christian points to Ruth's narrow existence and how it affects her relation to her father and son. She writes, "Ruth was bred to this narrow existence so thoroughly that all her passion is directed first to the father who gave her life, and then to the son whom she unnaturally nurses until late in childhood because she needs some physical contact" (Christian 1985: 56). Macon II felt inferior in the house of his wife and her father, due to their lack of interest in his economic goals and his personal history.

> "They made sure I remembered whose house I was in, where the china came from, how he sent to England for the Waterford bowl, and again for the table they put it on. That table was so big they had to take it apart to get it in the door. He was always bragging about how he was the second man in the city to have a two-horse carriage. Where I'd come from, the farm we had, that was nothing to them. And what I was trying to do they didn't have any interest in that. Buying shacks in shacktown, they called it." (Morrison 1977: 71)

Ruth, accustomed to her middle-class life standard, could not appreciate her husband's accomplishments or motivation to have a lot of money. Jill Matus contends that Ruth takes her identity from her position in relation to her powerful and respected father (Matus 1998: 82). Macon II felt displaced from his wife and her father. After Macon II witnessed Ruth kissing the fingers of her dead father he felt disgust and hate for his wife. For ten years he showed no interest in his wife till his sister Pilate came to town and gave Ruth funny things to do and some greenish gray grass stuff to put in his food (Morrison 1977: 125). Macon became interested in Ruth for four days, and Ruth became pregnant with her third child, but her husband tries to get her to abort the unborn child.

> But Macon came out of his few days of sexual hypnosis in a rage and later when he discovered her pregnancy, tried to get her to abort. Then the baby became the nausea caused by the half ounce of castor oil Macon made her drink, then a hot pot recently emptied of scalding water on which she sat, then a soapy enema, a knitting needle (she inserted only the tip, squatting in the bathroom, crying, afraid of the man who paced outside the door), and finally, when he punched her stomach (she had been about to pick up his breakfast plate, when he looked at her stomach and punched it), she ran to Southside looking for Pilate. (Morrison 1977: 131)

The violence that Macon demonstrates against his wife stems from the unwillingness of Ruth to convince her father to lend her husband money for property. Macon II, whose major goal in life his achieving economic wealth, cannot forgive his wife for not convincing her father to lend him money to buy land that he wanted to speculate on and sell to the Railroad company. Milkman's father tells him that

> Some track land was going for a lot of money – railroad money. Erie Lackawanna was buying. I had a good hunch where the tract would be laid. I walked all around over there, the Shore Road, the docks, the fork in routes 6 and 2. I figured out just where the tracks would have to go. And found land I could have got cheap and sold back to the railroad agents. He wouldn't lend me a dime. If he had, he would have died a rich man, instead of a fair-to-middling one. And I would have been way ahead. I asked your mother to talk him into it. I told her exactly where the Erie was headed. She said it had to be *his* decision; she couldn't influence him. She told me, her husband, that. Then I began to wonder who she was married to – me or him. (Morrison 1977: 72)

Macon is forever angry with his wife due to her unwillingness in the past to convince her father to lend him money. He cannot forgive Ruth for not helping him to get ahead financially. Macon's major goal in life is to own things because he believes it is the only way one can own himself. He tells his son, "(O)wn things. And let the things you own own other things. Then you'll own yourself and other people too" (Morrison 1977: 55). Macon believes that it was his possession of property that gave him the chance to marry Ruth, the only daughter of the most important African American in the city. Jan Furman writes that "(A) lifetime of acquiring property, collecting rents, and making deals has rendered Macon a greedy, self-absorbed, unforgiving (and unforgetting) man who is incapable of showing love or receiving it" (Furman 1996: 35). The difference in Ruth's and Macon's social class background contributed to the violent friction in their domestic affairs. Ruth is born into the comfortable social economic position, her father being the most important colored man in the city where they reside. Macon, who witnesses his father being shot for his property and he and his sister been forced to flee without anything, is obsessed with his goal to own things and people. Macon is alienated from his wife and sister too. He can only measure human relationship in terms of who is willing to aid him in his quest for money and property. His sister Pilate, he believes, stole gold from him and Ruth does not influence her father on his behalf, so he hates both of them.

Summary

Morrison shows that violence and alienation affect many aspects of African American lives. Morrison addresses the subject of domestic violence in Macon II's family. The violence in Macon II's family is caused by the difference between Macon's and his wife Ruth's social background. In the novel violence is used by Whites against Black Americans for economic gains as well as a controlling device over African American communities. As in Wright's representation violence is used by the dominant European Americans against African Americans for economic and political control. The violence used by White Americans against Black Americans has traumatic effects on many African Americans who are scared into accepting the oppressive racial social order. The inability of the character Hagar to fulfill the dominant cultural standard of beauty with its preference for 'limey skin color and silky hair' leads to alienation. Hagar is affected by the legacy of the slave culture, which used skin color and hair texture to distinguish slave from non-slave. African Americans are alienated from each other due to difference in social background and positions. The use of the European American clichés and stereotypical images of African Americans by members of the Black middle-class is to produce arguments to support their own view of superiority and distance themselves from other Black Americans.

4.4. Urban Collision and Resistance Images in African American Film: Spike Lee's *Bamboozled*

> You've been hoodwinked. You've been had. You've been took. You've been led astray, led amok. You've been bamboozled.
> (Malcolm X in *Bamboozled*)

In the fall of 2000 African American filmmaker Spike Lee released his fifteenth feature film, entitled *Bamboozled*. It tells the story of the African American television writer Pierre (Peerless Dalton) Delacroix who, after several of his scripts have been rejected by his White boss, comes to the conclusion that the network is only interested in producing shows that depict African Americans as buffoons. To get himself fired and prove how racist the television network is, Delacroix decides to create the most offensive and racist show possible, *Mantan: The New Millennium Minstrel Show.* To Delacroix's surprise the show is a national success. The American audiences and critics love it, even though there are sections of the African American public who reject it, disapproving the show's format and context.

Bamboozled was shot on digital video which, Lee points out, made sense to do since the film was about a television show, and there had only been a limited amount of time to shoot it. He said in an interview,

> (W)e had to run, and with the cameras just this big [holding his hand about six inches apart], there's a lot of flexibility. We were able to shoot eight, nine, ten cameras at a time. And it enabled us to put in the run-and-gun offense. So we are able to just shoot. (Fuchs 2002: 184)

Well known for getting his films made 'by any means necessary', Lee is often referred to as angry, brilliant, controversial, outspoken, 'racist', and the most prominent African American director in the American movie industry today. In 1986 Lee released his first feature film *She's Gotta Have It,* which won the Prix de Jeunesse Award at the Cannes Film Festival, the Los Angeles Film Critics Association's New Generation Award, and the Independent Spirit Award for Best First Feature (Fuchs 2002: xvi). To date he has directed over twenty films – almost one film every year – dozens of music videos and commercials. Moreover, he has published eight books and produced a number of films for other young directors. Even though Lee sometimes works for the major Hollywood studios he is still considered as an independent director, and he always has the 'final cut' of his films.

In *Bamboozled* Lee cites a number of films that have had an impact on his cinematic style. He points to screenwriter Budd Schulberg's *A Face in the Crowd* (1957) and *On the Waterfront* (1954) and also dedicates his film to screen writer and DVD pioneer Thomas Vinterberg. Lee makes a number of other cinematic citations to films such as *Network* (1976), *Ace in the Hole* (1951) and *Sunset Boulevard* (1950) (Goldstein in Fuchs: 2002). He also showcases performances from African American artists who made their living through diverse forms of minstrelsy and appearances in Black-cast musicals and race films, such as Bill (Bojangles) Robinson, Hatti McDaniel, Mantan Moreland, Amos 'n' Andy, Step 'n' Fetchit (Massood 2003: 208). In the 1950s the *Amos 'n' Andy Show* was presented first on the American radio and played by European American actors. Later, as the show moved to the television screen and the roles were taken over by African American actors, but the stereotype characteristics from the minstrel tradition remained here too. After angry protests in the 1960s the *Amos 'n' Andy Show* was taken off the air, it would take years before a wide spectrum of African Americans were represented in the television medium again.

In my analysis of *Bamboozled* I will demonstrate how Lee uses the 19th century minstrelsy genre to thematize alienation and violence in his cinematic representation of the persistent racist imagination in the United States. He uses a mixture of sharp satire, comedy, irony and 'cool' social criticism to examine some of the past, present and, possibly, future stereotypical images of African Americans on stage and in the film and television industries. Lee points out that he had wanted to do something about the images of Black people for a long time (Samuel in Fuchs 2002: 187). In his aspiration to comment on the images of African Americans Lee turns to the 19th century popular culture genre of minstrelsy. The concentration on minstrelsy indicates the importance he places on examining the legacy of slavery and its effects on how African Americans have been depicted in the visual media. As he puts it in an interview:

> Americans somehow fear going back and revisiting painful parts of history, nevertheless we need to do it. All we need to do is look at our fellow Jewish brothers and sisters and see how much they revert back to the Holocaust. Most blacks don't even want to bring up slavery. Why bring that up? But that's our legacy. (Judell in Fuchs 2002: 140)

It is not only the legacy of slavery which is painful to African Americans, but also the history of the failure of emancipation to truly liberate the former slaves as well as the failure of Reconstruction and the degrading experiences of the Jim Crow era. The film *Bamboozled* calls an African Americans to be aware of their cultural history and of the consequences of forgetting this history. According to film scholar Paula J. Massood, Spike Lee's main point of argument is that what might appear new in urban popular culture has its root in the forgotten history of African Americans' media representations. She writes that

> Pierre's choice of, and Dunwitty's enthusiasm about, the watermelon patch setting, combined with the performers' rag costumes, their blackface makeup, and their use of dialect suggest what is at stake when we either forget or are ignorant of this history. *Bamboozled* reminds audiences of the static boundaries of the antebellum idyll of black-cast musicals beginning in the late 1920s and showcasing performances by Mantan Moreland, Amos 'N' Andy, and Step 'N' Fetchit, all of whom made their living through various forms of minstrelsy, and some of whom appeared in black-cast musicals, race films, or both. (Massood 2003: 208)

Lee clearly points to the danger that can be caused by seemingly simple entertainment such as minstrelsy where a people's culture is appropriated and viciously misrepresented.

4.4.1. Minstrelsy

According to Orlando Patterson, minstrelsy

> (E)merged out of the blackface song-and-dance acts performed in the urban centers of the North during the first decades of the nineteenth century, first by Afro-American slaves and ex-slaves, then by Euro-American imitators, minstrelsy consolidated in the early 1840s into America's predominant popular genre. (Patterson 1998: 251)

With minstrelsy European Americans appropriated traditions of African American performance and added demeaning stereotypical images. Donald Petesch points out that the minstrel performance combines the plantation tradition, popularized in literature with the anti-tradition – the grotesque, comic doings of freed Blacks – and the graphic impact of such representations in material culture, e.g. in dolls and in lithographs (Petesch 1989: 100). He further indicates that the plantation type which got into the minstrel performance was apparently calculated to give the impression that all Blacks were lazy and shiftless fellows. In every facet of the minstrel performance and appearance the main emphasis was on the difference between Blacks and Whites. In the minstrel performance what was at 'center stage' was difference (Petesch, 1989). The classification of African and European Americans as different 'races' was emphasized through the dissimilarity between both groups' skin color and somatic features. As sociologist and scholar of African American studies Paul Gilroy states in his text *Against Race*, the history of scientific writing on

(...) "race" has involved a long and meandering sequence of discourses on physical morphology. Bones, skulls, hair, lips, noses, eyes, feet, genitals, and other somatic markers of "race" have a special place in the discursive regimes that produced the truth of "race" and repeatedly discovered it lodged in and on the body. (Gilroy 2000: 35)

The minstrel genre did not only emphasize skin color and other somatic differences between Black and White Americans; the popular cultural genre also depicted and claimed an imbalance in the level of intelligence between Black and White Americans, portraying African Americans as idiots, but good dancers. The stereotype of African Americans as good dancers but otherwise stupid reinforces the association of African Americans with Africa as the so-called primitive continent. As Patterson points out in his reference to symbolic anthropologist Victor Turner, "(M)instrelsy became a master symbol of nineteenth century American culture" (Patterson 1998: 253).

According to Donald Petesch the minstrel show became the site where difference was fixed. He states that "(A)s slavery evolved into segregation, to separate by law what had previously needed no separation, pictorial representation became caricature: to fix, to separate, to assert unequivocal difference" (Petesch 1989: 107). The minstrel show performances reinforced the mainstream American politics of segregation aiding in fixing African Americans as a separated group of people, as a separated 'race'. The emphasis on skin color and other somatic differences between African Americans and European Americans in the minstrelsy genre attempted to illustrate humanistic differences between these two American ethnic groups. According to Ron Eyerman it was after the re-narrating of the Civil War that European and African Americans were articulated as separated social groups. All Whites then could be identified with Western civilization, which was equated with civilization per se while African Americans were associated with Africa the "uncivilized" (Eyerman 2001: 18).

By discoursing on minstrelsy Lee refers to the negative stereotypical images of African Americans in the dominant American popular culture even today. I will go into this in more details in my analysis later as well as the appropriation of African American culture by European Americans. As Patterson mentions with the minstrelsy European Americans were able to appropriate African American creative production and at the same time deny their artistic creation. In reference to the dominant European American society's regard of minstrels, he writes, "most of all it could shamelessly appropriate and steal Afro-American cultural production while 'scientifically' insisting that Negroes never created anything of value" (Patterson 1998: 252).

Lee's choice to scrutinize some of the early stereotypical representations of African American images by European Americans in the United States indicates the cultural trauma that these images still have for many Black but also White Americans. Eyermann refers to the complexity of the problem of representation in African American culture. He writes that

> (T)he complex and problematic issues of representation have been of central concern to black Americans from the earliest period of the slave trade to the present. In what can properly be called "the struggle for representation" (…), black Americans have fought for the right to be seen and heard as equal in social conditions which sought to deny this. This struggle for representation occurred in literary, visual, and more traditional political forms. It encompassed a fight to be seen as well as heard and involved the question of who defined what was seen and heard. (Eyerman 2001: 13)

During slavery several Africans and their descendants struggled to represent the inhuman experiences of slavery in the Slave Narratives, but this was countered by the visual production of European American artists who produced paintings of the "happy slave myth".

Eyerman in his reading of Albert Boime points to the "visual encoding of hierarchy and exclusion"

> (…) "a sign system that was already in place" which supplemented written and oral justification for slavery. Especially in the nineteenth century, white artists produced paintings that reinforced belief about the "happy slave", contented in his/her servitude. This was filtered though popular culture in minstrelsy, where black-faced white actors parodied black dialect and behavior in staged performances. American culture was permeated with words, sounds, and images which "took-for-granted" that slavery was both justified and necessary, beneficial to all concerned, at the same time as there existed a counter-current which "remembered" the opposite. (Eyerman 2001: 15)

By thematizing minstrel portrayals of Black Americans, Lee re-enacts the history of demeaning images of African American visual representation in the United States. He draws attention to the continuing use of negative stereotypical images in the American media to describe Black Americans and demonstrates the negative effects of such misrepresentation on African Americans in the United States. The misrepresentation of Black Americans' images have been analyzed by other cultural critics (and the specific images that were produced). Writer Ishmael Reed, for example, sharply criticizes the overuse of African American images by television networks when dealing with subject matters such as violence, poverty, and crime in his essay "Airing Dirty Laundry".

4.4.2. Stereotype

> Stereotype – an unvarying form or pattern; specif., a fixed or conventional notion or conception, as of a person, group, idea, etc., held by a number of people, and allowing for no individuality, critical judgment, etc. (*Webster New World Dictionary*)

Stuart Hall points out that stereotyping tends to occur where there are gross inequalities of power (Hall 1997: 258). The inequality of power between African Americans and European Americans is reflected in the number and the quality of stereotyped images of African Americans in that society. Hall continues his argument drawing attention to the point that stereotypes reduce people to a few essential simplified characteristics and since slavery African Americans have been reduced to certain signifiers of their physical differences, be it thick lips, fuzzy hair or other indicatives (Hall 1997: 249). He also argues that stereotyping, as a signifying practice is central to the representation of racial differences (Hall 1997: 257). With stereotyping one has to bear in mind that what is real, or being said, is just as important as what is imagined in fantasy, and what is not being said. Hall writes that

> (T)he important point is that stereotypes refer as much to what is imagined in fantasy as to what is perceived as 'real'. And, what is visually produced, by the practices of representation, is only half the story. The other half – the deeper meaning – lies in *what is not being said, but is being fantasized, what is implied but cannot be shown.* (Hall 1997: 263)

In *Bamboozled* Lee uses telling names for his characters; e.g., one might read the name Dunwitty as dumb-wit. Lee demonstrates how Dunwitty's fantasies of African Americans are loaded with stereotypical images. I will return to this point when I analyze the character Dunwitty. Post-colonial critic Homi Bhabba points to the repetitive chain of stereotypes that are needed for successful signification. He writes that

> (A)s a form of splitting and multiple beliefs, the stereotype requires, for its successful signification, a continual and repetitive chain of other stereotypes. This is the process by which the metaphoric "masking" is inscribed on a lack, which must then be concealed, that gives the stereotype both its fixity and its phantasmatic quality – the same old story of Negroes' animality (…). (Bhabba in Baker, Diawara 1996: 100)

The implication of the negative stereotypical images of African Americans in the American visual media is that Black Americans are in some sense less human than White Americans. Bhabba also points to the ambivalence and fixture that gives the colonial[9] stereotype its currency. He writes that

> (I)t is the force of ambivalence that gives the colonial stereotype its currency; ensures its repeatability in changing historical and discursive conjunctures; informs its strate-gies of individuation and marginalization; produces that effect of probabilistic truth and predictability which, for the stereotype, must always be in *excess* of what can be empirically proved or logically constructed. (Bhabba in Baker, Diawara 1996: 88)

He also further points out that

> (T)he stereotype is not a simplification because it is a false representation of a given reality. It is a simplification because it is an arrested, fixated form of representation that, in denying the play of difference (that the negation through the other permits), constitutes a problem for the *representation* of the subject in significations of psychic and social relations. (Bhabba in Baker, Diawara 1996: 98)

The ambivalence and fixture of African American identities were represented in the minstrel genre, which has influenced the visual representation of African American images even today in the United States.

Lee in asserting to just how widely spread the minstrel images occupied American media culture, shows the lack of power that many African Americans have over how they are represented in the diverse visual media. According to Michele Wallace, Lee depicts a history of African American visual performers in his film. She writes that "(A)ll in all *Bamboozled* is an archive of Black performance history and visual culture, so tightly scrambled and compacted it is virtually inscrutable" (Wallace 2004: 488). The tightly scrambled and compact images that Lee presents in the final montage of the film, I would like to profess reflects the number of stereotypical images of African Americans in America's visual culture.

Spike Lee did not only showcase African American performers, he also shows black faced toys, dolls lithography, picture post cards, and European American Hollywood stars who did minstrel performances like Judy Garland, Mickey Rooney and Bing Crosby. In an interview Lee draws attention to the acceptance of minstrelsy in American television and film medium. He states, "we're showing that these images didn't just spring from the warped mind of D.W. Griffith, but reflected accepted behavior" (Spagow in Fuchs 2002: 196). Lee thus strongly criticizes the accepted practice in American popular culture of

---

[9] Even though I am aware that African Americans in the United States are not a typical example of a colonized people I am claiming that African American socio-economic and political history share a number of similarities with colonized and post-colonial subjects.

using negative stereotypical images of African Americans as a means of entertaining mainstream American audiences.

4.4.3. Analysis

In the characterization of *Mantan* played by tap dancer Savion Glover and *Sleep 'N' Eat* played by comedian Tommy Davidson, Lee shows how these two performers are entirely powerless as to how they are represented in the television medium. Manray and Womack (names will be changed to *Mantan* and *Sleep 'N' Eat* when they are given their minstrel roles) are two young homeless African American males that perform in the street in order to earn money for food. They are living in a dilapidated building that is raided by characters representing the New York City police. When the two performers are offered roles in a new television show, Manray is willing to change his name to Mantan as long as he earns enough money. As he said, "as long as the loot is good, I am down" (*Bamboozled*).

Even though Womack is more cautious and wants to know more about the new show, he accepts the role before he fully comprehends the show's context. At first the two performers are just happy to have money and new clothes, but the audiences see Womack (*Sleep 'N' Eat*) looking skeptical, as he is forced to blacken his face and paint his lips red. Each time Womack has to blacken up we see him becoming increasingly sad, even crying once while he is putting on his blackface make-up. Lee refers to the effects of the black facemask on the actors themselves. And said in an interview:

> The reality of black people putting this stuff on their face was devastating for Tommy Davidson and Savion Glover. It took away part of their soul, it took away part of their manhood, and it made us think of Bert Williams. Tommy and Savion did it for a couple of weeks, but Williams had to do that his entire career. (Crowdus and Georgakas in Fuchs 2002: 208)

The alienation that the actors and characters experience in putting on blackface make-up points to what Cornel West calls the modern Black diasporian problematic of invisibility. He writes:

> (T)he modern black diasporian problematic of invisibility and namelessness can be understood as the condition of black's relative lack of power to represent themselves to themselves and others as complex human beings, and thereby to contest the bombardment of negative, degrading stereotypes put forward by white-supremacist ideologies. (West 1999: 128)

The lack of power that many African Americans experience over how they are represented in the American visual media is a relevant topic up to this day. Even though Pierre Delacroix the African American writer creates the *Millennium Minstrel Show*, he does not have control over the show; his White boss and Finnish Stage director makes the script 'funnier'. As Delacroix asks "at whose expense", it is at the expense of African American identities. The masking of the two performers' identities and change of names demonstrate the lack of power that they have as actors over how they are represented in the television medium. As Patterson writes, "(T)he changing of a name is almost universally a symbolic act of stripping a person of his former identity (...)" (Patterson 1982: 55). The change from Manray to Mantan points to the displacement which some African Americans undergo when they are forced to change their own identities and represent African American identities in a demeaning fashion only so that they can practice their artistic craft in the American visual media. In the end Womack decides to quit the show pointing out that it is the same old story: "He has sung for Massa, tap-dance for Massa, anything to make Massa laugh, and in the end it is the same old bullshit" *(Bamboozled)*. Womack recognizes that by playing a coon[10] in a blackface minstrel show he is continuing and reinforcing the

> "Sambo" stereotype of Southern slave culture. "Sambo," the typical plantation slave, was docile but irresponsible, loyal but lazy, humble but chronically given to lying and stealing; his behavior was full of infantile silliness and his talk inflated with childish exaggeration. (Patterson 1982: 96)

Patterson further points to "the ideology of 'Sambo' the degraded man-child that, to the Southerner, constituted the image of the slave" (Patterson 1982: 96). Stuart Hall states that even though the invisibility of modernist cultural representations of African diasporic images has been replaced by limited visibility in post-modern global popular culture it does not accomplish much to call it the same (Hall in Dent 1993: 25). Even though I agree with Hall's argument that things have changed, there is a certain amount of repetitiveness when one examines the continual use of negative stereotype images of African Americans in the visual media. Patterson states that whoever is in a position to control the symbol of a culture is in a situation to control power. Patterson is referring to power in the situation of master over slave but there are also similarities in how contemporary power functions, when it comes to who controls images of

---

[10] "(T)he eye-popping piccanninnies, the slapstick entertainers, the spinners of tall tales, the 'no-account' 'niggers', those unreliable, crazy, lazy, sub-human creatures, good for nothing more than eating watermelons, stealing chickens, shooting crap, or butchering the English language" (Hall, 1997: 251)

African Americans in the United States. Pierre creates the minstrel show, but he is not able to control the visual representations of Manray and Womack; Manray's nose is made bigger than it is, and Womack's mouth is also larger. The big nose and mouth fulfill the existing stereotypical images of African American somatic features that are prevalent in the American society. As Hall points out these stereotypes are ritualized forms of degradation (Hall 1998: 245). Womack recognizes the demeaning images of big nose and lips and questions Sloan as to her and Delacroix's working position at the network. As he asks Sloan "where do you people work; in the damn lobby of the building" *(Bamboozled)*, Womack realizes the lack of power that Sloan and Delacroix have in the final visual representations of Manray and himself.

According to Patterson's reading of British anthropologists Meyer Forbes and Raymond Firth, symbols constitute a major instrument of power. He states

> (…) that symbols, both private and public, constitute a major instrument of power when used directly or indirectly. Herein lies the source of authority. Those who exercise power, if they are able to transform it into a "right", a norm, a usual part of the order of things, must first control (or at least be in a position to manipulate) appropriate symbolic instruments. They may do so by exploiting already existing symbols, or they may create new ones relevant to their needs. (Patterson 1982: 37)

In *Bamboozled* Dunwitty, the White boss, demonstrates his power and authority over the two homeless actors, by his ability to exploit negative stereotypical images of diverse sectors of African American communities. The *Millennium Minstrel Show* is made 'funnier' by its setting on a plantation in Alabama with a music band called *The Alabama Porch Monkeys*. The use of the watermelon and cotton patches, plus the over-sized lips of the mouth that opens, and out of which the actors Mantan and Sleep 'N' Eat emerge at the beginning of each show are all elements of existing stereotypical symbols of African Americans in the United States. The lack of control that African Americans as a group have historically had in how they are portrayed in the American media indicates a 'process of subjectification', which is reinforced by the diverse stereotypical representations of African American people in the United States.

Manray (Mantan) is at the beginning of the show only interested in getting paid. He does not question the possible negative effects of his role on the African Americans' identities. As he said, "as long as the loot is good, I am down" *(Bamboozled)*. At first he just thinks of his personal comforts, new clothes, new tap shoes, an apartment with scenic view; he is happy. It is only after his confrontation with Womack who points out that things have come full circle and in the end "it's the same old bullshit" *(Bamboozled)*; and Sloan, the main female character, Delacroix's assistant and the sister of Big Black African, questions as to whose puppet he is by showing him a wind-up tap dancing blackface toy, that Manray becomes aware that "he is tired of being a nigga". Manray tries to perform without the minstrel make-up, but he is pulled from the stage and thrown out by Dunwitty, who declares how ungrateful he is, and that niggers like him are "a dime a dozen", and he is able to replace him in no time. Dunwitty is aware of the countless hungry African American actors who are willing to play any role "as long as they are getting paid." As Delacroix states, "one line of advertisement in *Backstage* magazine was enough to have African Americans lining up around the block" *(Bamboozled)*. The shortage of versatile roles for African American actors plus the history of African American actors' willingness to demean themselves, so that they are able to perform their craft, are intensely critiqued in the film. Lee calls attention to the difference between today and the past where minstrel roles were the only roles available to African Americans. He argues in his film the importance of African American actors taking responsibility for their performances. Lee said in an interview:

> "With *Bamboozled* we really wanted to focus on media and its misuses and its abuses of people," Lee says "and the people that get co-opted and go along and fall for the okeydoke. As artists we all have to make choices. And there are consequences of those choices. This film is much more lenient with the generation of actors that includes Bill Bojangles [Robinson], Hattie McDaniel, Stepin Fetchit, Mantan Moreland, Willie Best, Bert Williams – they didn't really have a choice in the roles they were getting. Nowadays we have choices (…)." (Goldstein in Fuchs 2002: 185)

In the end Manray is kidnapped and killed; his execution is televised live on television and the Internet in what the executioners (Mau-Maus) called the "dance of death". In "the dance of death" Manray performs in the same shoes that Bill Bojangles wore when he died during a performance. Lee demonstrates the possible intertextual reference between these two performers. Bojangles, best known for acting with child actress Shirley Temple, was also not represented in his full humanity in the media; he performed in many minstrel type shows. The extreme violence of the Mau-Maus against Manray demonstrates the possible, bizarre and brutal consequences for African American entertainers who contribute to the distortion of their own images. Lee refers to the confusion and the wrong choice of the Mau-Maus rap group who executed Manray. The Mau-Maus, a pseudo-revolutionary rap group with names such as Big Black African, Mo Black, Jo Black, Double Black, Hard Black, Smooth Black, and 1/16 Black are convinced of their own profundity, even though their only demonstration of radicalism is to spell black 'b-l-a-k', according to Michael Wallace. The group feels they have to do something with the same sort of symbolism comparable to the African American athletes John Colts and Tommy

Smith who gave the Black Power salute at the Olympic games in Mexico in 1968, against the minstrel performances of Womack and Manray to demonstrate their revolutionary character. In the end they decide to kidnap and murder Manray, because he is an 'Uncle Tom'. Lee refers in an interview to the element of minstrelsy in today's gangsta rap in the genre of hip-hop music. He said "I mean, I don't condemn all of hip-hop; I've used a lot of it in my films starting, back in '89 with *Do the Right Thing* and Public Enemy. But I do feel gangsta rap has evolved to a modern day minstrel show, especially if you look at the videos" (Sragow in Fuchs 2002: 195).

The minstrel qualities of some African American performers are strongly criticized not only in the portrayal of the Mau-Maus rap group but also in the character of Delacroix. In his representation of the television writer Delacroix Lee depicts the self-hate and alienation undergone by this character. Delacroix, the only African American writer on the staff of CNS network station, does not want to end up like his father, Junebug, a stand up comedian, who due to his principles and dignity ends up playing in 'little nigger clubs'. Junebug has a pretty woman, money in his pocket, and by his own definition, is ahead of the game, but his Harvard educated son does not wish to end up like his father.

Even though Dela (Delacroix) is aware of the network's racist character, and his original goal was to demonstrate this racism, he himself gets intoxicated with the success of the show. The show is well received by the American audiences and critics. Dela begins to win diverse awards. Dela who wishes to continue working in the visual media performs different stereotypical actions attributed to some urban lower-income African American people. When he is given an award he dances and makes loud wows on stage, in the end he gives away one of his awards to an unknown European American actor. Lee makes direct reference to African American actor Ving Rhames who gave away his Golden Globe award to Jack Lemmon, and Cuba Gooding Jr. who did a head spin at one of the Oscar shows. Lee shows the effect of such actions on the African American actors' careers. He says,

> when you give your award to a man you never met in your life, what do you expect? That sent chills down my spine, to see him do that to an award he earned. The same with Cuba spinning on his head. What was that? But you notice neither has stopped working since. That kind of entertainment will keep you working. (Samuels in Fuchs 2002: 188)

Lee criticizes African Americans who are willing to contribute and reinforce certain stereotypical images of themselves and other African Americans by performing in a certain mode. Gladstone L. Yearwood points out that it is characteristic of Lee's films to offer an insider critique of institutions and personalities in the Black community (Yearwood 2000: 92). The fact that Dela is willing to dance and perform certain caricatures of low income urban African American people even though he himself is from a middle-class background shows his willingness to displace himself in order to fit into certain stereotypical modes. Although Delacroix embodies the diversity of African American communities, he plays along with cliché images of particular urban African Americans. He literally represents an alienated character. He changes his name from Peerless Dalton to Pierre Delacroix giving himself a French name with high status; he is uncomfortable with his own ethnic identity. Pierre's middle-class background and Harvard education are at odds with the stereotypical images of African Americans that he himself appears to have internalized. When he appears on a radio talk show he defends his position as creator of *The New Millennium Minstrel Show*, he claims that slavery has been abolished for over four hundred years now, and that Negroes have to stop blaming Whites for their lack of success. Delacroix accepts to some extent the conservative European and African American perspective of blaming the victims for their victimization. Ishmael Reed in his essay "Airing Dirty Laundry" talks of the literary scam of people claiming to talk openly about African American communities' problems and the reception that is given to such authors by the literary establishment. Even though his argument refers to literature I would like to suggest that his point could also be used when analyzing the character Delacroix. He writes that

> (T)he profitable literary scam nowadays is to pose as someone who airs unpleasant and frank facts about the black community, only to be condemned by the black community for doing so. This is the sure way to grants, awards, prizes, fellowship, and academic power. (Reed 2000: 179)

Before the success of the show Delacroix seems to be aware of the racism against African Americans in the media, he is the only African American on the staff at one of the biggest network stations in the country, but as he becomes successful with his show and more accepted by his White colleagues one witnesses his increasing distance from African American communities. Sloan, his African American assistance is suddenly 'the help', which he regrets having had a past romantic involvement with. At the beginning Delacroix wanted to demonstrate the racist character of the CNS network station and prove that the network only wants to see certain stereotypical images of African Americans on television. His own crisis of identity and quest for White approval becomes more important as the film progresses. Cornel West refers to the complication caused by gender and class in the initial response regarding the moralistic and communal aspects of African diasporians' reaction to social and psychic erasure. He writes,

(…) black diasporian responses to social and psychic erasure were (…) further com-
plicated by the fact that these responses were also advanced principally by anxiety-
ridden, middle-class black intellectuals (predominantly male and heterosexual),
grappling with their sense of double-consciousness – namely their own crisis of
identity, agency and audience – caught between a quest for white approval and
acceptance and an endeavor to overcome the internalized association of blackness
with inferiority. (West 1999: 129)

Even though West's comment refers to how some African American intellectuals have reacted to racism in the past, the character Delacroix shares certain
characteristics of West's description of (some) African American middle-class
male intellectuals regarding their response to psychic erasure. In an interview
Lee draws attention to the self-hate of Delacroix, saying "What makes Damon's
character unique is that Pierre Delacroix has a lot of self-hate. Here's someone
who's never been comfortable with his blackness: hence the name changed and
the diction and that type of stuff" (Sragow in Fuchs 2002: 193). Dela comes up
with different excuses when Sloan questions the ethics of the show; he compares what he is doing to the works of Dr. Martin Luther King. He points out
that Dr. King did not like to see his people being beaten on the 6 o'clock news
every evening, but it was necessary so that White America would wake up to
the reality of some African American communities.

Dela is not the only character in the film that invokes the memory of Dr.
Martin Luther King and the Civil Rights era. The Jewish publicist Myrna
Goldfarb, hired by Dunwitty to prepare the network strategy for dealing with
criticism against the *Millennium Minstrel Show*, tells Dela and Sloan that her
parents marched in Salem, Alabama with Dr. Martin Luther King. She then
continues by presenting what she calls the Mantan manifesto. In her policy for
dealing with critics of the network show Myrna suggests at first that everyone
should lighten up, because the show is about fun; she continues by telling them
that they should make sure they hired African Americans in all aspects of the
show before and behind the cameras, she asks who put these cultural policies in
charge anyway; who determines what is Black, who decides what is Black; even
though Mantan and Sleep 'N' Eat are lazy and unemployed they are not saying
anything about the whole African American community. Sloan and Dela should
always smile in public; they should wear kente cloth, and always use the word
community whenever they refer to *Mantan,* and invoke the spirit of Dr. King
(Bamboozled). Lee criticizes the uses of King's and Civil Rights' legacy by pseudo
liberal thinkers, be they European or African Americans. The twist of the Civil
Rights rhetoric and misuse of Afro-centric public images are signals of how the
Civil Rights language and strategies have been appropriated by neo-conserva-
tives in the United States. Myrna compares her experience of taking time off

after college to travel around European countries with the representation of
Sleep 'N' Eat and Mantan as coons in the *Millennium Minstrel Show*. She also
claims that she knows African American culture because she has a PhD in
African Americans Studies from Yale University. It is ironic that she then even
asserts that she knows African American culture, she still compares her
travelling around Europe after college with the portrayal of Mantan and Sleep
'N' Eat as 'slackers' representative of the African American communities. Lee
also ironically comments on the European critical tradition of studying the
other and claiming authorized knowledge while racialized or openly racist
perspectives are maintained. Lee's use of the minstrelsy genre to depict the misrepresentation of African American identities could also be read as a metaphor
for the claim of some European Americans, that they 'know African Americans
better than themselves'. The minstrelsy genre that developed in the mid-nine-
teenth century has at its core the imitation of African Americans by European
Americans; as Patterson points out in his reference to African American male
performances in the minstrelsy genre, "Afro-American men could imitate Euro-
American men imitating Afro-American men" (Patterson 1998: 254).

   In his creation of Dunwitty, the White boss, Lee draws attention to the
danger of cultural appropriation. Dunwitty is married to an African American
woman and has two bi-racial kids; he feels that this gives him certain cultural
rights. He refers to African Americans as 'Niggers', "he also thinks he knows
'Niggers' better than Delacroix with his Harvard education", his office wall is
decorated with a number of African American sport icons and famous personalities, which Dela is not aware of. Lee points out that culture is for everyone to
enjoy, but he also states:

> "(W)ell, as I've said in the past, and I'll continue to say it, culture is for everyone.
> Culture should be appreciated by everyone, but for me there is a distinction between
> *appreciation* of a culture and *appropriation* of a culture. People like Dunwitty are
> dangerous because they appropriate black culture and put a spin on it as if they are
> the originators of it. There's a big difference. This sort of thing is so powerful, though,
> that for many years I thought Bob Marley had covered Eric Clapton on 'I shot the
> Sheriff,' when it was really the other way around." (Crowdus and Georgakas in
> Fuchs 2002: 206)

The history of African diasporic musical creations being appropriated and
robbed can be seen in the example of Rock and Roll music of the past where
Elvis Presley is considered the king of Rock and Roll, and today in Hip Hop
music one asks when European American rapper Eminem will be casted as the
best rapper ever. Dunwitty not only thinks "he knows 'Niggers' better than
Dela", but he also thinks he is blacker than Dela. Dunwitty believes he knows

the African American community because of his marriage; he uses this identification whenever it fits his strategy. It is ironic that when Delacroix comes up
with the idea for the minstrel show, Dunwitty is happy, because he feels that
Delacroix has "dug deep into his black soul to come up with such an authentic
black show". Even though Dunwitty asserts that he knows African Americans
there is a certain amount of self-projection in his knowledge, and he does not
hesitate to use his 'knowledge' to produce the racist television show *Mantan*.
Cornel West points to the prestigious cultural authorities that were involved in
promoting Black inferiority. He writes that

> (W)hite-supremacist practices – enacted under the auspices of the prestigious cultural
> authorities of the churches, printed media and scientific academics – promoted black
> inferiority and constituted the European background against which black diasporian
> struggles for identity, dignity (self-confidence, self-respect, self-esteem) and material
> resources took place. (West 1999: 128)

Dunwitty with his claim of knowing Blacks still possesses a certain clichéd
ideology of African American identities. Dunwitty only believes and accepts
Delacroix as being truly Black at the very moment when Dela is demeaning his
Black self. As Frantz Fanon points out the colonizer is only truly satisfied when
the native accepts his own inferiority. Even though Dela is not a 'native' of any
colony, when one examines the African American past in America one sees the
connections of African Americans with the 'native' regarding their cultural,
political, economic and social class history. Delacroix is alienated because he
has internalized the association of blackness with inferiority and accepts the
stereotypical images of Dunwitty regarding himself and other African Americans. Dunwitty tells Dela that they are both aware that African-Americas set the
trends in the United States, but the irony is, he is only interested in trends
where African American identities are depicted in degrading stereotypical
fashion. Dunwitty rejects a number of ideas for shows that would represent the
African American middle class; he contends that Delacroix's proposals were too
white bread, that the characters were Whites with black faces. In this one sense
Dunwitty accuses Delacroix of creating "minstrels" of the White middle class.
He declares that even though the *Cosby Show* was revolutionary, the network
cannot go down that line again *(Bamboozled)*. When Dela pitches his ideas for
the new show declaring that the characteristics of Mantan and Sleep 'N' Eat
would be ignorant, dull wit, lazy, and unlucky Dunwitty is exhilarated. He
declares that this is exactly what he is looking for *(Bamboozled)*. Dunwitty then
rejects Dela's suggestion that the show should take place in the 'projects',
instead he proposes that the setting of the show should be on a plantation in
Alabama. Dunwitty wishes to separate European and African American

identities in the visual medium. He cannot accept Dela's ideas for new shows based on African American middle class. As he said about Dela's characters, "they are White people with Black faces" *(Bamboozled)*. Dunwitty himself profits from the existing White supremacist practices of depicting African and European Americans as two distinct "races". He does not want a television show which depicts similarities between these two American ethnic groups. Even though Dunwitty claims that the show is only about good wholesome fun, his choice of course has definite political and ideological dimensions since even in aesthetic representation of fictional persons and events there is a political and ideological motivation for the choice (Mitchell in Lentricchia and McLaughlin, 1995). Dunwitty's delight at Dela's ideas for the minstrel show demonstrates his interest in keeping certain stereotypical images of African Americans on the television. "It all goes back to how White-skin privilege operates in America, especially for White males" (Powell 2003: 131).

Big Black African, one member of the Mau-Maus group is angry at Mantan and Sleep 'N' Eat, because he feels "they are fucking things up for everyone" *(Bamboozled)*. He thinks that if one African American 'fucks up' other members of the ethnic community could be held accountable. West draws attention to two limiting ways that were used to combat racist cultural practices in the United States. One was the homogenizing impulse which claimed that all African Americans are alike, thereby obliterating differences. Another was that all African Americans were in the same situation and subjected to White supremacist abuse. He states:

> (S)imilarly, the insight in the second claim is that all blacks are in some significant sense "in the same boat" – that is, subject to white-supremacist abuse. Yet this common condition is stretched too far when viewed in a *homogenizing* way that overlooks how racist treatment vastly differs owing to class, gender, sexual orientation, nation, region, hue and age. (West 1999: 129)

Big Black African feels that Manray's and Womack's portrayals of some African Americans as lazy coons and buffoons are placing limitations on other African Americans who reject these images of themselves. Lee critizes the limits placed on African Americans, who tend to be seen as a monolithic group by many European and African Americans, and he also critizes the acceptance of these limitations.

In *Bamboozled,* Sloan the main female character is the only one skeptical of Delacroix's ideas for the minstrel show. Sloan tries in the beginning to warn Dela and Dunwitty about the racist elements of the show and the danger of representing African Americans in such negative ways. No one listens to her, and Sloan goes along with her boss Dela even though she uses every oppor-

tunity to educate Manray on the history of minstrelsy. Dela and Dunwitty fear
Sloan's influence on Manray, so in the end Delacroix fires her and tries to
convince Manray that Sloan only got her job because she slept with him in the
past. Sloan defends herself against such accusations questioning why is it that
whenever a woman is successful it has to be perceived in a sexually exploitative
way.

> "Why is it that every attractive woman who's successful, people always think that
> she slept with somebody to advance her career? I'm smart, I have drive, I worked my
> ass off, and that's how I got into the position. Did I go to bed with Pierre? Yes, I did.
> It was a mistake, we did it one time, and that was it. But that had nothing to do with
> me getting into the position that I am in." *(Bamboozled)*

Sloan is aware of the stereotypical representation of African American women
in the United States, which are oftentimes depicted as immoral, oversexed,
greedy for money and material things, and never to be trusted (Powell 2003:
122). The patriarchal and sexist structure of American society, which depicts
most successful attractive women as opportunists, is criticized and questioned
in the film.

At the end of the film Sloan kills Dela because the police kill her brother Big
Black African. She blames Dela for the death of her brother, and for his refusal
to listen to her regarding the creation of the minstrel show. Lee refers in an
interview to the possible deeper perception of some African American women
compared with men. He said that "because circumstances are often more difficult for African American women than for black males in other words, because
they're black and they're women, too, that might make them more perceptive"
(Crowdus and Georgakas in Fuchs 2002: 209). Yet though Sloan might have a
deeper understanding as to the ills of producing such a show as *Mantan* she still
goes along with Dela.

In the film *Bamboozled* the extremely violent action taken by the Mau-Maus
against Manray points to a possible link in Spike Lee's cinematic representation
and Toni Morrison's characterization of Sethe in her novel *Beloved*, who also
committed a violent crime by killing one of her children and trying to kill two
more to prevent them from being taken into slavery.

In both cultural texts the director and the novelist thematize the extreme
violence that some African Americans are willing to utilize to right certain
wrongs, even to the extent of trying to play God. It is not only in their
representation of extreme violence that I claim an intertextuality between the
works of Morrison and Lee, and even Wright. Both writers and the filmmaker
interrogate African American communities and offer an insider critique of
institutions and personalities in Black communities that are willing to demean

themselves in order to please members of the ruling White society. In
Morrison's novel *Sula* one witnesses how Nell's mother smiles even when the
White conductor on the Jim Crow train is insulting her. In *Black Boy* Wright also
writes of his perplexity regarding the character of Shorty. Even though Shorty
takes pride in his African American ethnic affiliation he has no problem with
letting a White man kick him in the ass for money. All three cultural artists
criticize the willingness of some African Americans to demean themselves and
contribute to their own degradation.

Summary

One of the contributing factors of the emotional alienations undergone by
characters in the film is the lack of power and authority they have over how
they are represented in the media. The use of stereotypical images of African
American somatic features by Dunwitty points to the signifying practice of
racial differences and the gross inequalities of power between African Americans and European Americans that is represented in the film. Dunwitty's
approval of the minstrel show demonstrates his wish to emphasize the racial
difference between African and European Americans. Dela changing his name,
which always means a change of identity, wants to distance himself from his
African American heritage. His internalization of negative stereotypical images
of some urban African American people leads to his self-hate and emotional
alienation. Dela is caught in his own crisis of identity and his quest for approval
and acceptance from the dominant European American society.

The Mau-Maus' use violence against Manray because of the demeaning
African American characters which he portrays. They fear that the lazy coons
and buffoons that Manray portrays could be seen as homogeneous of African
American people.

Dela's self-alienation and recreation of negative stereotypes of African
American identities lead to different forms of violence and alienations for him
and other characters in the film.

5   Jamaica: A Historical Overview

In this chapter I will summarize the numerous rebellions in the Jamaican slave society as well as the major uprisings that took place after emancipation. The relevance of focusing on the number of slave rebellions and uprisings in Jamaican history is to establish the point that violence and alienation have been structural features of the island's society from its inception. I will refer to some of these revolts in Jamaican history, drawing attention to how the first Maroons established a precedent of "counter-violence" (Walla 2005) in gaining their freedom and in combat against the brutal violence of the British slave masters. Later in my analysis of the novel *The Harder They Come* I will demonstrate the psychological importance of the Maroon history of resistance for Ivan's grand-mother and maybe for Ivan himself in dealing with the alienation that he confronts in the urban center of Kingston. I will also show how the slaves and later the peasants have used their religious beliefs in their fight for freedom in a colonial and post-colonial world.

Another focus in this chapter is to show how Marcus Mosiah Garvey and his influence on Rastafari, a distinctively Jamaican phenomenon, is still continuing a tradition of cultural resistance, using and fusing the specific elements they have found in the large African Jamaican peasant culture. The relevance of focusing on the role of the Rastafarian culture in the Jamaican society will be demonstrated in the colonial and post-colonial texts, *The Children of Sisyphus* and *The Harder They Come* to be analysed later in my study.

According to the sociologist Orlando Patterson, rebellion or the threat of it was an almost permanent feature of Jamaican slave society (Patterson 1967: 266). One reason for this may be the mountainous surface of the island, used as a protective hideout for the rebellious slaves. Aside from the topography, one might argue that the overwhelming numbers of different religious denomina-tions have also played a major part in this tradition of resistance. According to the social cultural anthropologist Barry Chevannes, in his study *Introducing the Native Religions of Jamaica*, there are seventeen large religious denominations along with a great number that make up the category of "Others" in Jamaica today (Chevannes 1995).

The island nation of Jamaica shares a common history with a number of island states in the so-called New World; it is said to be 'discovered' by the Italian-Spaniard Columbus in 1494. Before Columbus came upon the Island, Amerindians from South America known as Arawaks Caribs peopled the Island. The Spaniards started to settle on the Island of *Yamaye* in 1509. By 1611 only 74 Indians remained from the approximately 60,000 Indian population. As

Orlando Patterson states in his revised doctoral thesis, *The Sociology of Slavery* (1967), where he examined the social structure of the Jamaican slave society: "The Spaniards with the ruthless cruelty that characterized their treatment of the indigenous Indian people had wiped out the entire native population" (Patterson 1967: 15). Bartolomé de las Casas, the Spanish priest, in his text, *A Short Account of the Destruction of the Indies* (1542), also documented the atrocity committed by the Spanish on the native Indian population in South America and today's Caribbean islands. Regarding Jamaica he wrote:

> In 1509, the Spanish, with the same purpose in mind as they had when they landed on Hispaniola, found their way to the two verdant islands of Puerto Rico and Jamaica, both of them lands flowing with milk and honey. (…) Here they perpetrated the same outrages and committed the same crimes as before, devising yet further refinements of cruelty, murdering the native people, burning and roasting them alive, throwing them to wild dogs (…) and then oppressing, tormenting and plaguing them with toil down the mines and elsewhere, and so once again killing off these poor innocents to such effect that where the native population of the two islands was certainly over six hundred thousand (and I personally recon it at more than a million) fewer than two hundred survive on each of the two islands. (De las Casas in Griffin 1992: 26)

The Spanish then neglected the island because of its lack of mineral resources. In 1655 Jamaica was seized by British troops after their disastrous attempt to take Santo Domingo; the Spanish resistance continued for five years. In 1660 the Spanish withdrew from Jamaica leaving behind 1500 African slaves some of whom had been fighting the British troops along with the Spanish, and some run-away slaves, who had been hiding in the mountains. From 1655 to 1670 the British were largely engaged with fighting these ex-slaves of the Spaniards under the leadership of Juan de Boles and Juan de Serras (Sherlock and Bennett 1998: 80). These former Spanish slaves formed the first group of Maroon fighters on the island. In 1660 the English granted de Bolas and his band of Maroons full civil rights and 30 acres of land each (Sherlock and Bennett 1998: 81).

The British established civil government on the island in 1663, and in 1670 the British planters started commercial production of sugar. With the establishment of sugar production the demand for more African slaves to cultivate the fields increased. In 1658 there were 1400 African slaves on the island, by 1664 their number increased to 8,000, then in 1703 to 45,000 with 8,000 Whites. From 1701 to 1810 the Jamaican society imported 662,000 slaves (Sherlock and Bennett 1998: 133). According to the historians Philip Sherlock and Hazel Bennett in their *Story of the Jamaican People,* many of the slaves came from the region of modern Ghana, Nigeria and Benin, and were shipped to Jamaica from British slave holding forts on the Gold Coast.

One of the first major slave rebellions in Jamaica under British rule took place in 1690 in the parish of Clarendon and involved over five hundred slaves (Hart 1985). Many of the slaves that escaped from the sugar plantations during the rebellion found refuge in mountainous Cockpit Country. The newly escaped slaves joined the Maroons already living there under the command of Cudjoe, himself an escaped slave. The term 'maroon' is taken from the Spanish word Cimarron and it was first used to describe domestic cattle taken from the hills of Hispaniola. The term was further used to refer to Indians who escaped from the low lands in the 1530s; later the word was used to describe African run-aways (Sherlock and Bennett 1998: 16)

According to Patterson between 1700 and 1722 not a year passed without rebellion, and Sherlock and Bennett point out that uprisings following the English occupation were organized by plantation slaves, and involved slaves that were already in revolt.

In 1713 in the Treaty of Utrecht Spain granted England a contract for supplying Spanish America with slaves. According to Sherlock and Bennett, Kingston became a major port for ships leaving to England, Latin American ports, North America and other Islands (Sherlock and Bennett 1998: 135). By this time the maroon bands were formed into two major groups. The Leeward Maroons who were based in the central mountains and the Windward Maroons in the northeastern mountains. Cudjoe commanded the Leeward Maroons with his two brothers Accompong[11] and Johnny. The Windward Maroons were commanded by the guerrilla leader Cuffee, with Quao, Kishee, and "dreaded by the whites, the rebel tactician leader Nanny" (Sherlock and Bennett 1998: 137). Patterson refers to the historical records on Jamaica and draws attention to the fact that in 1722 rebellions were taking place all over the island.

By 1739 the British were forced to seek peace with the rebels. The British signed a fifteen points treaty with Cudjoe and the Leeward Maroons. They were given 1500 acres of land, plus they were free to hunt where they choose, except within three miles of any White settlement. One very disheartening fact of the treaty that Cudjoe signed with the British was the agreement to fight alongside with the British against the stubborn Windward rebels if they refused to accept the treaty. He also agreed to help the British with any rebellions, and send back all runaway slaves, and hunt down runaway slaves for a fee in the future (Patterson 1967: 271; Sherlock and Bennett 1998: 141). Cudjoe's agreement with the British government proved to be disastrous for other Africans still in bondage, because the British government from this point on always had an ally whenever the Africans still in bondage revolted (Hart, 1985).

---

[11] Up to today there is a maroon town with the name Accompong.

In 1740 the Windward Maroons signed the same treaty with the British, only they had to return all slaves who had joined them in the last three years (Sherlock and Bennett 1998: 141). Patterson states that between 1730 and 1734 the British government spent 100,000 pounds in attempting to suppress the rebellions (Patterson 1967: 270). The economic damage to the British slave-holders in Jamaica forced the British government in Jamaica to seek a peace treaty with the rebelling Africans. I will refer again to the importance of economic destruction against the British slave holding property in Jamaican in influencing the British government decision in granting the African slaves any form of freedom when I examine the Sam Sharp rebellion.

The first major rebellion, rousing European suspicion about the slaves using their religious beliefs to organize a revolt, was the "Taki Rebellion" of 1760. A Coromantee slave named Tacky lead over 1000 slaves in rebellion with his goal of "a total massacre of the whites and to make the Island a Negro Colony" (Patterson 1967: 271). The rebellion lasted from April to September. One month after the insurrection was put down there was another uprising in St. Thomas in the East. During Tacky's rebellion over sixty Whites were killed and between three to four hundred slaves were either killed or committed suicide (Patterson 1967: 271).

Barry Chevannes calls attention to the significance of the Taki Rebellion as perhaps being the first time that a revolt was planned on a Pan-African level involving slaves of different tribes (Chevannes 1994: 17). The African religion the slaves were practicing appears to have been Myal. Myal is believed by many scholars today to have originated in Central Africa and is credited for its ability to absorb foreign influences (Chevannes 1994: 6). Nicole Waller points out in *Contradictory Violence: Revolution and Subversion in the Caribbean* that

> Myalism, which developed in eighteenth-century Jamaica, goes back to the Akan distinction between healer (embodying what will become the métier of Myalism) and obeahman. Growing from this distinction, Myal became a multicultural system of belief (…) the first Jamaican religious movement which addressed Africans of various different groups and even incorporated elements of Christianity. (Waller 2005: 165)

Barrett states that "(t)he word *myal* has come to mean 'being in a state of posses-sion,' and the ritual which accompanied it was a rigorous dance now known as *Kumina*" (Barrett 1977: 18). Barrett also mentions that kumina means to be pos-sessed by an ancestor. It appears that the myal man, later known as "Shepherd" or "Daddy" and myal woman, "Mada" (Jamaican Patois for Mother), were what in an African context might have been considered priests and priestesses, who were at the same time healers. These myal men and women were not sorcerers, but ironically this is how the Europeans in their lack of understanding and in their disrespect for the African cultures saw the myal men and women. I will demonstrate the relevance of examining myal religion in my analysis of Orlando Patterson's novel *The Children of Sisyphus,* when Dinah, one of the main characters, turns to Shepherd John to aid her in her determination to leave the life of poverty in the Dungle behind her.

In 1807 William Wilberforce and his followers in England won the battle to abolish the slave trade in the British colonies; many African slaves in Jamaica concluded that this meant the abolition of slavery (Sherlock and Bennett 1998: 200). This belief in the legality of their freedom would form the basis for one of the largest and most ambitious slave revolts in Jamaica, which broke out two days after the Christmas holiday in 1831. This revolt is known as the Sam Sharp Rebellion or the Baptist War. The revolt lasted less than two weeks, but according to Patterson it was the most damaging to the property of Whites and the institution of slavery. Sam Sharp, a domestic slave born in Montego Bay, planned the rebellion. The revolt was concentrated in the Western part of the island (St. James, St. Elizabeth, Trelawny, and Hanover), where thirty percent of the slave population was consolidated (Sherlock and Bennett 1998: 213). Patterson estimates that at least 20,000 slaves were involved in the revolt, and the number of sympathizers was even larger. Sam Sharp was deacon of the established Baptist religious denomination and at the same time a "Daddy" of the myal-influenced Native Baptist Church. "Sam Sharpe was a man whose active brain devised the project; and he had sufficient authority with those around him to carry it into effect having acquired an extraordinary degree of influence among his fellow-slaves" (Barrett 1977: 41). When Barrett quotes Henry Bleby, an eyewitness of the insurrection, Bleby fails to take into account Sam Sharpe's role as "Daddy". "Leadership under Myal was a function not of training but of gift, hence the obedience, deference, and respect leaders received" (Chevannes 1994: 19). Practicing a dual religious membership Sam Sharp incorporated Myal and Christian beliefs in his planning of the rebellion.

Sam Sharp, who organized the rebellion, convinced other slaves to agree by oath not to work after Christmas as slaves. If the Whites' masters agreed to pay them wages, yes, they should work. But if they were forced to continue working as slaves then they should fight for their freedom. According to Sherlock and Bennett the uprising was different from other revolts because it was a call to slaves everywhere not to arms, but a call for the slaves to withdraw their labor (Sherlock and Bennett 1998: 212). Involved in the rebellion were a wide cross section of Africans and colored population. As Bennett and Sherlock state

The leaders formed the elite of the labour force, men who had exercised as much authority as a slave could exercise, some of them deacons of the Baptist Church, literate, aware of events in Britain, and especially of the works of the abolitionists. (Sherlock and Bennett 1998: 213)

Even though the rebellion failed to accomplish the immediate purpose of its authors it helped to strengthen the hands of the abolitionists in England (Patterson 1967: 273). The revolt also demonstrated to the imperial government that the question of emancipation could not be postponed. Bleby states that

> (T)he revolt failed of accomplishing the immediate purpose of its author, yet by it, a further wound was dealt to slavery which accelerated its destruction for it demonstrated to the imperial legislature that among the Negroes themselves, the spirit of freedom had been so widely diffused as to render it most perilous to postpone the settlement of the most important question of emancipation to a later period. (Bleby: 1868, in Sherlock and Bennett 1998: 227)

On August 28, 1833 the British parliament passed the Act of Emancipation, it came into effect on August 1, 1834. The Act of Emancipation mandated that the former slaves were no longer slaves, but they were not free neither, they were considered "apprenticed labour"; full freedom was granted in 1838 (Sherlock and Bennett 1998: 230). During the four years period of apprenticed labour many masters took out their bitterness on the slaves; according to Walker cited in Sherlock and Bennett:

> In Jamaica, however, "Many masters in their bitterness of heart, vented their wrath upon their unfortunate labourers (…) within a period of two years 60,000 apprentices received a total of a quarter of a million lashes and 50,000 other punishments by tread-mill, chain-gang work, or some other device (…)." (Sherlock and Bennett 1998: 234)

Even though the reprisals for the slaves after rebellions were brutal and inhuman, the Jamaican slaves fought and continued to fight for their freedom up to the day of emancipation.

Patterson claims that even though one might speculate that the reason for the amount of slave revolts in the Jamaican slave society sprung from the fact that the Jamaican slave society failed to reproduce itself compared with the American slave society. He shows that in the Sam Sharp Rebellion even Creole slaves who had never known freedom were willing to die for it. He writes:

> (B)ut in the last days of slavery even the Creole slaves, who had never known what it was to be free, began to organize revolts against their masters, and the last and most damaging of all the rebellions remains a living memory of their struggle for something they had never experienced but for which they felt a need sufficiently strong for which to die. (Patterson 1967: 283)

After the rebellion Jamaica became a crown colony, but the system was still based on the doctrine of White superiority and imperial control. Due to the great difference in number between the African slaves and English masters there was a great fear among the White population in Jamaica. Sherlock and Bennett draw attention to the barbaric reprisals from Whites after Black uprisings and to the quick resort to violence as a means of enforcing authority (Sherlock and Bennett 1998: 193). They point out that an adult African slave had a very short working life span of seven years under slavery. The violence of working the African slaves to death is made clear in the short working life span of an adult African slave who was forced to labor on the sugar plantation. Sherlock and Bennett quote Hearne in his reference to the rigid and energy consuming life of the sugar plantation. He states that "(T)he society created by sugar was rigid, base and greedy. It consumed life, energy and thought, and manured the industrial revolution of England with the profits from its labour" (Sherlock and Bennett 1998: 192). One might speculate that with such short life span the African slaves in Jamaica were more willing to die in rebellion instead of being worked to death. Patterson points out that with the possible exception of Brazil no other slave society experienced such intensive and continuous revolts. He compares the number of revolts in Jamaica to American slave societies, demonstrating with Nat Turner's revolt that involved only seventy slaves; in Jamaica in comparison in the seventeenth and eighteen centuries there were approximately four hundred slaves involved in every major rebellion (Patterson 1967: 274). Patterson points to the difference in the ratio of Blacks and Whites in both slave societies.

> In the case of the American South we find that of the fourteen slaves states only two – South Carolina and Mississippi – had slave populations which slightly outnumbered the whites. In nine of the other states the slaves population varied between 1.5 and 33 per cent; and in three, between 44 per cent and 47 per cent of the total population. Thus, of all the British slave societies Jamaica had by far the highest ratio of slaves to whites. (Patterson 1967: 274)

The high ratio of African slaves in the Jamaican society compared with Whites forced the British government to make peace with the Maroons and strongly influenced the emancipation date in the Jamaican slave society.

Sherlock and Bennett show that even though Whites were split into classes of distinction, they were united by race. In reference to Whites they state, "Their superiority was institutionalised in law as well as in social terms" (Sherlock and Bennett 1998: 193). I will demonstrate how 'race' and class continue to be represented in the cultural texts as deciding factors in the Jamaican society when I examine the novels *The Children of Sisyphus* and The *Harder They Come* as well as the film with the same title.

The next rebellion that was again planned with the help of the Native Baptist as well as the Baptist Church was the Mordant Bay Rebellion in 1865. A post-emancipation uprising lead by the African Jamaican Paul Bogle, a deacon of the Native Baptist Church, and George William Gordon, a Jamaican of mixed African European heritage and elected representative of the parish of St. Andrew. He was also a deacon in the Native Baptist Church. Nicole Waller states that according to Edward Kamau Brathwaite, "Myalism was the underlying energy of the Morant Bay Rebellion and is fuelled, beneath Christian doctrine and concerns for legal rights, by an explosive African politico-religious core (…)" (Waller 2005: 165). The Jamaican peasants in the Morant Bay Rebellion fused together politics and religion in their struggle for legal rights as well as for economic freedom from the precapitalist plantocracy economy that still dominated the Jamaican society after emancipation. Quoting Robotham, Chevannes states that

> (t)he root of the crisis (…) lay in the precapitalist forms of relations that the planto-cracy sought desperately to maintain, so that the "working people, the entire post-emancipation economy, the social and political system remained bound to slavery, even in freedom." (Chevannes 1994: 13)

Another factor contributing to the post-emancipation rebellion was the high taxation on the poor. (This might be compared today to the high interest that Jamaica's government has to pay to the World Bank for the economic loans.) There were tollgates placed in strategic locations on roads leading to towns where the poor sold their products. One assembly member of the government commented in 1861 on the different taxes that the poor peasants have to pay. He states "they were taxed on their bread, their salt, their Lucifers, their clothes, and everything else they used" (Sherlock and Bennett 1998: 252).

In the early 1920s Jamaican rural unemployed population began relocating to Kingston, the urban center in the hope of finding employment. From 1880 to 1920 about 146,000 Jamaicans migrated from Jamaica in search of employment (Sherlock and Bennett, 1998). During the 1930s, the years of the American depression, the socio-economic situation became desperate for Jamaicans; there was a no entry sign to countries such as Panama, Honduras, Costa Rica, Cuba and the United States of America. According to Sherlock and Bennett these no entry barriers to countries where Jamaicans had migrated in the past transferred the population from the rural areas to the city. I will point to the relevance of examining the Jamaican demographic shift from the rural areas to the urban when I analyse the novel *The Harder They Come*.

On May 1st in 1938 a strike in the newly built West Indies Sugar Company in Frome, Westmorland turned violent. The workers were protesting against wage deduction and inefficiencies in the payment office (Sherlock and Bennett 1998: 365). During their confrontation with the police four strikers were killed, fifteen wounded and over one hundred arrested. Three weeks later violence broke out in Kingston as docks workers went on strike, according to Sherlock and Bennett the strikers and the mob brought Kingston to stand still (Sherlock and Bennett 1998: 365). It was out of this crisis that the two political parties emerged. The People's National Party (PNP) was formed by Norman Manley, the young British educated Jamaican lawyer who represented the striking workers; the Jamaican Labor Party (JLP) four years later by Alexander Bustamante, who had formed the Jamaica Workers' and Tradesmen's Union in 1934, then after the strike the Bustamante Industrial Trade Union. Bustamante was also involved in representing the striking workers. It was not only the political parties and trade unions development that were influenced by the strike and protest. The report conducted by the West Indies Royal Commission with Lord Moyne as chairman, and the devastation of England during World War II, lead Britain to grant self-rule to the colony of Jamaica. In 1944 Jamaicans gained adult suffrage, and the beginning of self-government with the reforming of the constitution in November. In 1962 a non-violent Independence was desired after Trinidad and Jamaica had rejected the confederacy and chosen their respective independence instead.

5.1. Cultural Aspects: Marcus Garvey and Rastafari

In the following pages I will focus on the Jamaican national hero Marcus Mosiah Garvey and Rastafari. The reason is the relevance of the UNIA and Rastafari in the novel and film *The Harder They Come*. The Rastafarian culture is also strongly thematized in the novel *The Children of Sisyphus* to be analysed later in my text. Reading Garvey's work, one cannot help but notice that Marcus Mosiah Garvey, prophet, Black Nationalist, and Pan Africanist, has a deep knowledge of the Bible. In most of his writings he uses either biblical quotations or allusions, as for example in his poem "Tragedy of White Injustice" from 1927: "a salvation from man's hypocrisy" or "great thunderbolts he has hurled" (Tafari 1996: 25). Garvey, a man who follows the Jamaican tradition of spiritual/ cultural resistance was founder and leader of the Universal Negro Improve- ment Association (UNIA) from around 1916 to about 1930. The UNIA was later based in Harlem – Garvey had emigrated from Jamaica – from 1919 to 1927, with branches in the Caribbean, in North, South, and Central America as well as in several African countries. In New York Garvey gave the following descrip- tion of the UNIA in 1924:

> The Universal Negro Improvement Association represents the hopes and aspirations of the awakened Negro. Our desire is for a place in the world; not to disturb the tranquility of other men, but to lay down our burden and rest our weary backs and feet by the banks of the Niger and sing our songs and chant our hymns to the God of Ethiopia. (Barrett 1977: 79)

Even today there are still branches of the UNIA in Jamaica.

The Africans in the New World who were taught to believe that Africa was a continent of darkness, came to realize with the reading of the King James' version of the bible that the name Ethiopia was already mentioned in Genesis chapter two.

> Black preachers though for the most part unlearned discovered in the only book to which they had access (the Bible) that Egypt and Ethiopia were in Africa, and that these countries figured very importantly in the history of civilization. (Barrett 1977: 68)

In addition, Ethiopia was the only African country to have remained free of colonial domination throughout its history. Ethiopia managed successfully to defend its borders twice when Italy tried to conquer its territories in 1896 in the battle of Adowa and again in 1935. Haile Selassie, the king of Ethiopia, turned to the League of Nations in 1936 after the Italian army led by Benito Mussolini invaded Ethiopia. The famous speech given in Geneva by Haile Selassie after the European nations denied Ethiopia military assistance warned that "God and history would remember your judgement, if you do not bow before these accomplished facts. You have struck the match in Ethiopia, but it shall burn Europe" (Mack 1999: 55). This speech is still quoted by the Rastafarians today, because it proves to them the prophetic powers of Selassie, who according to them foretold the Second World War.

> *Ethiopianism*: The advocacy or idealization of Ethiopia as "the motherland" and the hope, held by a group of Jamaicans, to be repatriated there; also symbolizes a system of belief in the positive cultural consciousness of African roots that first surfaced in the Americas. (McFarlane, Murrel, Spencer 1998: 6)

When Garvey adapted the Ethiopian national anthem for the UNIA, he was trying to connect the Africans in the Diaspora and at home with their great African heritage. To strengthen this he coined the motto "Africa for the Africans at home or abroad". Garvey thought that one of the reasons why the people of African descent failed to overcome the brutal and dehumanizing colonial structures was because of the lack of a centralized government to fight for the rights of Black people. Garvey thought that he could help to create a central government in Africa with his movement. "A return to Africa was not in Garvey's mind a sort of mass exodus to right past wrongs. 'We do not want all the Negroes in Africa,' he said. 'Some are no good here, and naturally will be no good there' (…)" (Chevannes 1994: 41). Garvey preached unity and self-reliance for the people of African descent. As a migrant worker Garvey traveled the West Indies as well as the Americas and saw that conditions under which the people of African descent were living were not much different compared to Jamaica. He thought that the African people lack the necessary self-confidence to pull themselves up from their oppressive conditions, so he tried to instill that confidence in the Black masses.

> We, as Negroes, have found a new ideal. Whilst our God has no colour, yet it is human to see everything through one's own spectacles, and since the white people have seen their God through white spectacles, we have only now started out (late though it be) to see our God through our own spectacles. The God of Isaac and the God of Jacob let him exist for the race that believes in the God of Isaac and the God of Jacob. We Negroes believe in the God of Ethiopia, the everlasting God – God the Son, God the Holy Ghost, the one God of all ages. That is the God in whom we believe, but we shall worship him through the spectacles of Ethiopia. (Barrett 1977: 77)

In 1919 Garvey founded the shipping company known as the Black Star Line in order to give Africans living in the Diaspora the possibility to return home to

Africa, the motherland. Even though this venture failed, it still has a lasting impact on the consciousness of African people; we can see this in the symbol of the black star, which is represented in the national flag of Ghana. Although Garvey died half a century ago his teachings and ideology are still part of the belief systems of the Nation of Islam in America and the Rastafarian movements. According to Joseph Owens in his book *Dread – The Rastafarian of Jamaica*, Garvey engaged the unconscious, the repressed desires of Black people. I think Garvey's words still continue to do so up to the present day.

"Look to Africa, when a black king shall be crowned, for the day of deliverance is near" (Augier, Nettleford, Smith 1988: 5). These words are believed to have been uttered by Marcus Garvey. Aside from this celebratory statement, there is the careful differentiation between realms of truth: "Truth has two levels in social affairs. There are actual events, and there are statements about actual events" (Augier, Nettleford, Smith 1988: 5). The Rastafarians who took the words of Marcus Garvey literally saw his prophecy being fulfilled when in 1930 the Ethiopian Emperor Haile Selassie was crowned king of Ethiopia.

The Rastafarian movement is a unique phenomenon with its origins in Jamaica. Some people consider the Rastafarians a religious sect, others see Rastafari as a philosophy, to most of the Rastafarians themselves Rastafarianism is a way of life. It is believed that the Rastafarian movement started in 1930 with the coronation of Ras Tafari, Emperor Haile Selassie I of Ethiopia, who took the biblical titles King of Kings, Lord of Lords, Conquering Lion of the Tribe of Judah, placing himself in direct lineage of the biblical King Solomon, descendent of King David. Without doubt, the Rastafarian movement stands in the Jamaican tradition of spiritual/cultural resistance. The culture of Rastafari did not just manifest itself with the crowning of the Ethiopian Emperor, instead there are many aspects of Rastafarian ideology stemming from almost three hundred years of slave, ex-slave, peasant, spiritual culture of resistance in Jamaica. Yet, when Garvey said that Blacks should start seeing God in their own image he did not imagine that some of his fellow countrymen would find the representation of God in the Ethiopian Emperor.

Four people who were decisive in the spreading of Rastafarian ideology were Leonard Howell, Joseph Hibbert, Archibald Dunkley and Robert Hinds. To them the crowning of Emperor Haile Selassie was the fulfillment of the prophecy allegedly made by Marcus Garvey. On the request of the Rastafarians a report of the Movement was published and carried out by the University of the West Indies, by three well-known scholars, M.G. Smith, Roy Augier and Rex Nettleford. Especially in the 1950s the Rastafarians were suffering from maltreatment by the police and the general public, due to what the 'brethren' thought was a general misunderstanding of their way of life. The report stated that Leonard P. Howell appeared to have been the first to preach the divinity of Haile Selassie in Kingston. Archibald Dunkley started preaching the divinity of Selassie first in the Parish of St. Andrew and by the time he got to Kingston Howell was already praising Selassie as the returned messiah. The Rastafarians believe Emperor Haile Selassie I is the living God. While God lives in man, God manifests himself most eminently and completely in the person of Haile Selassie I. As mentioned in the Old Testament, the Rastafarians believe that they are the true children of Israel. They are made to suffer in Jamaica (the equivalent to Babylon) because of the sins of their forefathers. And they also believe that they will finally be repatriated back to Zion – the equivalent to Ethiopia. They consider the capitalist system as the Babylon system, which oppresses the children of Israel, the Rastafarians.[12]

The Rastafarian movement is a non-violent movement, believing in the power of the spoken word as manifested in their concept 'word, sound, and power', "that the spoken word as a manifestation of the divine presence and power can create and bring destruction" (McFarlane, Murrel, Spencer 1998: 6). Since the Rastafarians regard themselves as part of the divine order, the body is also treated as a holy temple. Therefore they refuse to eat any kind of artificial food as well as salt. Because the Rastafarians believe in the natural order of things, they believe in the protection of the environment. The Rastafarians are afrocentrist in their outlook of life. As a decentralized movement the Rastafarians do not have one single leader.

The official language in Jamaica is Standard English. From colonial times onward the Rastafarians have addressed different issues, which they see as relevant to the Jamaican peasant society, language being an important issue. The language of the majority of the Jamaican population is Creole. In order to achieve upward mobility in the Jamaican society, one has to master Standard English. Failure to do so has been one way of keeping the people down. In the process of changing the language system the Rastafarians try to develop their own system of 'Dread Talk', an example is the concept of 'I' words.

(...) "me" of Jamaican Creole speech as in "Me have mi book" (to mean "I have my book") is seemingly perceived by the Rastafarians "as expressive of subservience"; and so the pronoun "I" not only replaces it but takes on special significance in Rastafarian utterance giving to Jamaica a new vocabulary of "I-words" which indeed "express the individualism that characterises the Rastas and the unity they see among themselves." (Owens 1976: x)

---

[12] The Rastafarians use the word 'downpress' in order to visually express the term oppression, because in their understanding there is nothing 'up' – uplifting – in the term oppression.

Thus, individualism and unity, quite often regarded as mutual opposites become coexistent in Rastafarian culture. A lot of Garvey's ideas have been taken
up by the Rastafarians and have been given a new interpretation. Garvey's
ambition of 'Back to Africa' for the Rastafarians has become repatriation to
Ethiopia, which many of them consider a divine act. According to Chevannes, if
repatriation is regarded as a concept of justice, the Europeans must also leave
and go back where they came from. "As a theological concept Repatriation
serves as critique of White racism against Africans and other 'coloured races'
and a call for a new order of justice in the world" (Chevannes 1995: 31). Over
the last seventy years there have been four attempts at repatriation, and at no
time were these attempts supported by all the Rastafarians of Jamaica. Two of
the dates were set by Leonard Howell, one in 1934 and another one in the 1940s.
According to Chevannes, there was another event in 1958, when Prince
Emmanuel Edwards held an all-Rasta convention, where a lot of the brethren
thought that at the end of the convention repatriation would take place. This is
the event that Patterson fictionalizes in his novel *The Children of Sisyphus.* In his
chapter "New Approach to Rastafari", Chevannes mentions that these events
took place at a time when migration was very high in the wider Jamaican
society, so it might be misleading to look at these events in a purely Rastafarian
mode.

Another Rastafarian concept that I would like to briefly focus upon is the
idea of God. In their acceptance that Haile Selassie I is God, the Rastafarians see
the Black race as sharing this divinity, after all, 'God created man in his own
image'.

> Two things follow. First is the rejection of the hegemonic system of values whereby
> "if you are White, that's right; if you are Black, you stay back." Second, the alienation
> between God and man need no longer exist, because there is a profound way in
> which God shares a part of his being with those who were once poor. Man, that is
> Black Man, is also divine. (Chevannes 1995: 31)

According to Chevannes, in the Rastafarian concept one does not convert to the
Rastafarian faith, one manifests Rastafari, because it is already in oneself. He
goes on to point out that Rastafarians do not see all White people as evil; Whites
can reach the same divinity as Blacks, if they reject the evil of the White
'Babylon system'.

There are other elements of the Rastafarian movement like the ritual
smoking of the holy herb (marijuana, referred to as ganja), the gathering in
camps for reasoning and the celebration of different dates that are important to
the Rastafarian brethren and sistren, for example November 2nd, the coronation
date of Haile Selassie.

Within the Rastafarian movement there are also different houses – groups – as the Bobo Shanties started by Prince Emmanuel Edwards, the Twelve Tribes of Israel, a more middle-class oriented branch and the house of the Nyabinghi. Membership in one of these groups is not obligatory. Other than these three main organizations, the Rastafarians meet for reasonings in different houses, yards, or camps, the only requirement is that one is truly interested in Rastafari-anism.[13]

Within Jamaican society the attitudes towards the Rastafarians have changed over the years. Especially the outer appearance of Rastafarians no longer shocks the established Jamaican society, where as before the symbol of the dreadlocks meant, "'(w)hen you are Dreadlocks you come like a outcast.' Locks had a shock value, but they were also a way of witnessing to faith with the same kind of fanaticism for which the prophets and saints of old were famous" (Chevannes 1994: 158). Today this is no longer true, dreadlocks have become a part of the established 'haute couture'.

One of the reasons why Rastafari for a lot of people is identified with reggae music is because of the young urban musicians who started to spread the message of Rastafari from the 1960s onwards. Young Rastafarians like the singers Bob Marley and Peter Tosh used reggae music to tell the life-story of the urban poor – the sufferers, the effects of colonialism, post-colonialism and capitalism on Jamaica. These musicians made Jamaica famous for its musical culture. Reggae music is a form of cultural resistance, I will analyse later on in *The Harder They Come*, a film that became especially popular for its outstanding soundtrack. Even today reggae/dancehall music is used to communicate and comment on the cultural, political, social and economic conditions of Jamaican society.

"(…) *Rastafarianism* – a still developing system of religious thought and a style of practical living that summon a groping and equivocating society to honesty and moral certitude" (Owens 1976: vii).

---

[13] 'Reasoning' is a form of philosophical discourse, where the Rastafarians exchange ideas on different subject matters as well as world politics pertaining to their ideology. A reasoning session can be a very lively experience.

6 Aspects of Existentialist Alienation in *The Myth of Sisyphus and Other Essays* by Albert Camus

> The myth in a primitive society, that is in its original, living form, is not a mere tale told but a reality lived … the assertion of an original, greater, more important reality through which the present life, fate and work of mankind are governed (…) It was the recognition of the link between past and present established by myth in daily life. (Cotterell 1980: 10)

> Absurdism (…) bears a close relationship to EXISTENTIALISM. (…) Albert Camus's *The Myth of Sisyphus* offers the most familiar presentation of the movement's central ideas: in a world without God, human life and human suffering have no intrinsic meaning. (Childers and Hentzi 1995: 3)

Another theoretical basis which I will ground my interpretations of Jamaican cultural texts upon is taken from two essays of Albert Camus' volume *The Myth of Sisyphus and Other Essays*, first published under the French title *Le Mythe de Sisyphe* in 1942. The relevance of using Camus' arguments on absurdity will be demonstrated when I analyse Patterson's novel *The Children of Sisyphus*.

In "An Absurd Reasoning – Absurdity and Suicide" as well as in his other essay, "The Myth of Sisyphus", Camus touches upon a lot of aspects that I see reflected in post-colonial literature and film. The theme of alienation seems to correspond to Camus' theme of the absurd.

> A world that can be explained even with bad reasons is a familiar world. But, on the other hand, in a universe suddenly divested of illusions and lights, man feels an alien, a stranger. His exile is without remedy since he is deprived of the memory of a lost home or the hope of a promised land. This divorce between man and his life, the actor and his setting, is properly the feeling of absurdity. (Camus 1959: 5)

When Camus talks about a "world that can be explained even with bad reason," he refers to a human state where the absurdity of life has not been realized. In contrast to that, "a universe suddenly divested of illusions and lights" (Camus 1959: 5) is the state of mind after the insight into the absurdity of life. One has recognized one's state of being alienated. For Camus, one arrives at this state of alienation through the process of thinking, which is the beginning of what he calls "to be undermined" (Camus 1959: 4). To be undermined is the moment when one sees life without illusions; one recognizes that the daily routine of life has no hidden meaning or purpose. This means to Camus the crucial point is the gaining of insight into the meaninglessness resp. absurdity of life, which inevitably leads to the feeling of alienation. Therefore it remains to be examined how one gains this insight.

According to Camus, one arrives at the state of recognizing the meaninglessness and absurdity of life in the moment when one is not actively taking part in the daily routine of suffering, which Camus sees in his portrayal of Sisyphus in the moment he descends from the mountain towards the stone, which again and again rolls back.

> It is during that return, that pause, that Sisyphus interests me. (…) That hour like a breathing space, which returns as surely as his suffering, that is the hour of consciousness. At each of those moments when he leaves the heights and gradually sinks toward the lairs of the gods, he is superior to his fate. He is stronger than his rock. (Camus 1959: 89)

It is the moment of consciousness that leads to the insight of life's absurdity. When Camus talks of the superiority of one's fate, he sees the insight as the end of illusion, which for Sisyphus means that he no longer believes that he one day will fulfill his task.

To Camus the insight into the absurdity of life leads to three possibilities of dealing with it: to accept absurdity and live with it, to commit suicide or to live on hope. "Tenacity and acumen are privileged spectators of this inhuman show in which absurdity, hope, and death carry on their dialogue" (Camus 1959: 8).

At first sight hope seems to be rather irrelevant in dealing with absurdity. How can one remain hopeful after realizing the meaninglessness of life? While Camus in the first chapter of his essay "Absurdity and Suicide" names hope as a possible way to deal with absurdity, in his last essay about Sisyphus hope is no longer mentioned as a possible alternative. Sisyphus knows that there is no way out of his rolling the rock up the hill. For Camus, Sisyphus is the absurd hero, because he realizes the absurdity of his life, accepts it and can even be happy in it.

> Sisyphus, proletarian of the gods, powerless and rebellious, knows the whole extent of his wretched condition (…). It makes of fate a human matter, which must be settled among men. All Sisyphus' silent joy is contained therein. His fate belongs to him. His rock is his thing. (Camus 1959: 90)

I will substantiate the relevance of Camus' thought on absurdity when I examine the novel *The Children of Sisyphus* later.

7   Diasporic Popular Culture and Urban Space: Jamaican Cultural Texts

7.1. Perry Henzell's *The Harder They Come*

For many years *The Harder They Come* had a representative status as "the" Caribbean film. It was the first feature film to be produced, directed, and shot in Jamaica by Jamaicans. Trevor Rhone, a Jamaican play-writer, and Perry Henzell, who also directed and produced this film classic, wrote the script. When the ban which the first independent government of Jamaica had placed on the film for "(…) its potentially incendiary effect on the ghetto 'sufferahs' a version of whose experience it expressed so power-fully" (Cham 1992: 177) was lifted in 1972, it is believed that over 40,000 people turned out to see it.

> Instead of the elite, from their cars moving (complimentary) into the Carib Cinema watched by the poor and admiring multitude, the multitude took over – the car park, the steps, the barred gates, the magical lantern itself – and demanded that they see what they had wrought. (Brathwaite 1984: 41)

The Harder They Come is based on the life of Ivanhoe Martin, maybe the first media-created star in Jamaican history. "Ivan Martin", "Ivanhoe Martin", "Ivan Brown", "Rhyging" or "Rhygin" – meaning rage – was a small-time criminal who held the whole nation's attention in the fall of 1948. The conservative Jamaican daily newspaper *The Daily Gleaner* gave in to a "sensational, tabloid-style news coverage" (McFarlane, Murrell, Spencer 1998: 285) of Rhyging, a desperado gunman, whose robberies and shooting had Robin-Hood style bravado, according to Kavin J. Aylmer in his essay *Towering Babble and Glimpses of Zion: Recent Depictions of Rastafari in Cinema*. In the movie's updating of Rhyging's story, he is not only a criminal, but also an aspiring young reggae singer, who has to deal with the exploitation of a monopolist music producer.

The film depicts the odyssey of a country boy, named Ivanhoe Martin (a role played by the young reggae superstar Jimmy Cliff) who comes to town after the death of his grandmother. Before finding his mother in the city of Kingston, he is robbed of all his belongings. Ivan's mother, astonished to see him, learns of the death of her own mother and advises her son to return to the country. But Ivan is determined to become a singer and stays in the city. On his very first night he becomes the victim of exploitative strategies of urban survival by getting to know Jose, a young hustler, who takes him to a famous cinema, the

"Rialto". Here Ivan is introduced to American Western movies and learns that the hero – 'star boy' – cannot die until the last reel.

On his own without money we see young Ivan trying to survive in the slums of West Kingston. He finally arrives at Preacher's church, an address given to him by his mother. Here he meets Elsa, a young Christian girl, who has been the ward of Preacher since her parents' death. However, after Ivan is caught practicing his 'devil music' in the church, he is thrown out, and a dispute erupts between Ivan and Longha, his senior co-worker in Preacher's workshop. A violent fight takes place where Ivan slashes Longha's face with a knife. Ivan is then subjected to punishment by the law.

When Ivan finally gets his chance to cut a record, he experiences the exploitative practices of the music market and learns that he will receive no more than twenty dollars. But without the seemingly omnipotent music producer, he cannot sell the record. On his outing to celebrate the release of his record, Ivan again meets Jose, who offers him a chance to sell marihuana. Ivan realizes that local marihuana traders are being exploited and refuses to accept this. When one of the corrupt policemen tries to arrest Ivan, he shoots him, an event that marks the beginning of Ivan's 'sensational' life as an outlaw. In the end Ivan is brutally killed by the police.

Music plays an important role throughout the narrative, and the soundtrack of the film achieved legendary fame. Some of the songs support the storyline; e.g. "You can get it if you really want (…) persecution you must bear, win or lose you gotta get your share, you can get it if you really want, but you must try, try, and try (…) you succeed at last (…)"[14] – is first played at the beginning while the credits are rolling, and the bus is driving from country to town. We see a young man driving a white convertible in the city, and Ivan in the bus laughing and waving as if he knew the person. The song is played again when Ivan enters the ganja trade, and the camera shows marihuana plants, the marihuana trade being one of the few ways to survive the economic hardships of this post-colonial society. The song is played for a third time when Ivan steals a white convertible and cruises around on a golf course. Here the motto seems to be "it does not matter how you get it as long as you do". We finally hear the song almost like a fading wind when Ivan is lying on the beach after he has missed his last chance to escape to Cuba. Can you really get it even if you try?

"The Harder They Fall" – the title of the song is a supplement[15] to the elliptic film title – is the tune that Ivan sings in the studio. He seems to be willing to live up to the words of his song: "I would rather be a free man in my grave than

---

[14] Cliff, Jimmy, "You Can Get It If You Really Want". In: Various, *The Harder They Come* (Jamaica, 1972).

[15] In the Jamaican culture there is a proverb that says 'the harder they come, the harder they fall'.

living like a puppet or a slave" *(The Harder They Come)*, and decides to rebel against the oppressive treatment experienced by large parts of the population. Phrasing his refusal of deferred gratification in traditional metaphors, he tells Elsa that he is not going to wait for any milk and honey up in the sky. Right here and now he wants to have his share of the sweetness of life.

To the lyrics of the song "Pressure Drop", we see Ivan chasing Jose out of the slum, the neighborhood which Jose "controls since birth" *(The Harder They Come)*. The song is sung by the well-known Jamaican early reggae stars "Toots and the Maytals".

"Many Rivers to Cross", another Jimmy Cliff song, is being played while Ivan is wandering through the streets of Kingston. First we see him looking for work in uptown Kingston, where he is humiliatingly turned away by an upper-class woman, then the camera shows him at the market, where he almost gets his hand cut off for stealing a fruit, finally he is at the garbage dump, where he watches a large group of people trying to find something to eat.

The Harder They Come addresses the themes of alienation and violence in different ways. There are moments when we see the protagonist suffering from hunger and other basic human needs, and alienation is the consequence of the overall oppressive post-colonial condition in which Ivan finds himself forced to live. Starting with a panoramic view of West Kingston, we see him on his first days in the city wandering through the slums of West Kingston. The camera depicts the degradation that people are forced to undergo in seeking their daily bread in the dump. We encounter Ivan looking onto this misery before turning and finding his way to Preacher's church. Ivan starts venting his frustration by taking out his anger on Longha whom he resents for bossing him around and challenging him. While he has walked away from provocations and possible confrontations before, he reacts violently after being excluded from the security of living under Preacher's care. When Ivan claims a bicycle which he has repaired himself in Preacher's yard, Longha refuses to give it to him, and Ivan warns him not to play with his own life. The erupting fight shows that this warning was meant literally. In the end Ivan is able to overpower Longha, slashing his face with a pocket-knife and repeating: "Don't fuck with me (…)" *(The Harder They Come)*. According to Fanon "(…) you will see the native reaching for his knife at the slightest hostile or aggressive glance cast on him by another native; for the last resort of the native is to defend his personality vis-à-vis his brother" (Fanon 1963: 54). Because of the disempowerment faced by Ivan as a post-colonial subject, he takes out his anger on the nearest person representing any kind of authority.

"The violence which has ruled over the ordering of the colonial world" (Fanon 1963: 40) is enacted in the ensuing punishment. Ivan is tied up like an animal, stripped of all his clothing and is beaten by a representative of post-colonial authority. The degrading and dehumanizing character of this punishment is drastically demonstrated when Ivan, lying across a barrel with his underwear taken off, loses control of his bladder while he is been whipped. The violent methods of the post-colonial society seem to be a continuation of the colonial order. Even though the camera does not show a courtroom we are made to understand that Ivan is caught within the legal system with the showing of a police van. The judge who sentences Ivan to the punishment that evokes the experience of slavery still wears the wig, a representation of the British legal system that is enforced in Jamaica even in the post-independence years. While Ivan is being punished we hear the judge's voice talking in so-called Standard British English, a further demonstration that signals very little change in the power structures.

The violence that Ivan suffers at the hands of the post-colonial authorities will continue to perpetuate itself. When he feels threatened by the corrupted police authorities, he again reacts violently. Since there is no money to be made in the music industry, which is under the control of a member of the ruling class, for Ivan, an unskilled young man, trading ganja seems to be the only alternative. But, as already mentioned, Ivan has to realize that this trade is exploitative, too, he and refuses to pay the neighborhood hustler Jose the fifteen dollars protection money. Jose, himself controlled by the power structure in the form of the police, wants to teach Ivan a lesson. When the police on the motorbike try to stop and arrest Ivan on his way back from buying ganja in the country, we see Ivan recalling in the form of flashback technique the brutal and humiliating way he was treated by the court. To avoid being punished in that manner again, Ivan, riding on a motorbike, shoots the police officer who is chasing him. For Ivan this signals the start of a life of 'freedom', as an outlaw: "The colonized man finds his freedom in and through violence" (Fanon 1962: 86).

Ivan who always wanted to be a star as a singer, visualized in the star jersey he wears while he records his song "The Harder They Come", finally achieves this status by stepping outside of the social space contained by law.[16] After shooting the policeman Ivan is seen having sex with a woman in a hotel room, Jose's girlfriend as we later learn, who engages in helping to trap Ivan for the police. Yet, Ivan is able to shoot his way out of the hotel, killing three police officers. He then goes to his girlfriend Elsa, asking her if she has heard about his

---

[16] In Jamaican culture the role of an outlaw is often glorified, which is exemplified by the rude-boy culture, an urban youth subculture often identified with the willingness to defend their standpoint violently. For a more detailed account of the rude-boy culture see my analysis of the film *Dancehall Queen* in chapter 7.4.

deeds on the radio. Ivan helps to create his own glamorous outlaw persona by bringing the news of his deeds personally to the newspaper, and letting himself be photographed in different Western movie type poses. With his violent actions Ivan is actually able to achieve what most of the traders did not even dream of, a share in the export business for some of the local ganja traders. "(B)y an ironic turning of the tables it is the native who now affirms that the colonialist understands nothing but force" (Fanon 1962: 84). In post-colonial Jamaica the police as executive force enacts the part of the colonizer and Fanon's words still ring true.

"At the level of individuals, violence is a cleansing force. It frees the native from his inferiority complex and from his despair and inaction; it makes him fearless and restores his self-respect" (Fanon 1962: 94). Fanon's comment, though heavily contested, indeed seems to characterize Ivan. We see him dressed in Western style clothing moving around a hotel, where he appears to be the only guest of African descent. We also recall Ivan outside this same hotel begging a 'brown' guest ten cent for watching his car. It remains as post-colonial irony that with the help of the gun Ivan is able to achieve entrance to most things he was excluded from before. We see the ease with which he moves around in the hotel, his self-confidence, and no one seems to dare questioning whether he belongs there or not. As an outlaw he is able to achieve respect, self-respect as well as respect from others, including the children of the ghetto. Respect is ritually granted as well as denied when Jose, who has received a gun from the corrupt police officer, goes to the slum looking for Ivan in order to kill him. When he does meet with him, Jose is forced to run away from his own neighborhood, chased by Ivan with all the children following him and looking up to him as a hero. Again, Fanon's words seem to capture the post-colonial condition:

> For example, the gangster who holds up the police set on to tract him down for days on end, or who dies in single combat after having killed four or five policemen, or who commits suicide in order not to give away his accomplices – these types light the way for the people, form the blueprints for action and become heroes. (Fanon 1962: 69)

It is not only the children who see Ivan as a hero. In a scene at a photo studio a man comes to visit the photographer and, realizing who Ivan is, wants to have a picture and autograph from Ivan. Ivan is also respected by most of his fellow ganja traders for his violent action against the authorities. That the film itself is based upon the real life story of Ivanhoe Martin, indeed affirms that respect, a basic word-concept in so many communities of African descent, is given to someone who willingly takes on the authorities. Fanon mentions that the colonized person has experienced from the beginning that the colonizer is armed with a gun in order to achieve his goal. This helps to spread the illusion that violence is the only way to gain respect.

> The colonial regime owes its legitimacy to force and at no time tries to hide this aspect of things. Every statue (…) – all these conquistadors perched on colonial soil do not cease from proclaiming one and the same thing: "We are here by the force of bayonets (…)" The sentence is easily completed. (Fanon 1962: 84)

The principle of 'divide and conquer' is repeated in the film. Thus, the police is able to get the information, which finally leads to the end, the death of Ivan, by stopping the ganja trade. "They 'use the people against the people.' We have seen with what results" (Fanon 1963: 80). After trying to track down Ivan for weeks, Detective Ray Jones finally gives up looking for him. But he will only allow the ganja trade to start again when Ivan's fellow traders tell the police where to find him. The traders who have family to feed cannot afford to be faithful to Ivan any longer, while their own children are starving. Ray Jones is aware of this, so he forces the traders to betray Ivan and, since Ivan is one of them, also themselves. We see this happen in the person of Ivan's lover Elsa, who is no longer able to watch Pedro's young Rasta child whom she is taking care of, suffer anymore. She finally goes to Preacher and tells him where Ivan is hiding, which Preacher immediately reports to the police. It is the women who are accused of betraying him, which might be read as a reflection of patriarchal claims in Jamaican society. "(…) and those who most claimed to love him are those who most thoroughly betray him, starting with his mother and ending with his lover" (Cham 1992: 212).

In the film we see Ivan wandering the streets of the slum with nothing to eat, and he finally arrives at Preacher's church. Since colonial times the church has played an ambiguous role for people of African descent. The church was sometimes used as a protective, disguised space where rebellions could be planned. Fanon, evoking Karl Marx's metaphor of religion as opium for the people, points out:

> The colonialist bourgeoisie is helped in its work of calming down the natives by the inevitable religion. All those saints who have turned the other cheek, who have forgiven trespasses against them, and who have been spat on and insulted without shrinking are studied and held up as examples. (Fanon 1962: 67)

Even though people take religion and syncretize it into something distinctively African Jamaican, religion has lent itself as a weapon in the hand of the colonial as well as the post-colonial masters. Fanon's statement, encompassing painful truths about the colonial and post-colonial world, is again evoked, when at the end of the first sermon given by Preacher, he tells his congregation that the 'master' record from America has not yet arrived for the rally. The term 'master record' may be read as a metaphor for US control over Caribbean and West Indian politics as well as its cultural hegemony shaping people's daily lives.

However, it is the flexibility of a colonized people that enables them to turn the founding text of Christian belief, the Bible, into something revolutionary. This is the power of the Rastafarian community, which is not as graphically demonstrated in the film as that of the established religion, but at least it is alluded to. The Rastafarian Pedro "(…) lives simply, upright, eats fresh foods with no salt or preservative, eschews violence, reads the Scriptures, and besides daily praising Jah Rastafari, tends to his family" (McFarlane, Murrell, Spencer 1998: 288). Pedro who has most of the non-violent characteristics lacking in Ivan could be seen as a figure that resists the final pitfall of selling out Ivan. Like Ivan, Pedro would like to see the local traders earn more in the ganja business, and he does not give in to the pressure of the corrupt police. Even though Pedro's son Rupert is sick and suffering, because of Pedro's inability to sell ganja, he is not willing to tell the authorities where Ivan is hiding. Pedro as Rastafarian thus becomes a symbol of resistance and of integrity in post-colonial Jamaica.

If the film grants an eminent status to music, it shows how Ivan's and other musicians' artistic talents are dealt with as profit-generating commodities to be bought at the cheapest possible price by the music producer, Mr. Hilton. Ivan and the other musicians are reduced to their function in a capitalistic context, they become commodities themselves. We are first introduced to Mr. Hilton, the music producer who seems to control the entire music industry in Jamaica via a radio commercial. We see Ivan looking into a display window with music instruments, while the voice on the commercial tells that one can get all musical needs fulfilled at Hilton's. "Hilton has everything in music" (The Harder They Come). We see and hear Ivan calling Mr. Hilton outside his gate, and Hilton, a well-fed and confident European with a touch of African blood, drives a white convertible, very similar to the one that has impressed Ivan in the opening sequence of the film. Leaving his home after noon to get to his studio, Hilton is stopped by five would be star singers, who have been waiting for him since 11 o'clock. They were sent by someone to see Mr. Hilton, who seems to have forgotten about the appointment and cares very little about the fact. Sitting in his car with one hand still on his steering wheel he asks the young men if they have a song to sing for him. The five singers quickly gather themselves together and start singing, "We are all one big family (…)" (The Harder They Come). They are just as quickly dismissed with the words "I can't use it, too the slow" (The Harder They Come), before Hilton drives away. Ivan, who has been looking onto the scene, starts to realize that it will not be easy to become a recording artist. He finally gets his chance to see Hilton's recording studio after Preacher sends him there with the 'master record' from America.

Ivan is deeply impressed by the recording studio, but also aware of the commodity quality of his talent as singer. He tells Hilton that he has a 'boss' song that will surely sell. Hilton's Chinese engineer gives him an off-handed appointment for either tomorrow or next week. Even though the appointment is given in less than business-like manner, for Ivan this is the big chance he has been waiting for. While Ivan is singing his song "The Harder They Come" – referred to in the film as "The Harder They Fall" – and emphasizes the lines "I would rather be a dead man in my grave, than living like a puppet or a slave" (*The Harder They Come*), Hilton and his engineer, seem to be amused at the passion demonstrated by Ivan while he's singing. At the end of the song Ivan enthusiastically wants to know when the record will be released. He is stopped by Hilton who first gives him a contract to read and sign. Ivan is told that he will only be paid the tiny amount of twenty dollars once for the record. When Ivan refuses to sign Hilton sarcastically wishes him luck as a new producer. We can hear the song "The Harder They Fall" while Ivan is desperately trying to get his record played independently from Hilton. So he visits various important people in the music industry and media, among them a famous radio person-ality, a record distributor and a club DJ. All these individuals tell him that without Hilton's approval the record will not be played. Therefore Ivan is forced to go back to Hilton and accept the twenty-dollar contract. Hilton who has always been sure of the outcome of the situation tells Ivan, "You damn right you will take the twenty dollars" (*The Harder They Come*). Ivan's record is finally released, but not promoted, as Hilton tells Ivan the producer is the one who makes hits, not the public or the singer. Ivan is only able to make his record into a hit when he becomes an outlaw. Then Hilton is also interested in capitalizing more on the record. Therefore he tells the police that before they 'string up' Ivan, he would like to make one or two more hit songs with him.

Towards the end of the film when the two controlling powers meet, the police – the intermediary – and the record producer, Hilton asks about the ban that is put on the record and the ganja trade. The police detective Ray Jones is surprised at his interest. But Hilton is only concerned about the trade because it is the only source that brings money into the slum communities of West Kingston, money that is spent to buy Hilton's music products, as Hilton points out when ganja and music – maybe two of the comforts for the poor – are not available, "then law and order soon finish in this part of town" (*The Harder They Come*).

Summary

The film addresses the subject of violence and alienation in many ways. The physical alienation that Ivan experiences in the city is caused by the overall oppressive post-colonial condition in which the character finds himself forced to live. Ivan uses physical violence against his senior co-worker Longha when he is excluded from the security of Preacher's home. Ivan uses violence against Longha the nearest person representing any kind of authority because of his own disempowerment as a post-colonial subject. The police – the representative of the post-colonial authority – use degrading and dehumanizing physical violent methods to punish Ivan after he cuts Longha. Ivan himself uses physical violence against the police to protect himself from being arrested and brutally beaten a second time and frees himself from his inferiority complex and regains his self-respect. Ivan also uses physical violence to accomplish his goal of securing a share of the profit for the local ganja traders.

7.2. The Novel *The Harder They Come* by Michael Thelwell

Michael Thelwell, professor of African American studies at the University of Massachusetts at Amherst, emigrated from Jamaica. Aside from the novel *The Harder They Come* his published work includes a collection of essays entitled *Duties, Pleasure and Conflicts: Essays in Struggle* (1987).

According to Thelwell, he was invited by Kent Carroll, an editor from Grove Press, to do a novelization of Perry Henzell's film *The Harder They Come* in 1978. Thelwell mentions that the film had become a cult movie for a certain counter-cultural group within the American public, even though he seems to have had some ethical misgivings about the project which at first seemed to be in his eyes "(…) singularly ill-considered, rife with the possibility – nay inevitability – of trivialization and cultural rip-off and altogether a project to be discouraged" (Cham 1992: 178). But in the end he was nevertheless interested, because he had been thinking of doing a book on 'Jamaican working class life' for a long time. Michael Thelwell envisioned a text for his novelization of the film from which the film script could have originated, if the situation was reversed, as is usually the case. He wanted to give the hero Rhygin – Ivanhoe Martin – a social, cultural, political, economic and psychological background, which was missing due to the limited scope of the film medium. Thelwell states that he wanted to compress some sixty years of social history and cultural changes into one generation's lifetime. He writes:

> I have created characters and situations, as well as a personal and social history for the hero, in such a way, one hopes, as to preserve, and indeed deepen, the essential character and vision of the film while expanding its historical and cultural range. (…) I have for reasons of irony and sharpness compressed some sixty years of social history and cultural change some would say – "progress" – into one generation. (Thelwell 1980: 7)

Carolyn Cooper in her essay "Country Come To Town" states that Thelwell's text "explore(s) the intertextuality of oral and written performance" (Cooper 1993: 98).

Thelwell's novel *The Harder They Come* comprises nineteen chapters, which are separated into four books. The reader gets first person perspectives from different characters of the novel with most of the first person narration coming from the hero Ivanhoe Martin – Rhygin. The text opens with Ivan's grand-mother, Miss Mando thinking of her young grandson that he is turning into a big boy now, wandering further away from home, not knowing when supper time is anymore, but she hastens to add what a loving child her grandson is. Thelwell gives an almost pastoral representation of the life in the country for the young boy Ivan – Rhygin. The title of book one, "The Hills Were Joyful", evoking biblical connotations, reflects the romantic character of Ivan's fictional childhood and also places Thelwell's narrative in connection with Jamaican novelist Roger Mais' novel with same title. We follow young Ivan hunting in the hills, fishing, swimming, falling in love for the first time with the pretty young village girl Miriam, having dreams of becoming a fisherman, then an entertainer after he is been taken to the café of Miss Ida – 'the sporting lady' – by his friend Dudus. From Mass Nattie, a Garveyite like Ivan's grandmother, he learns about the African Jamaican peasant culture and history. In Book One we learn about the death of Ivan's grandmother with a detailed description of a traditional African Jamaican funeral. After the funeral, Ivan is determined to put into action his wish to leave for the city, find his mother and become a famous entertainer.

Book Two "Another Generation Cometh" narrativizes the opening scene of the film where we meet Ivan on the bus going to Kingston. Thelwell provides a very authentic description of what it means to travel in Jamaica. The quarrels, the laughter, the lively discussions in an always overcrowded bus are all part of the Jamaican 'public-private' transportation experience. In Book Two we also get an in-depth study of Ivan's arrival in the city, how he is swindled by a young pushcart driver as well as by Jose, whom we already encountered in the movie. We follow Ivan to a slum in West Kingston, where he visits his mother and afterwards we follow him wandering through the city in loneliness and desolation with nothing to eat.

In Book Three, "By the Waters of Babylon", Ivan arrives at Preacher Ramsey's church, where he learns that his mother is dead. Thelwell gives a long depiction of Ivan's development into a movie fan, never missing a Western show at the Rialto. Here the text comments on the influence of American violent movie culture on young urban Jamaican males. Ivan meets and becomes friends with other inner-city youths with nicknames like Bogart, Cagney, Peter Lorre, names taken from movie stars. Here Hilton, the wealthy music producer is introduced as a macho-man who picks up or who is picked up by American tourist women at the Sheraton hotel bar. In this chapter we again meet Jose as a small time criminal who got his prison sentence shortened by six months in exchange for becoming an informer for Mass Ray – Ray Jones, one of the first graduates of the special police school set up by the Americans in Panama.

"Presshah Drop" is the title of book four, where we encounter Ivan laying in bed for three days after his punishment for cutting up Longha, his back torn up from the beating. Instead of one track as in the film he cuts two tracks for

Hilton, one for each side, "The Harder They Come" and "You Can Get If You Really Want". Ivan then meets Ras Pedro – Petah, a very conscious non-violent man. Thelwell hints at the possible connection of the ganja trade with the Jamaican government. He also mentions a possible conflict between the army and the police in Jamaican society; a non-fictional chapter of contemporary Jamaican history is fictionalized here. Both the army and the police force use those who are involved in criminal activities to get their information.

The first major difference between the film and the novel is Thelwell's use of the songs we hear in the film. First of all we read some of the lyrics when someone is supposed to be listening to a radio or jukebox. Sometimes the lyrics are used as quotation at the beginning of a chapter or book. Next to the song lyrics Thelwell gives Rastafarian versions of different songs common among the Jamaican Christian peasant culture where in the film we listen to different songs from the soundtrack.

The language of the book changes back and forth between so-called Standard English and Jamaican Patois.

> The work done in the film by the camera – narrative and description – would be rendered in standard English, as would be much of the speech of middle-class characters. The patois would be introduced gradually (…). Also, I would try to represent the vernacular on the page in such a manner as to suggest the rhythm and poetry of the sound and cadences of the spoken language. (Cham 1992: 193)

In the appendix of the novel Thelwell also includes a "Glossary of Jamaican Terms and Idioms", as aid for readers not familiar with Jamaican Patois. The language used anchors the film as well as the book in Jamaican life and provides a feeling of authenticity for audience and reader.

Besides the representation of music, another major difference between the novel and the film is the childhood narrated in the novel. Up to the point where Ivan is sitting in the bus – where we meet him in the film – we as readers of the novel have already read almost 130 pages about Ivan's family life and his plans for his future in Kingston. We know that most of the money he is carrying is in one of the boxes that will be stolen later on in Kingston. The bus is described as more crowded in the novel, and we get to meet the bus driver whose name is Collie Man, an Indian drunkard. We also learn that the name of the bus is 'Fervent Prayer' and that God is the co-pilot.[17]

---

[17] There are many more slight differences between film and novel. At his first personal encounter with Rastafarians, Ivan helps a Rasta man whose name is 'Sufferah' to push his cart full of bottles. Further small details not mentioned in the film are Ivan getting mangoes from a garden boy and his being attacked by dogs while looking for work in uptown Kingston.

The novel also tells us that almost seven years passed between Ivan's arriving at and his leaving of Preacher's yard. During this time he gets to know a gang of youths of his own age and develops into a dedicated fan of Western movies. They hang out in the West Kingston slum at a place called the "Salt Lake City Ranch" with the motto "Death before Dishonour". He and his friends acquire the habit of interpreting aspects of their everyday life according to scenes seen in movies. "For these impressionable young men adrift in the city, local events acquire the resonance of spectacle and are interpreted in terms of film metaphors" (Cooper 1993: 106).

Various forms of alienation are experienced/suffered by Ivanhoe Martin – Rhygin, forms of alienation, which encompass location, culture, and individual psyche. I will concentrate on the alienation endured by the hero in his quest to become an entertainer as well as in his attempt to satisfy his basic human needs, and I will only focus on those aspects of alienation that I have not yet pointed out in my interpretation of the film.

One of the first moments of alienation experienced is the displacement caused by the dichotomy of country and town. Ivan has spent all his life living in the security of his grandmother's house and community where everyone knows and helps each other.

> "Lawd, what a way 'im grow big? But Ah would know 'im anywhere; 'im is the dead stamp of 'im grandfather.' And Miss Mando would continue on, assured that should the boy be in difficulty or need, there was one more adult obliged by custom and friendship to come to his aid. (Thelwell 1980: 36)

It is from such security of the country that Ivan leaves to go and live in the city. Ivan, not used to the customs of the city, gets all his belongings stolen and is later deceived by the city slicker Jose, who seems to have taken an interest in him at his first night in the city.

> "Town people dem *different,* different bad (…). All kinds a people you a go meet dere. Some whe' no know no law at all, *at all.* Lie? Mi Gawd! T'ief? Ha' mercy! You no see t'ief yet. Wait, you see! Dem *love* fe work dem brain fe get what is not fe dem, to reap where dey have not sown, to pick up what dem no put down." (Thelwell 1980: 110)

These are the people that Ivan according to Mass Nattie's words first encounters in the city. Because the young hero lacks experience and guidance, he becomes victim of the town people's 'wicked' ways. We see Ivan wandering the streets, hungry and forced to think of sleeping in a tree, although a more experienced city sufferer gets up the tree before him.

There was a rustling of the leaves and the gnome's bearded face grinned down at him, cracking with malicious triumph. "He, he heaw, young bwai! Ah firs' you – you t'ink Ah never see say you was out to capture me resident, no?" "Who me? You mad?" Ivan's indignation was as genuine as the quick flush of shame that burned his cheeks. "After me is not a fowl? Man no sleep a tree!" (Thelwell 1980: 160)

Ivan is ashamed to admit to himself or even to someone else that he was contemplating sleeping in a tree like a bird. In the end the young hero is forced to sleep on a piece of cardboard on the concrete floor in the market reflecting that sleeping in the tree might have been the healthier thing to do. The displacement suffered by Ivan during his first weeks in the city will continue, even though he might find temporary stability in between the phases of feeling alienated.

Having grown up in the country, Ivan has learned from his grandmother and the community around him the value of the land. "One of Mass Nattie's favorite sayings was 'Tek care of the land and you wi' nevah hungry' (…)" (Thelwell 1980: 45). Even though Ivan has rejected the land and has chosen to go and live in Kingston he still knows the land's value. Almost at the end of the novel after Ivan has recorded his songs only to have them boycotted by Hilton and after he has made a success of himself in the ganja trade, we see him going back to the country with presents for his old friends. Like most people who leave the country Ivan did not want to go back before he has achieved some sort of success. On returning, Ivan expected everything to be the same with the exception that a few people might have gotten older and the birth of new children. To Ivan's surprise everything has changed, his childhood friend Dudus has not become a fisherman like his father, but works nights at the café that used to belong to Miss Ida. "The only black face he saw belonged to a white jacketed waiter who emerged from the café with a tray (…)" (Thelwell 1980: 314). This is the café where Ivan as a youth devised his plan of becoming an entertainer. Mass Nattie the well-traveled Garveyite had died the same year Ivan left for Kingston, his beautiful house and garden that had "an African sense of colour" (Thelwell 1980: 45) is taken over by white Rastas who run around the house naked. After seeing all this Ivan goes to visit the site of his childhood home without finding anything familiar. He is forced to ask himself "'Lawd Jesus, a whe' me deh?'" (Thelwell 1980: 320). Ivan finally realizes that he now has lost everything, even the last possible stability that has always given him strength even in his worst alienated moments in the city.

He felt rootless and adrift in a world without rules or boundaries. 'Ivanhoe Martin, you no come from nowhe',' he told himself bitterly, and knew the pain of losing something important, but unexamined and taken totally for granted, so that the first awareness of its importance came only with its loss. (Thelwell 1980: 323)

Ivan had gone to the country looking for something beautiful and familiar, but instead "(…) of the joyous and triumphant homecoming of the mind, he had learned, abruptly and with no preparation, that he had no home to come to. *'G'way bwai, you no come from nowhe'*" (Thelwell 1980: 323). Like most people who leave their home in the country, Ivan had always found strength to carry on knowing there was the possibility, even if he did not make use of it, to go back to his peasant roots, to go back to the land. "For a colonized people the most essential value, because the most concrete, is first and foremost the land: the land which will bring bread and, above all, dignity" (Fanon 1963: 44). Ivan is completely lost when he realizes that this last security is no longer there for him. He begins to even doubt his own childhood memories after realizing how the countryside of his childhood and youth has changed. This change of the countryside becomes drastically visible in the description of the polluted rivers caused by bauxite factories. Regretting that he did not stay in the country in order to take care of the family land, he will now have to suffer the

> (…) worst insult that people had [which] was the sneering "Cho, you no come from nowhe'." For the first time he was feeling what that really meant. Now he realized just how important this sense of place was to his most fundamental sense of himself. (Thelwell 1980: 321)

Ivan has completely lost himself or at least his idea of self. It is this experience in the country that leads to Ivan's change. After coming back from the country, Ivan takes to his bed for three days. According to Carolyn Cooper's reading of the novel he suffers a ritual death, and has to recover from the shock of his experience. He then goes and buys the guns from Midnight Cowboy, but the guns do not restore Ivan's sense of self, "for what was gone could not be restored, but there was something in its place" (Thelwell 1980: 326). Ivan seems to realize the absurdity of his life. We see Ivan – Rhygin – undergoing personal changes, according to Elsa they are good at least in one way: Ivan now starts to tell the stories of the African Jamaican peasant history to Man I, Pedro's son. Yet, apart from this, according to Elsa he seems unable to find peace in himself. Then Ivan actually starts living up to his name Rhygin – raging and turns to violence in order to fight his feelings of absurdity. In his choice for violent (re)action against the police, the intermediaries of oppression, he chooses his own death. Thus, in a sense Rhygin decides to commit suicide when he takes on the system. His "friend" Jose whom Rhygin tries to convince that they could sell ganja directly to the Americans refuses to do so. Jose, born in the city, is more aware of the danger of such a plan. "The townspeople [such as Jose] are 'traitors and knaves' who seem to get on well with the occupying powers, and do their best to get on within the framework of the colonial system" (Fanon

1962: 112). Rhygin 'takes on the system' alone and in doing so, decides and answers one of Camus' questions about the absurdity of life. "Does its absurdity require one to escape it through hope or suicide (…)" (Camus 1959: 7). Even though Rhygin does not commit suicide in the classical sense of pulling the trigger on himself, he kills himself in taking on the colonial and post-colonial system all by himself. He could not have possibly hoped to get away with this. We realize that the only time Rhygin imagines himself accomplishing his goal is in the unreal moment as a 'star-bwai' in the movies. There he imagines himself being looked at by African Jamaican children as a movie hero and gives up his life as a simple human being in order to become a transcendental movie hero.

In the novels *The Harder They Come* and later *The Children of Sisyphus* we see the theme of 'madness' being repeated. We learn that Solomon in *The Children of Sisyphus* was defrocked from the Church of England on the grounds of insanity. In *The Harder They Come* we learn that Izaac, a bright and friendly young man who left his village to become a parson, returns home with a broken spirit after a short stay in the lunatic asylum shortly before he was to finish his studies.

It is revealing that both Izaac and Solomon should have to leave the Church of England seminary because of insanity. In trying to study the Anglican catechism both men end up being so alienated from themselves that they lose their mental sanity. Even though these two men, Solomon and Izaac, seemingly succumb to madness in the world of the colonizer they are able to return or find home in peasant communities. In the case of Izaac the inhabitants of the village have different theories as to the cause of his madness. Some believe it is caused by an evil spirit which has been set against the young man, others think it was due to ganja, referred to as the wisdom weed, then again there are others who think the young man's sickness is due to Izaac himself seeking supernatural power only to have it turned against him. The last opinion is that Izaac's troubles were caused by the "'white and brown man dem'" (Thelwell 1980: 80). According to this school of thought, the cause of Izaac's trouble was not obeah or anything mysterious, but the accumulation of gratuitous and ingenious insults (Thelwell 1980: 80).

> Because it is a systematic negation of the other person and a furious determination to deny the other person all attributes of humanity, colonialism forces the people it dominates to ask themselves the question constantly: "In reality, who am I?" (Fanon 1962: 250)

Izaac is only able to answer the question of his personal identity of who he is within his own ethnic community. In the closed world of the colonizer he is lost because he lacks an identification model.

The defensive attitudes created by this violent bringing together of the colonized man and the colonial system form themselves into a structure which then reveals the colonized personality. This "sensitivity" is easily understood if we simply study and are alive to the number and depth of the injuries inflicted upon a native during a single day spend amidst the colonial regime. (Fanon 1962: 250)

Summary

In the novel one form of alienation that Ivan experiences is the displacement caused by the dichotomy of country and town. Ivan suffers emotional alienation when he realizes that he no longer has any land in the country to return to. This emotional alienation leads to violence for Ivan and other characters in the novel. Ivan uses physical violence to fight his own feelings of emotional and mental alienations. In the novel the police forces the local traders to choose between emotionally alienating themselves from Ivan or suffering physical alienation themselves. The police forces the traders to betray Ivan and since Ivan is one of them, also themselves. In the novel mental alienation is caused by the systematic negation and the denial of colonized humanity by the colonizer and colonial system.

7.3. Alienation and Violence in the Novel
The Children of Sisyphus by Orlando Patterson

Horace Orlando Patterson was born on June 5, 1940, in the parish of Westmoreland, Jamaica. In January 1953 Patterson attended Kingston College High School. Five years later he was awarded a scholarship for the University of the West Indies in Kingston. Before he entered the university Patterson taught at Excelsior High School. He studied economics, but developed a keen interest in sociology during his first years of studying. In 1962, he was awarded another scholarship to do his Ph.D. at the London School of Economics. During his first year at the London School Patterson wrote his first novel *The Children of Sisyphus*, which was published in 1964. In 1965 he finished his dissertation on *The Sociology of Slavery*, and was able to publish it as a book along with his second novel *An Absence of Ruin*. After finishing his studies he taught at the London School of Economics. One year later he returned to the University of the West Indies in Kingston, where he continued his teaching profession. After two years Patterson left the UWI to become a Professor at Harvard University, where he still is considered one of America's leading scholars in history and sociology. He has published various novels and has also written short stories for Jamaican daily newspapers.

In *The Children of Sisyphus* Orlando Patterson confronts us with different characters, most of them are living in the slum of West Kingston, which is called the Dungle. It used to be a swampland where faeces were dumped. Now the place is 'respectable', only garbage is dumped there. The Dungle is situated between the garbage dump and the cemetery. In twenty-three short chapters told by five different characters in first person narrative, we get a picture of different people trying to survive against all possible odds in Jamaica's urban center. One of the main characters is Dinah, a thirty-year-old prostitute who has spent half of her life living in the Dungle. For six years she has lived with Cyrus, an unsuccessful Rastafarian fisherman, whom she supports with her earnings as a prostitute. Dinah is tired of living in the stink of the Dungle; therefore she leaves Cyrus and their child. "She never saw the reason why she should have to be burdened with the care of another human being when she could hardly take care of herself" (Patterson 1964: 19).

Another character, Mr. Solomon or Brother Solomon, was defrocked from the Church of England after three years of theological seminary on the grounds of insanity. Since then he has joined up with the Rastafarians living in the Dungle, where he seems to be more prosperous than most of the other inhabitants. He runs a shop and his house is the only comfortable one with a floor.

Some of the inhabitants of the Dungle see Solomon as the reincarnation of Marcus Garvey, another Black Moses. They believe that Haile Selassie, their God, has sent Solomon to guide and lead them. Everyone respects and fears Mr. Solomon, because he is said to have mystic powers. Most of the novel's philosophical reflections on the human condition are voiced through Solomon.

Rachael maybe the oldest one, or rather the person who has lived in the Dungle the longest, making it her prerogative to know everyone's intimate affairs. She thinks that no one is able to leave the Dungle for long, once they have landed there. Rachael is a character who sees life in a fatalistic manner.

The remaining characters play a minor role in the novel. Mary, another prostitute, lives only for her mulatto daughter, Rossetta. Marbel, who tries to run away from the Dungle, is beaten and taken back by her Rastaman. Before she is taken back to the Dungle she puts an evil spell – obeah – on Dinah. So no matter how hard Dinah tries she will have to go back to the Dungle. On the recommendation of her Jones Town neighbor (Jones Town is another poor West Kingston inner-city community, but is considered more civilized compared to the Dungle) Dinah visits Shephard John, the revivalist leader, to take off the obeah that Marbel has put on her. Obeah is a word used to describe witchcraft practice and may have its origin in the Twi language according to Diane J. Austin-Broos in her book *Jamaica Genesis: Religion and the Politics of Moral Orders.* She writes:

> Obeah, the word for witchcraft practice, possible derives from the Twi meaning "witch" or "witchcraft person" (…) in Jamaica, obeah deployed wandering ghosts of Jamaican construction and elicited its own ritual response. Jamaican "myal" evolved overtime to combat the effects of obeah. (Austin-Broos 1997: 43)

Additionally, the novel provides short perspectives on other characters. In the opening chapter we are introduced to three garbage men. One of them, Sammy, is a sometimes customer of Dinah when his wife leaves for the revivalist church. We encounter Sammy not only at the very beginning of the story, but also at the end. The other garbage men are convinced that the inhabitants of the Dungle are not really human beings. Another character, Mrs. Walkins, is depicted as the rich uptown woman for whom Dinah works for a short period of time. Finally, there is Seymore Nathaniel Montesaviour, the experienced politician, who knows how to infect the people with 'politricks'.

Patterson situates his novel in the Jamaican society of the late 1950s and early 1960s. In the introductory notes of the Longman Caribbean Writers edition (1986), Victor L. Chang states that the novel thematizes the year 1959, that is the time immediately preceding independence which was achieved in 1962. I do not think one can claim any specific year, however, because there are some episodes of Jamaican history which Patterson fictionalizes, for example a revealing joke told by the university student: "(…) not very long ago the island of England obtained its independence from Jamaica" (Patterson 1964: 99).

In my analysis I will take a closer look at the role of skin color, a role that I consider decisive for one's social position and therefore one that helps to perpetuate the alienation process in colonial and post-colonial Jamaican society. The characters I will focus on are Big White Chief and Mary.

> When you examine at close quarters the colonial context, it is evident that what parcels out the world is to begin with the fact of belonging to or not belonging to a given race, a given species. In the colonies the economic substructure is also a superstructure. The cause is the consequence; you are rich because you are white, you are white because you are rich. (Fanon 1962: 40)

Big White Chief is a Black man living in the Dungle. Strangely enough, he is convinced that he is White and it is only because one of his forefathers committed a sin in England that he turned Black as a punishment. The text suggests that Big White Chief used to hold a high position in the civil service,

> (…) an' was due fe some big promotion an' it get to 'im 'ead. 'Im fall in love an' wanted fe married English gal. T'ief government money fe impress her. When them sen' im to prison an' 'im lose both de gal an' 'im job 'im go off 'im 'ead same time. (Patterson 1964: 73)

Big White Chief seems to suffer from insanity, but I will argue that Patterson uses this character to represent alienation of Black selfhood. Because Big White Chief sees the hardship and human degradation suffered by the masses of Black people at the hands of the White colonial masters, he wishes to be White, to become the oppressor instead of the oppressed. "'They want to take our place.' It is true, for there is no native who does not dream at least once a day of setting himself up in the settler's place" (Fanon 1962: 39). Big White Chief

> (…) was short and black, jet black, with a flat face, a broad heavy nose and thick lips (…). As he passed the laughing Rachael he glanced down at her with pitiful disdain and shook his head in resignation. "These natives," he was saying. (Patterson 1964: 70)

Even though under normal circumstances he is in no position to pity anyone, Big White Chief can pity Rachael, because he has elevated himself to the superior status of the White colonizer, who is in control of everything. Thus, he savors to look down upon the native the way the colonizer has been looking down on him.

Big White Chief provides the often-repeated mythical explanation for the enslavement of Africans, 'a sin committed by our forefathers'. Whether it is the Rastafarians who see themselves as the true children of Israel or the White biblical exegesis claiming that African Americans are the Children of Ham. There seems to be a constant seeking for a biblical context of sin to explain the human atrocities suffered by the people of Africa and those in the African diaspora.

> Forms of social and psychic alienation and aggression – madness, self-hate, treason, violence – can never be acknowledged as determinate and constitutive conditions of civil authority, or as the ambivalent effects of the social instinct itself. They are always explained away as alien presences, occlusion of historical progress, the ultimate misrecognition of Man. (Bhabha 1994: 43)

Mary, an older prostitute, lives with her mulatto daughter Rossetta in the Dungle. She is proud of her daughter, because of her light skin color. Against all obstacles, Rossetta does well at school, which Mary explains with the color of her skin. "'Yu no' see she 'ave backra blood in her. Is her father she got de brains from. Me black an' stupid, but her sailor father give her all de brains she need'" (Patterson 1964: 72). The reader can assume that Mary does not really know anything about the father of her child, but nevertheless she feels elevated because the father is White. Mary does not take any credit for herself, that she as the mother is able to send her child to school and look after her. "In the colonial context the settler only ends his work of breaking in the native when the latter admits loudly and intelligibly the supremacy of the white man's values" (Fanon 1962: 43). Mary rejects the ability of children of African descent to perform well, thus negating her own blackness. Rachael also states the belief that people of African descent are not able to achieve educational merits.

> "Higher dem studies? Den is wha' yu an' yu pickney business wid dat for? That is backra business. Wha' de rass yu goin' sen' yu pickney fe higher her studies fo'? Is bust yu wan fe bus' de pickney brain? Education no mek fo' neager people, yu know." (Patterson 1964: 72)

Here the text stresses the stereotype that higher education is not for people of African descent. This is again a moment when, according to Fanon, the native admits the superiority of the White man. In Mary we see a person who firmly believes one "is white as one is rich, as one is beautiful, as one is intelligent" (Fanon 1967: 51). The character Mary is convinced that her daughter Rossetta will one day marry a rich White man who is going to take Rossetta to live in a palace, then her "sweet-sweet brainy, brown daughter" (Patterson 1964: 75) will take her, Mary, to go and live with them. Mary who wishes to become White, but knows that she herself does not have any chance of achieving her goal, thus invests all her efforts and hope in her daughter.

Mary, metaphorically a child of Sisyphus, does not achieve her goal; her daughter Rossetta is taken away from her by the Child Welfare Institution and Mary finally ends up in a mental hospital. Both Mary and Big White Chief are alienated from themselves because of their identification with white skin as being equivalent to a happy and successful life. They believe that because of their black skin color, they will never be able to live a happy and meaningful life. Exemplifying the colonial as well as the post-colonial condition, these two characters confuse social and economic oppression with skin color; the legacy of the colonial system, the self-hate of the characters, is one aspect of Jamaican society. One could compare the characters Mary and Big White Chief with Hagar, in Toni Morrison's novel *Song of Solomon*, who suffers from what Jill Matus calls 'insidious trauma', "(…) effects of oppression that are not necessarily overtly violent or threatening to bodily well-being at the given moment but that do violence to the soul and spirit" (Matus 1998: 28).

Patterson's novel enacts the Manichean world imaged by Frantz Fanon. The description of the Dungle with its socially deprived and poverty-stricken characters contrasts with the description of the uptown residential area, where Dinah works as a maid for Mrs. Walker, a representative of the colonizing class.

> Now in the vicinity of the Dungle, Sammy felt more than ever like cursing. Once more he became frightened by the thought of encountering them again. The cart moved slowly forward. The mean, derelict smell of human waste mingled with the more aristocratic stink of the factory chimneys. Towards the right of the highway several meagre cows strayed in a dry, scorching common. And on the left were the shacks: dreadful, nasty little structures – a cluster of cardboard, barrel sides, old codfish boxes, flattened tar drums and timber scraps. A few, the more luxurious, consisted of the carcasses of old cars. (Patterson 1964: 7)

Uptown is the spatialized and visualized opposite:

> Her eyes roamed over the bright new concrete walls – blue, light green, black, pink and white; oh, the white one was so pretty – completely white outside except for the two black clay pots with the long, slender green ferns in them. And the housewives with their brown and olive-skinned legs pouring out of their Bermuda shorts and their gardener boys with their black torsos gleaming in the sun. (Patterson 1964: 110)

The settler's world is a world of beauty, a place of rejuvenation, whereas the native's world is less than human. In the Dungle the people follow the garbage man to see what kind of 'goodies' he has brought for them:

> It was a free-for-all. A mad, raging, screaming, laughing, angry, hungry scramble. A wolf-pack at war. Men and women and children and beast all joined in snatching and grabbing and biting one another for any new prize they found in the garbage. (Patterson 1964: 9)

This is where the natives pick up and eat the leftovers that are discarded from the settler's part of town:

> (…) they ate fantastic little sandwiches that Ruby had so skillfully prepared, and they nibbled delicately at the cakes and biscuits. They left most of the sandwiches and cakes behind them. Dinah, who was not hungry, could consume only a little of what remained. (…) So like most of the other meals, the greater portion went to the garbage-box. (Patterson 1964: 119)

The figurative language enacts the oppositeness of the two worlds: the delicate way in which the settler eats his meal in comparison to the beastly way in which the native acts out his needs. "At time this Manichaeism goes to its logical conclusion and dehumanizes the native, or to speak plainly, it turns him into an animal" (Fanon 1963: 42). This Manichaeism in the colonial and post-colonial world ensures the perpetuation of the poverty of the 'have nots'. Thus, a woman from the Dungle with seven children has been able to find work but is unable to keep it.

> "The missis come out same time an' ask me if is true dat me come from Dungle, an' when me tell her yes she fire me same time an' never even give me a penny 'cause she say me lie to her an' dat she could'n' keep somebody dat come from a den o' thieves and cultists like de Dungle (…)." (Patterson 1964: 44)

The woman's employer rejects her poverty and thereby condemns her to a continued life in the slum.

The examples pointed out above show how these two different worlds clash. In the native's part of town we see people eating the food that was meant for vultures and other animals. If one is forced to live like a beast one naturally starts acting like one in the end. "A youth plucked the bread of another and kicked him in the pit of his stomach for snatching his piece of bread and stuffing it down before he had time to get it back" (Patterson 1964: 9). The inhuman condition of life in the Dungle is depicted through the eyes of Sammy the garbage man who is not rich, but at least has a job, something most of the people in the Dungle do not have, except for the prostitutes and the few fishermen. Sammy feels threatened, being afraid that one day he will be attacked by the inhabitants, the same way they attack the garbage looking for something to eat. "They made his blood run cold. And the young ones with their bellies and their mouths. They were going to eat him up when they couldn't find anything in the cart. Those ugly, inhuman little bitches you see there. And the dogs beside them" (Patterson 1964: 8).

In the colonized world people often physically fight against each other. When the text introduces Sammy and his colleagues, we also encounter two women fighting each other, one of them completely naked, and the other one only wearing her underwear. "The colonized man[18] will first manifest this aggressiveness which has been deposited in his bones against his own people" (Fanon 1962: 52). These two wretched souls are fighting because of jealousy.

> The two women scratched and bit and tore each other's flesh till the blood gushed down their skins. The woman with the underwear got on top of the other, held her by the hair and battered her head on the asphalt. Each time she smashed the other's head she screamed: "You dirty black bitch, you; trying to tek me man from me! You nasty niggering dog you!" The battered nude barked and bellowed and scratched the other in her face, screaming back: "Ah never trouble you man, you damm' liar. Who would want a ugly runt like dat?" "Call me man ugly! Call me man ugly!" She pommelled the other across her face. "At least it better fe live with him then fe pregnant fo' a dirty Yankee sailor!" (Patterson 1964: 21)

The women are engaged in what today is referred to in the Jamaican context as matey war. According to the Jamaican sociologist Imani Tafari Ama women fight each other to win the right to have a relationship with the man they both desire. She states that these fights between women "have become infamous as 'matey wars', an appellation that derives from the understanding that the adversary of the woman who is perceived to be the first choice of the man in question, is designated the *mate* – hence *matey*" (Tafari 2002: 234). Tafari also points to the spectacle and public entertainment quality of these fights between women, she further mentions that even though violence is often associated with the male gender in the Jamaican society some women tend to imitate violent practice to escape "the inequality in material relations of power that they have to negotiate in their everyday lives" (Tafari 2002: 237). The expressions of violence among women seem to be a reflection of how a great deal of poor Jamaicans deal with diverse conflicts. In the patriarchal structures of the Jamaican society some men tend to demonstrate their hegemonic masculinity in the form of violence against each other. There are women who also tend to internalize and reproduce the masculine mode of power.[19] Even though some

---

[18] Again, the problem of a gendered terminology arises in this description.

[19] I am aware of the history of Jamaican women fighting alongside men in slave rebellions (the famous Maroon leader Nanny) and other major violent conflicts, but daily use of violence in the Jamaican society is more associated with the male than the female gender.

women gain materially, and characterfully from the matey wars, these confrontations do not address the social alienations that produce the expression of the matey wars. As Tafari points out,

> (A)lthough not addressing the taproot of their experiences of symbolic and social exclusions, the power gained in the matey competitions contributes significantly to their reputations and also in some cases enables them to gain some material advantage from their prize men. Nevertheless, in this configuration it is apparent that the dominant discourse informs behaviour insomuch as behaviour informs and substantiates the cultural norm. (Tafari 2002: 237)

Although the matey conflict, with its possible material and character gains, strongly influences the forceful confrontation between some women, women fight each other for a number of different reasons. One is to demonstrate her own personal power to compel another person to respect one's biddings. I will demonstrate this element of violence through the fights between Dinah and Mabel, and the beating of Mabel by her boyfriend.

The character Dinah after finally managing to leave prostitution and the inhuman life circumstances of the Dungle does not want her new neighbors to know about her past. One of her new neighbors turns out to be Mabel, a former rival of Dinah from the Dungle. Mabel, who realizes that Dinah wishes to hide her past, tries to provoke her. As Dinah points out she has left the Dungle behind her so she wishes to have no talks or reminders of her past. Mabel who opens her mouth to tell of Dinah's past is forcefully beaten by her.

> Lifting up the shirt she had been washing, Dinah swung it behind her and with all her might whacked Mabel on her mouth with it. She howled with pain and held her mouth for a few seconds. Then she sprung on Dinah, pushing over the tub as she did so. The two women fell to the ground, drenched all over with soap-water. Dinah was the first to spring to her feet. She snatched Mabel by her short, straightened hair, dragged her a few feet to the side of the fence and hit her head on one of the posts to which zinc was nailed. (Patterson 1964: 79)

Dinah brutally attacks Mabel to accomplish her goal that Mabel keeps her secret. Dinah's demonstrative physical power over her opponent forces Mabel to abandon her haughtiness and respect her wish to have her past living circumstances concealed. Mabel is beaten a second time when her boyfriend found out where she is living after she left him for another man who could minimally improve her social standard. As Mrs D said:

> Mabel man come fo' her from down ah de Dungle. My God, Dinah, you know dat with all the style dat dat gal pull 'pon we is down ah Dungle she come from! Her

man is a terrible bearded man, look like a Rasta. 'Im come with gang an' haul Mabel out ah de room an' gi' her one piece ah beatin'." (Patterson 1964: 146)

The physical force that Mabel's boyfriend uses against her demonstrates his power as male in controlling how and where she lives. Even though Mabel's boyfriend lacks certain material power, he has the physical power as a patriarch to dominate Mabel. Mabel is suppressed physically by her boyfriend and Dinah.

The violent physical confrontations have one similarity. The aggressive undressing of the enemy is represented in the two fights between the women, but also in the domestic violence between Mabel and her boyfriend. The tactics of shaming one opponent by making them a public display is an element that connects all sets of violent conflicts in the novel. In the conflicts between women, the pulling of the hair, the beating of the opponent's head against some hard surface and the beating in the face are brutally expressed. The pulling of the hair reminds one of the biblical figure of Samson whose extreme physical strength was connected to his hair. The wish, and the desire of these women to destroy each other physically are even more vividly demonstrated in the last representation regarding the physical destruction of Dinah. I will refer to this later in the text. In taking out all her aggression on someone whose life circumstances equal her own, Dinah is able to release her suppressed feelings. She proves to Mabel, to the neighbors and also to herself that she remains in control of her life. As pointed out in my theoretical considerations, in the colonial as well as post-colonial situation the natives' readiness to use violence against each other is grounded in the inability to attack the settlers, who are responsible for their miserable conditions. "The native's muscular tension finds outlet regularly in bloodthirsty explosions – in tribal warfare, in feuds between septs, and in quarrels between individuals" (Fanon 1962: 54).

It is not only in Jamaican society, fictionalized in *The Children of Sisyphus*, where we see internal violence, but also in African American inner-city urban community spaces in the US. Toni Morrison also fictionalizes the violence in her novel *Song of Solomon*; I am referring here to the force demonstrated by Guitar against Milkman, and Macon Dead against his wife Ruth as I pointed out above in my interpretation.

In his reading of the colonial and post-colonial world Fanon continually stresses the destructiveness of the natives fighting each other. However, once violence is enacted, the natives might sooner or later use this violence against the oppressive system. In the novel, this does happen at the unemployment office where Dinah first goes to seek work after leaving the Dungle. The narrator tells us about the crowd suffering too at the unemployment office who fight back against the police.

> The symbols of social order – the police, the bugle calls in the barracks, military parades and the waving flag – are at one and the same time inhibitory and stimulating: for they do not convey the message "Don't dare to budge"; rather, they cry out "Get ready to attack". (Fanon 1962: 53)

These people are 'fed up' with the system, they are angry and hungry, therefore they have nothing to lose. They have listened to enough promises from the politicians. "An angry murmur waved through the crowd as two mesh-wired jeeps from the police riot squad, each with around twelve policemen, all helmeted and ready with their tear-gas bombs, arrived" (Patterson 1964: 84). In seeing the police vehicles with their intermediaries of the oppressive system the people's anger is stirred. A policeman has to retreat:

> The pregnant women around him advanced menacingly. One of them came forward and slapped him across his neck, another spat on his trousers. He took one long look at their eyes, swallowed, and retreated to his car. The crowd scattered before it as it drove off rapidly. (Patterson 1964: 90)

Since civilians are never as well armed as the controlling system, they can only use violence against the system in a rather spontaneous, disorganized manner. The internal violence and the small-scale spontaneous violence are both expressions of alienation, and violence becomes the only outlet, even if it is only for a brief moment. Often times these reasons are not touched upon by so-called experts from outside, who are not themselves forced to live under these oppressing conditions. The difference to the so-called civilized world where the majority of the people do not have to constantly struggle for their basic daily needs – food, shelter and warmth, becomes obvious. People who are constantly preoccupied with satisfying their basic needs do not have time to reflect upon their alienated social condition. This leads to the shortsightedness of only seeing their neighbors who are – in their eyes – trying to take away their daily bread. One begins to realize why some governments in the colonial and post-colonial world have little interest in feeding the masses, since then these masses would reflect and act upon their social condition. Instead, a large part of the population is kept in a state of constant material deprivation. This, one might argue, is how the 'civilized' few keep the 'un-civilized' masses in a constant state of alienation.

Even though Albert Camus, on whose writings I ground my argument, does not use the term alienation when questioning the meaning of life, his theory of absurdity contains elements that I consider similar to various aspects of alienation. According to Victor Chang, Patterson admired Camus' essays relating to the myth of Sisyphus. "He read it, he says, obsessively 'over and over, almost like a bible' so that he knew whole chunks of it by heart" (Patterson 1964: x). In titling his own novel *The Children of Sisyphus* a close connection between the works of both authors is suggested. In Patterson's novel we encounter characters living in situations that are true to their fatherly name "Sisyphus". In the novel the living circumstances of the characters could be seen as a metaphor for the rock that Sisyphus has to push up the hill eternally only to have it rolled back just before he reaches his goal, the peak of the mountain.

> "Oh, WHAT a life, what a worthless, lousy, dirty life" one of them cursed beneath his breath, staring at the tick that was sucking the life from the hoary grey ear of the donkey that pulled the cart. (Patterson 1964: 17)

One of the garbage men comments on the lack of value of life. He sees nothing of worth in life, for him life is "worthless, lousy and dirty", as he gazes at the parasite sucking the blood from the donkey. Patterson confronts the reader in the first four lines of his novel with a narrative voice that tells us from the onset, that life is worthless and dirty. The tick sucking the blood of the donkey is a metaphor that the author uses to point to the exploitative quality of life for the characters in the novel. The voice is that of one of the three garbage men who the author tells us

> (...) sat upon the wooden seats of their carts, quietly grunting the fears of their thoughts over the boisterous black heads of the teeming blazing city. Their wide black faces, the bars of their brows were dreary portraits of restrained anxiety. They sat up there, necks droopily outstretched, eyes half awake, askance, mouths permanently half open in some strange, prolonged astonishment, they sat up there like condemned men being hauled by the asses to a fate unknown, unthinkable. (Patterson 1964: 17)

The three garbage men on their way to the Dungle to dump their refuses are anxious about their fate. These three men seem to be condemned to fates that terrify them. Even though they doubt the existence of fate, they fear that if fate does exist then they already recognize their fates.

> They were like men possessed, up there above the city, wretched and lost. Abandoned to a fate which seemed to terrify them, partly because they were perpetually plagued with doubts of its existence, partly because they felt that if indeed it did exist, then in some bizarre way they already knew what it was. (Patterson 1964: 17)

The garbage men seem to recognize their individual fates but the alienating quality of their fates frightens and appalls them. The omniscient narrator's voice tells us that "dismal blankness of their faces seemed to say, perhaps it was nothing more than the workings of the moment" (Patterson 1964: 17). The three men are horrified at their lot and apparently wish to postpone the acceptance of their conditions. The possible acceptance of the garbage men regarding their faith is one of the themes that Patterson develops further in his novel. I mentioned Patterson's fascination with the French existentialist thinker Albert Camus: He responds to Camus' philosophical reasoning regarding the absurdity of life by demonstrating the connection between the lives of the poor in urban Jamaica and Camus' absurd hero Sisyphus. Sammy the second garbage man felt particular moody this morning, he reflects on his domestic strife with his wife or his unfaithfulness as reasons for his foul mood. But, there is another reason for his ill disposition "this morning", as he said, "(…) it was just the Monday morning that was getting him down" (Patterson 1964: 19). Sammy hates Monday mornings, because it seems to signal a repetition of another week of work. As Camus points out in his essay *The Myth of Sisyphus,* regarding the gods' punishment for Sisyphus: "there is no more dreadful punishment than futile and hopeless labor" (Camus 1959: 88). Sammy the garbage man recognizes the absurdity of his labor and he hates the Monday morning that makes him conscious of the preposterous quality of his life and the lives of fellow lowly workers. As he said himself:

> Jesus Christ, how he hated Monday-morning time! It had something about it that positively made him want to vomit. All those weary men pulling themselves out to work with their pick-axes and shovels, their hammers and saws. He hated the sight of those stiff khaki drills with sharp-starch-press threads sticking out all parts of their behinds. He hated, he hated; great Lucifer, how he hated! (Patterson 1964: 20)

Sammy hates all the symbols representing a new week of work. One might compare him to Sisyphus who after pushing the stone up the summit sees the reality of his position as the stone rolls back down from whence it came. Sammy is not as happy with his fate as Camus' Sisyphus.

The third garbage man was hunching his shoulders and constantly trying to hide his head in them because he could not accept his low station in life. As he said, "A street-cleaner. A garbage-man (…). The lowliness of his position weighed down upon him like a boulder" (Patterson 1964: 20). The third garbage man's low station in life is compared to the weight of a big stone. One could compare the weight of the garbage man's low social status with Sisyphus' stone.

To deal with his despair, terror and humiliation the narrator tells us that he seeks refuge in "every incident, every object" that can hide him away from the consciousness of the moment. The station of the garbage man is one of the lowest positions that one can achieve in a class society. The Jamaican society is a class society and the third garbage man is fully aware of this fact, so he seeks to hide himself away from life. The three garbage men represent each a different aspect of Camus' theory as to how the absurdity of life can be dealt with. According to Camus there are three possible ways of dealing with the absurdity of life: One accepts the absurdity of life; one can live on hope or one can commit suicide. The first garbage man looks for signals or maybe hopes. As he says, "after ten years of looking at a tick sucking the blood of a donkey he had never seen it move before this morning. It was some kind of a sign. Sure as God it was" (Patterson 1964: 20). He hopes that the movement of the parasite will indicate a change that he yearns for. The second garbage man recognizes the absurdity of his life and swears at the Monday morning that maybe reminds him too strongly of this absurdity. The third garbage man hides from the moment. He wishes to conceal himself from his reality. He metaphorically wishes to commit suicide. Patterson uses the three garbage men to introduce the reader to the displacement and absurdity of the lives of his characters that we will meet later in the novel

It is especially the depiction of Dinah which suggests such a metaphorical reading. Dinah attempts to escape out of her predicament with the help of "'a Special Constable. While 'im should be on 'im job prosecutin' me 'im fall fo' me. Now 'im wan' me fe live with 'im all de time'" (Patterson 1964: 22). Dinah hopes to finally have a solid roof over her head, solid walls surrounding her and a floor under her feet, to eat 'normal' meals and to have a chance to live like other women, giving up her life of prostitution. Despite her success in leaving the Dungle and finding domestic work, she does not understand why one person should have to work for another. But in her quest for a 'civilized' life, she puts up with the humiliation imposed on her through the upper-class employer, Mrs. Walker. Reflecting on her degrading experience, Dinah believes that the obeah Mabel has put on her is now working. Therefore she decides to visit the revivalist leader Shepherd John to seek help, which is granted under the conditions that she give up her secular life and join the church. Shepherd John who has been waiting for his 'chosen' one, Dinah, cleanses her in three ritual bathings and baptizes her. Taking Dinah as his lover, Shepherd John decides to leave for England and take her with him. 'De Moder', the older woman who trained the Shepherd, rejects his leaving, because of his popularity among the flock. In the last service given by the Shepherd, 'de Moder' turns out the lights and kills him with a butcher knife and puts it in Dinah's hand. She is physically torn apart by the women of the congregation.

> Then they all burst out screaming again. They dashed in upon her. They ripped the clothes from her. They bashed her head against the floor. They ripped the hair in large chunks from her scalp. Fingernails clawed her. Teeth fastened down around her

ear and ripped it half apart. More teeth upon her belly. Upon her back. Then deep into her breast they sunk. A head jerk sidewards and the breast ripped out from the base of her chest. They kicked her. They pinched her. They spat upon her. She begged. She winced and turned and screamed. But there was no mercy. There could be no mercy. (Patterson 1964: 196)

The ripping, biting, pinching of Dinah's body by women of the congregation remains one of wild animals feasting upon the body of their prey. Dinah is physically torn apart, her body is violently annihilated. Even though one would expect that the congregation would have mercy there is no mercy. The boundless violence that is represented in 'the house of God' points to the dominant character of violence in the Jamaican society as represented in Patterson's novel. It can also be connected to contemporary violence where in early 2006 there were a number of violent acts committed against victims after they left churches or on church grounds. The representation of one of the most physical violent scenes in the novel in the environment of the church can be connected to how many Africans were killed by Europeans, in their mission of bringing enlightenment and the word of god to the so-called Dark Continent. The violent hypocrisy of the members of the church is well demonstrated in the destruction of Dinah. The African American writers Fredrick Douglass and Richard Wright also point to the hypocritical quality of the church. Patterson did not only demonstrate the pretentious nature of the Revivalists but the pretentious character of all churches. The character Solomon is also led to madness due to his inability to cope with the contradictory nature of the English church doctrine.

When she is left almost dead, the garbage man Sammy helps Dinah. According to Kenyan writer and cultural critic Ngugi Thiong'o, Dinah becomes garbage (Thiong'o 1973: 85). "She crawled. The breast was now almost completely ripped off. It dragged on beside her as she made her way up the mound. She was almost there. She knew he would be waiting for her (…)" (Patterson 1964: 188). Dinah is a true child of Sisyphus repeating his interminable quest: "As for this myth (…), one sees the face screwed up, the cheek tight against the stone, the shoulder bracing the clay-covered mass, the foot wedging it, the fresh start with arms outstretched, the wholly human security of two earth-clotted hands" (Camus 1959: 89). Like Sisyphus, Dinah almost reaches her goal, but fails in the end, shortly before fulfilling her dream, she is killed. Unlike Sisyphus, however, she has no more tomorrows. As a mythological figure, Sisyphus goes on living only to beget more children like Dinah. It is impossible to imagine Dinah to be happy; the way Camus can imagine Sisyphus as being happy.

Yet, even in such seemingly inescapable conditions as portrayed in the novel as well as in the larger Jamaican society, there are those who attempt radical change. "The Rastafarian movement is one of the organizations helping the wretched of the earth to rise above the absurdity of their situation" (Thiong'o 1973: 86). In the hopeless society of the Dungle it is brother Solomon who is aware of the absurdity of the situation and he is able to voice it. Repatriation to the Promised Land, Ethiopia, is the only hope that some of the inhabitants of the Dungle still have. We learn during a conversation between Cyrus, the unsuccessful fisherman, and Solomon that the Rastafarian brethrens have sent a delegation to Ethiopia to seek their return. Brother Solomon explains that in a letter from the delegation, repatriation is considered a true possibility. In this moment, Cyrus who has been abandoned by Dinah feels some hope in an otherwise hopeless life. "'So when we hear from them the next time we will hear the good news and know just when we'll be leaving this land of Babylon'" (Patterson 1964: 33). Repatriation date is set for October 25, and the Rastafarian brethren are overcome with happiness. "So now all was happiness. All was the release of pain and the anticipation of more release. All was joy" (Patterson 1964: 104). At the close of the novel with the gathering of Rastafarians from throughout the country in the Dungle, we learn that another letter from the delegation has arrived.

> "It say dat de whole delegation was a flop. Dat de only person they manage to see in Ethiopia was some subordinate official in de public-relations department. No body in Ethiopia seems to tek dem seriously. Dat las' letter dat they write 'bout seeing de Emperor was jus' a pack a damn' lie." (Patterson 1964: 182)

After that, Solomon admits: "'I made up that letter. It wasn't the delegates that write it. I invent everything about the ship coming. It was necessary'" (Patterson 1964: 183). Brother Solomon's explanation for lying to his fellow brethren is that he wished to give the poor some moments of hope and happiness. "'Look! They have before them one hour, two hours, five, no twelve, before the ship come. Twelve hours of unreality. Twelve hours of happiness. Who else but the gods could enjoy such happiness? For the moment they are conquerors'" (Patterson 1964: 186). Brother Solomon clearly realizes the Sisyphusian element in the life of the poor. The novel's depiction of the sufferers shows that there is nothing but a few hours of happiness for those forgotten children of Sisyphus. For a few hours these Rastafarians are happy in their anticipation of the ships that are supposed to come to take them back to Ethiopia. "'I still say it can't happen. Nobody can leave de Dungle fo' good'" (Patterson 1964: 166). These are the words spoken by fatalistic old Rachael, when everyone told her that the Rastafarian brethren were preparing to leave for Africa, repeating what she already said shortly before Dinah left the Dungle. The hopeless life of poverty does not let anyone go free. One cannot imagine that one day these people will repeat the words of Oedipus put into Sisyphus' mouth by Camus: "'Despite so

many ordeals, my advanced age and the nobility of my soul make me conclude
that all is well'" (Camus 1959: 90).

Brother Solomon, the analytic voice of the Dungle expresses it thus:

> "So now him whip is poverty and his claim to superior culture and the Slave Driver
> is the dirty black lackeys who lap up his myths and the Slave Master is the filthy
> white capitalist from abroad. Development! Economic development that is the new
> Sermon on the Mount, Brother. Hear it well. It enslave the white man long time. It
> enslave the brown lackeys and black traitors long time. And it keep us in perpetual
> damnation, Brother. It's our sweat that made England. It's our poverty it smothering
> over now." (Patterson 1964: 34)

The text uses Solomon to reflect on Camus' thoughts about the connection
between absurdity and suicide. At the beginning of the novel Solomon tries to
live on hope, as a Rastafarian he believes that God is inside him. Night after
night he has tried to reach Zion[20] – though not physically but spiritually. After
having given his fellow brethren some moments of happiness, Solomon decides
that his life is no longer worth living. "Does its absurdity require one to escape
it through hope or suicide (…)" (Camus 1959: 7). At this moment he reflects
back on his life and on the last section of Henry King's *Sic Vitae* sonnet, which
he had found in a book on metaphysical poetry during his studies as parson.
This sonnet had kept reminding him of the happier days of his childhood, and
it was the only spiritual support he had while at college. "That little book was
to become his savior during the three years he remained at the wretched
college. Three years with all those hypocrites. Studying their catechism, praying
to their gods and quarrelling with their whores" (Patterson 1964: 45). The
sonnet was the only spiritual support Solomon had in his early moments of
cultural and emotional alienation. Now shortly before he takes his own life, his
mind goes through the last part of the sonnet:

> The wind blows out, the bubble dies;
> The spring entombed in autumn lies;
> The dew dries up, the star is shot.
> The flight is past – and man forgot
> (Patterson 1964: 189).

To Solomon the writer of the sonnet appears foolish, thinking that his despair
could be taken seriously. Now Solomon takes one last look out of his window at
his Rastafarian brethren as Dinah is returning to Cyrus to die in his arms. "He
burst out laughing. It was a deep wild soul-consuming laugh. It mocked the

---

[20] In Rastafari mythology Zion appears to resemble the state of Nirvana.

shanties and hovels in front of him. It derided the many mounds of filth. Far, far into the night it could be heard" (Patterson 1964: 189). Only the rotten rich or the desperately poor, Solomon thinks, can truly contemplate on suicide. Even though he is poor he still has one choice left open to him, one last moment to act freely, choosing when to die. Patterson like Camus seems to accept that there is very little one can do when confronted with the absurdity of life, but to accept this absurdity and be happy with it or to commit suicide.

As pointed out before, language and education are crucial to the process of alienation. "Every colonized people – in other words, every people in whose soul an inferiority complex has been created by the death and burial of its local cultural originality – finds itself face to face with the language of the civilizing nation (…)" (Fanon 1967: 18). In a post-colonial society like Jamaica the native Creole is seen as 'bad talk' and 'broken tongue'. Even though the majority of Jamaicans understands so-called Standard English, most of them have not incorporated it into their daily lives. Those who master 'Standard' English are often alienated from fellow country men and women because they are then accused of 'talking like books' or like the 'white man' (Fanon 1967: 20). This can lead to double alienation for the educated person in a post-colonial society. On the one hand, one remains alienated from the European cultural educational system in which one has been educated, on the other hand, even though one is respected and sometimes feared by one's community for achieving a 'good education', one is estranged from that same community.

The language spoken by the different characters in the novel reflects different educational levels. Solomon, maybe the most educated inhabitant of the Dungle, had to leave the Church of England because of his alleged insanity. For Solomon, his familiarity with English culture and Anglican catechism seem to contribute to his alienation. His fellow members of the Dungle community fear him:

> Only the most privileged of the cultists dared to address him as Brother Solomon; to everybody else he was Mr. Solomon. Yet, as far as the garbage-man knew he never did anything bad for anybody to fear him. He never cut up anybody, he never murdered anybody. For all he knew he had not even the distinction of having spat at an American tourist. Still everybody feared and respected him. (Patterson 1964: 8)

Solomon is not feared for the usual reason of being dangerous, but for his status as an educated person. The ambivalence of large parts of the population towards education is intensely reflected here and a part of the older generation still believe in the White man's stereotypical vision that education is not for people of African descent.

Big White Chief is another well-educated person who suffers from self-alienation. Even though he has all the features of an African he is convinced of his Englishness. One can understand why the less-educated regard higher education as something which in the end works against people of African descent.

> "Ah still don' believe in too much a dis studying 'fe black people. Look 'pon Mr. Solomon him, yu see 'ow funny-funny 'im gwan. Them say dat 'im was big-big Anglican parson, 'im try fe study more dan wha' 'im teacher dem could teach 'im. Send 'im stark mad. Dat is why 'im 'ad fe leave de Church an' join up wid de Rastafarian them. An' look 'pon Big White Chief, yu did know dat 'im is a very educated man. I knew fe certain dat 'im was big-big in de Civil Service an' was due fe some big promotion an' it get to 'im 'ead." (Patterson 1964: 73)

These are words of warning and an example that Rachel tries to give to Mary, when Mary mentions the possibility of her daughter Rossetta applying for a scholarship to high school. After winning the scholarship Mary's daughter is taken away from her mother by the government, because Mary is unable to take proper care of her child. Rossetta too seems willing to leave her mother for a better life and Solomon comments:

> "Well, you going have to buy good clothes for her to go to school; you have to give her good food, people can't study on hungry belly, you know. But that is not all. When Rossetta go out an' see how Babylon live, when she meet new friends, what you think going to happen? Here will satisfy her no more." (Patterson 1964: 92)

Both quotations bear witness to the spectrum of the spoken word, coming from the old woman Rachael in Jamaican Creole, the other from Solomon the ex-parson. At the unemployment office we encounter a minor politician who is unable to speak the language of the masses. The people in the crowd repeatedly interrupt him. "He tried to speak in the dialect, but unfortunately he had been too well bred and it came off stiltedly" (Patterson 1964: 85). The politician knows the power of language and wants to connect with the people through the Creole language. This would naturally give the impression of him being one of the people, but because of his upper-class upbringing he has no command of the language.

In his novel Patterson deals with the theme of mental illness; he uses the characters Mary, Big White Chief and Solomon to represent diverse forms of mental insanity. After the prostitute Mary is beaten by a drunken sadistic American sailor, who is aware of the value of his "Yankee dollars" (Patterson 1964: 142), and by the police, she is incarcerated for a few days. Mary is offered to sign over her daughter for adoption in exchange for her own freedom. As the "light skin" welfare worker said to Mary

> "Now listen, girl," the lady said more firmly, "you're on a serious charge. You realize you could get years for this. In any case we would be in charge of the girl and even if in the unlikely event, you were set free we could press the issue for keeping her. Now if you are sensible and sign for this adoption perhaps we could arrange something for you." (Patterson 1964: 177)

Mary, who is even more frightened of the brown woman representing the English colonial power than the Black policeman who beats her, agrees to sign the papers; she hopes she will have time to get to her daughter before the welfare worker. Mary successes in getting to her daughter, but the police come and take her daughter from her. "They smashed the door open and went inside. 'No!' Mary's voice broke out. Then again the heavy, muffled thuds, the screams, the shaking of the huts. Suddenly the girl runs out. Mary dashed out after her" (Patterson 1964: 84). Mary loses her "sweet-sweet" daughter. She is unable to live without her only hope; she loses her mind. She is taken to a mental hospital by the same system, which causes her madness. The story of Mary's mental displacement is told by urban Rastafarians to their country brethren as an antidote as to the evilness of the colonial 'Babylon' system. "Did they not witness the agony of the poor slut Mary who was not even one of them, how they maimed and twisted her, then came back for her in the black van and took her off to the asylum?" (Patterson 1964: 189). The physical and emotional violence committed against Mary leads to her insanity. The violence and alienation of the oppressive colonial system that is represented in the novel robs the colonized of their children and even their mind. The acts of violence committed against Mary due to her color and class is one of the burden of the poor African Jamaicans in the colonial/post-colonial society. As Fanon points out it is during the calm times of colonialism that one witnesses mental pathology. He states that "(T)here is thus during this calm period of successful colonization a regular and important mental pathology which is the direct product of oppression" (Fanon 1962: 251). Madness caused by alienating violence is a theme also represented by Michael Thelwell in his novel *The Harder They Come*, and by Rick Elgood in the film *Dancehall Queen*. I will point to the character and the specific circumstance that cause the mental illness, when I examine the film later.

Big White Chief is another character in the novel who suffers from mental illness. He became mentally ill according to Rachael when "'Im fall in love an' wanted fe married English gal. T'ief government money fe impress her. When them sen' 'im to prison an' 'im lose both de gal an' 'im job 'im go off 'im 'ead same time'" (Patterson 1964: 89). Big White Chief steals money to be able to afford a life with an English girl; he wanted to live an English life. In the end he is caught and destined to live among the poor Black sufferers. Big White Chief now finds his 'English life' and heritage in his ill mental state. The alienation that Big White Chief suffers in losing his English love and having to spend time in jail contributed to his mental illness. As I argued above Big White Chief also represents alienation of Black selfhood in the novel.

Summary

In the novel both characters Mary and Big White Chief experience emotional alienation because they both negate their Black selfhood. Both characters believe that one is rich because one is White or that only Whites are rich. The Manichean world imaged by Fanon leads to alienation for the characters forced to live in the social deprived and poverty stricken space of the Dungle. As represented in the character of Solomon the emotional alienation is caused by the cultural displacement he underwent when he studied at the Anglican seminary. The physical violence between two women over a man of common desire is conditioned by the social alienations of these women. The material gains strongly influence the violence between these two women, but the social alienations which are responsible for the violent confrontation are not ad-dressed. The number of physical confrontations in the novel is conditioned by the inability of the colonial and post-colonial subjects to use violence against the controlling powers that are responsible for their miserable conditions. Violence is then transferred onto a member of one's own social position. The physical emotional violence used against Mary, when the police beat her and then had her daughter taken away from her leads to mental insanity for the character. Mary's mental pathology is conditioned by the oppressive racial conditions she is forced to live with.

7.4. Don Lott's and Rick Elgood's *Dancehall Queen*

The film *Dancehall Queen* (1997) is a 'modern-day Cinderella' tale that tells the story of Marcia, *the mystery lady*, a poor struggling street vendor and single mother raising two daughters on her own. When her 'street protector' Sonny is killed by 'rude boy', 'bad man' Priest, her brother Junior, 'the only man in the house' becomes temporarily insane. Marcia is also forced to deal with the loss of financial support by Larry, Tanya's so-called godfather, when Tanya, her fifteen year old daughter, rejects Larry's sexual proposes. Marcia sees a possible solution to her economic problems when she recognizes the 'ordinary' beauty of the reigning dancehall queen Olivine without her make-up and costume.

Rachel Mosely-Wood points out in her doctoral thesis *Look at Women: Representation of Women in selected Examples of Popular Culture in the Caribbean* (2002), that officials at Place Amusement Company, one of the largest entertainment centers in Jamaica, claimed that when the film *Dancehall Queen* was released it was their longest running film to date. The Jamaican film *Dancehall Queen* was written by Suzanne Fenn, Ed Wallace, Don Letts, and directed by Rick Elgood and Don Letts.

The film was advertised as a modern day Cinderella story with no prince charming, but with one strong Black woman. Carolyn Cooper, professor of literature at the University of the West Indies and Caribbean and cultural critic, points to the stereotype of the superhuman Black woman and the derelict Black man in the way the film was advertised. She states that, "the Caribbean stereotypes of the superhuman Black woman and the delinquent Black man meet the European fantasy of the nurturing Prince Charming; and part company" (Cooper 2004: 127). The cliché that Black women do not need any male support in raising their children is questioned and problematized in the film. According to feminist critic Belinda Edmondson in her essay *Public Spectacles: Caribbean Women and the Politics of Public Performances* (2003), the image of the strong Black woman, too strong to be protected by Black men, goes back to the 19th century English male travelers' representations of Black Caribbean women. She writes that "black working class women were usually described as loud, lewd, and not respectable because they were too strong to be 'protected' by Black men and also because they were always 'in the street'" (Edmondson in Scott 2003: 4). The centering of the story around Marcia, a strong African Jamaican street vendor raising two children on her own, calls to mind the 19th century English travelers' representations of Black Caribbean women. It is maybe ironic that one of the film directors is an English male who migrated to Jamaica and has experiences in the advertising industry. As Edmondson points out in her essay,

"(I)t is therefore critical that any discussion of contemporary Caribbean women in popular culture be historicized" (Edmondson in Scott 2003: 2).

Before starting with the analysis of the film there are a number of concepts which I will examine due to the relevance that these terms have for my analysis. I will also indicate what role they play in the discourse on violence and alienation in a Jamaican cultural context.

7.4.1. The Rude Boy

> At its worst it is a "world of violence, suffering and deprivation, police brutality and the cruelty of the poor to poor." (Nettleford 1998: 97)

According to Obika Gray in his study *Radicalism and Social Change in Jamaica, 1960–1972* (1991), in the early 1960s a rebellious youth movement erupted as a distinct force among the urban unemployed. They called themselves 'rude boys' or 'rudies', and devised their own form of resistance culture (Gray 1991: 73). The rude boys were young inner city unemployed males, who used violence against their fellow social class at first and then later at the wider society. Their favorite weapons were the German ratchet knives or handguns. Characteristic of the rudies were to select and invert moral codes that were cherished by upper and middle-class Jamaican society. Whether it was speech patterns or code of dress, the rebellious youth reversed the official codes. Even though the rudies were influenced by some of the same ideologies of Rastafari, for example Rastafarian notions of Black emancipation, they did not adapt all Rastafarian ideologies. "Instead, they drew haphazardly on Rastafarian ideology, borrowing those notions they found useful in indicting their antagonists or in affirming the legitimacy of ghetto culture" (Gray 1991: 74). The rudies did not establish any clear political thoughts or alternatives for social changes; they were also influenced by the Americanization of Jamaican society, which brought them into contact with American cultural exports such as the 'westerns', cowboy movies. These 'western' films were shown almost exclusively in working class neighborhoods (Gray 1991). Gray further points out that the rudies model themselves on the marauding outlaw gangs of these films, turning fiction into facts; their imitation of western film heroes culminated in juvenile gang warfare by the mid 1960s. Gray writes that

> (T)he emerging pattern of gang warfare, combined with a marked hedonism and materialist ethic, set the youths off sharply from the Rastafarians. Protest among urban ghetto youths assumed a distinctive form, as their antagonism reflected the double cultural impact of Rastafarianism and American outlaw dramaturgy. Western

forms of outlaw culture, materialist values, racial assertiveness, and susceptibility to the perils of ghetto culture all were fused in the rebellious youth's identity. (Gray 1991: 75)

I will demonstrate later in my analysis of the character Priest how the rude boy culture continues to grow and change in contemporary representations of Jamaican urban culture.

In his text *Cut 'N' Mix: Culture, Identity and Caribbean Music* (1987), Dick Hebdige states that the rudies were anywhere between fourteen and twenty-five years old and came from all over West Kingston. They were above all very angry because of the ill social conditions. (Hebdige 1987: 72) He writes that "(R)ather than buckle under to a life spent doing menial work or no work at all, the rude boys took to streets and crime" (Hebdige 1987: 72). Even though the rudies came into existence during the 1960s their style of violence and crime has continued up to this day in the filmic representation of Jamaican inner city culture. I will indicate where I see this taking place later in my analysis.

Imani Tafari-Ama examines the rude boys' identity construction from a gender perspective and asserts that the rudies ideology was a prevailing masculinity of cool, tough *badness*. She states that

(M)en in the inner-city communities develop this identity construction as a hegemonic discourse of masculinity, as well as an embodied resistance strategy to countervail the social disadvantages into which they have been constructed. However, this version of violence, as a trope of identity polities, also contains ominous elements of nihilism. (Tafari 2002: 120)

The violence characteristic of the rude boys' identity is represented in the film with the character depiction of Priest, which I will also demonstrate in my analysis.

Tafari further shows that some of the rudies were courted by politicians to act as their clients in the urban grass roots (Tafari 2002: 120). Some of the rudies returned to their ordinary lives of crime after working for the politicians. Tafari quotes Terry Lacey who connected the rudies with the two Jamaican political parties. She cites that

In the period 1966–7 many were armed to provide the "soldiers" for a battle between the PNP *(People's National Party)* and JLP *(Jamaica Labor Party)* in western Kingston. After this short introduction to polities within the system, some of the gangs reverted to ordinary criminal activities, others turned to more revolutionary polities and used their newly-acquired guns to terrorize the rest of society. (Lacey in Tafari 2002: 121, italics added)

The employment of the rude boys by the politicians and members of the upper class to perform violence and antisocial behaviour has also been traced by Laurie Gunst in her text *Born fi Dead* (1995).

In the film Priest defines himself as a 'rude boy' who does not fear. His comment calls to mind lines from different rocksteady records that were released during the 1960s in Jamaica to represent the notoriety and fearlessness of the 'rude boy' culture. According to Rex Nettleford,

> The anarchy and violence of the mid-sixties were reflected in the rocksteady songs of the rudies. Comment on the injustices of the system, on confrontation with the law courts and tragic-comic representations of personal experience in the depressed gully courses characterized the rudies songs. (Nettleford 1998: 98)

The character Priest, identifying himself as a rude boy who does not fear anything is placing himself in lineage with this nihilistic rebellious phenomenon. I will examine further the connection between the character Priest and the rude boy culture later in my analysis.

7.4.2. Dancehall

> Dancehall is the most potent form of popular culture in Jamaica. (Stolzoff 2000: 110)

Dancehall is considered and accepted by many Jamaicans as the latest genre of reggae music. The anthropologist Norman Stolzoff in his published doctoral thesis *Wake The Town and Tell The People: Dancehall Culture in Jamaica* (2000), connects the contemporary Jamaican dancehall culture with the Saturday night dances from the Jamaican slave culture. He points out that even though the slave masters tried to control the slaves' "plays" or "dances", the slaves continued to beat their drums late on Saturday nights. He further states that the slaves in their refusal to let their masters fully control their amusement tried to advance their own cultural agenda. He writes that

> (I)n refusing to let the masters dictate their every move, the slaves advanced their own cultural agenda and political autonomy, gaining a sense of freedom and spiritual transcendence. (Stolzoff 2000: 30)

Even today in some inner city communities in Jamaica members of the poor economic class continue to advance their own cultural and economic agenda through the dancehall culture. I will illustrate this fact later in my analysis. Dancehall is also considered by some Jamaicans as an indigenous music form.

Stolzoff cites Winston Blake, one of the pioneers of Jamaican's sound systems, regarding the indigenous quality of the dancehall culture. He states that

> Dancehall is a culture in itself. In a land where our influences came from the English – or those people – it is something that would seem to be very indigenous to us, something we have created. It basically answers to itself; it answers to nobody. (Winston Blake, sound system pioneer, in Stolzoff 2000: 20)

Hedley Jones, another dancehall pioneer, "builder of the first sound system," points out to Stolzoff in an interview that dancehall has always been with Jamaican culture. He states that "Dancehall has always been with us (…) because we have always had our clubs, our marketplaces, our booths (…) where our dances were kept. And these were known as *dancehalls*" (Stolzoff 2000: 23). The continuing popularity of Jamaican dancehall culture at home and on the international music scene today indicates the still vibrant quality of the dancehall culture.

Stolzoff in his discourse on the roots of dancehall argues that dancehall as a music and performative style underwent several developments in the 1970s. He refers to the emergence of the DJ style, which was to become a very important genre in dancehall music culture. This DJ style would split the local dancehall style, which was associated with DJs and sound systems, and the "international style" which was associated with Rastafarian inspired reggae of artist such as Bob Marley (Stolzoff 2000: 97). Stolzoff writes:

> (D)ancehall was a creative means of reasserting a distinctive black lower-class space, identity and politics. That is, the dancehall itself became a symbol of the division between uptown and downtown, between a music that was increasingly oriented to an international market (roots-reggae) and one that spoke to the local sensibilities of a younger generation of dancehall fans. For example, the dancehall-style DJs relied on Patois to a much greater extent than did roots reggae singers. (Stolzoff 2000: 103)

The division which is sometimes made between uptown – the home of the Jamaican middle and upper class – and downtown – the home of the poor – is demonstrated in the film by the representation of the Larry. As Stolzoff points out the dichotomy of uptown and downtown is very often a description of social difference rather than social space. He states that

> (…) the uptown downtown dichotomy is more of a metaphor of social differentiation – one carved in the social imagination – than an accurate description of the way that space is divided by social difference. While this binarism applied to the rural areas as well to such a degree that the term 'downtown' is transferred onto poor blacks no matter where they live. (Stolzoff 2000: 231)

Dancehall culture as shown in the film represents a distinctive downtown space. I will indicate where I see these factors being depicted later in my analysis.

According to Stolzoff in the 1980s dancehall with its DJ style emerged as the dominant form of dancehall culture, eventually becoming the basis of a new dancehall culture, which openly celebrated the physical space of the dancehall (Stolzoff 2000: 97). I will refer again to the openly celebratory depiction of the dancehall space when I examine the characters Marcia and Olivine later.

7.4.3. The Dancehall Costume

The costumes worn by some female dancehall patrons have triggered a number of comments from diverse cultural critics. I will examine a few of the critical comments and point to the relevance of these comments for my analysis of the character Marcia.

Carolyn Cooper draws attention to the transformation of the female body once one is dressed in the dancehall costumes. She states:

> (...) the styling of the body – the hair, makeup, clothes, and body language that are assumed – enhances the illusion of a fairy-tale metamorphosis of the mundane self into eroticized sex object. The "fantastic" undress code of the dancehall, in the original Greek sense of the word "fantastic," meaning "to make visible," "to show," is the visualization of a distinctive cultural style that allows women the liberty to demonstrate the seductive appeal of the imaginary – and their own bodies. In an elaborate public striptease, transparent bedroom garments become Theatrical Street wear, somewhat like the emperor's new clothes. And who dares say that the body is naked? Only the native. (Cooper 2004: 125)

The use of the dancehall costume to transform the ordinary self into the eroticized sexual object and the metamorphosis of the mundane self are both thematized in the representation of Marcia in the film. I will demonstrate how costumes aid Marcia in her quest to improve her economic situation.

Norman Stolzoff points to the women's physical "ass-et" which is demonstrated with the dancehall costumes. He writes in reference to the female dancehall participants that

> (T)hese "donnettes" demonstrated their physical and financial "ass-ets" by wearing clothes labelled "batty riders", which Chester Francis-Jackson defines as "a skirt or pair of shorts which expose more of the buttocks than it conceals" (...) "Puny printers" (pants that showed the outlines of a woman's genitalia), wigs of all colors,

mesh tops, large jewelry (gold bangles, rings, earrings, nose rings), and elaborate hairdos all became part of the new fashion ensemble. (Stolzoff 2000: 110)

The demonstration of their body as physical and financial assets and the meta-morphosis of the mundane self into eroticized sex objects are thematized with the representation of the character Marcia, who uses the costumes to presents her physical 'assets' and at the same time conceals her everyday identity. I will refer to this matter later in more detail.

Tafari comments on the subversive quality and the class-specific structure of power that inner city women defy with their bearing of the body. She writes that

The cultural rebelliousness of the Dancehall Queen is symbolised by the practices of elaborate *undressing* (…) Dancehall Queens who emerge from the inner-city environment, defy bourgeois norms of morality by *daring to bear* their bodies as a bold appropriation and transformation of stereotyped notions of the *exotic* African body as primitive and/or vulgar in its nakedness. Reclaiming (near) nudity as a subversive discourse of dress in the Dancehall space has been an effective mechanism for these Queens to discursively proclaim the death of bourgeois ideological domination in the domain of self-representation, and the re-creation of embodied subjectivity in their own terms of reference. Thus, Dancehall Queens who bear their bodies embody a disruptive regime of discursive power that presents a direct challenge to class-specific structure of power. (Tafari 2002: 307)

I will point out how Marcia challenges the race-class-specific structures of power with her 'elaborate undressing' later in the analysis of the film.

7.4.4. Analysis

In my analysis of the film *Dancehall Queen*, I will focus on diverse themes of alienation and violence depicted in the movie. I will also emphasize how the themes of alienation and violence can be tied to the historical, economic, political and cultural history of Jamaica. One of the first themes of violence that the film addresses is the force perpetrated on characters accused of being informers. In the film the character Sonny is killed because he informed the squatters on his boss Larry's land of his plans to remove them from the property. Priest, Larry's paid killer, tells Sonny when he stabs him to death to "walk and live and talk and bombo-claat dead" *(Dancehall Queen)*. Priest's comment is said for Sonny, but more importantly for the people witnessing Sonny's murder. Sonny is made to pay the consequences of talking with the penalty of his life. As Larry declares to Marcia in the guise of the mystery lady, informers have to die. The Jamaican sociologist Imani Tafari Ama calls attention as to how poor urban dwellers are further oppressed by discourse of silence as a power mechanism. She writes that

> (w)hile there are obviously deadly consequences for those who are known to talk back to those who prescribe the discourse of silence as a power mechanism, keeping silent ultimately protects the perpetrators of antisocial acts of hegemonic gender power. (Tafari 2002: 231)

The act of silencing the poor who informs is motivated by power mechanisms as well as economic concerns. In the film the major reason for Larry 'delegating' to Priest the death of Sonny is the financial loss he suffers when the squatters rebelled and burned up two of his bulldozers. In the end Sonny is killed not only because he talks, but also because his talking caused Larry a major financial loss, and the price for this is death. Carolyn Cooper also refers to the element of power that is involved in informing. She writes that

> Giving information to authority figures such as the police is not a simple matter of good citizenship. Information is power that can be abused. So the informer is often perceived as a threat to his or her community, disclosing its vulnerabilities. (Cooper 2004: 13)

By being informed the squatters on Larry's land had enough time to prepare an offensive against their forced removal. Even though Sonny did not talk to the police, his information to the squatters gave them some power. The squatters used their force to destroy Larry's property and defend themselves against been forcefully removed from his land.

The fact that Priest killed Sonny on Larry's order points to the possible con-tinuing cliental relationship between the inner-city rudies and members of the upper class in putting forward their own kind of social justice. Larry, a finan-cially wealthy person and economically a member of the upper class, is able to hire Priest to kill Sonny. As Chalice, a friend of Marcia from whom she seeks help in dealing with Priest, said: "Priest is a blood claat terrorist who has killed more than ten people", so he has to move slowly (Dancehall Queen).

In the film Priest stabs Sonny to death with a knife. It is interesting that even though today in Jamaica the favorite weapon of the "bad-man" is the gun; Priest the bad man uses the ratchet knife. As I pointed out above one of the favorite weapons of the rudies is the German ratchet knife, in using the knife to kill Sonny Priest connects himself with his mode of violence with the rude boy culture.

After Priest kills Sonny he further intimates both Marcia and her brother. Priest wants to make sure that neither one of them talks to the police. Junior, the only person who remains at the scene of Sonny's death when the police siren is heard, finds himself in a dilemma. The police who want to know who killed his friend, beat him. Junior is aware that if he talks to the police he risks being killed by Priest. As Marcia makes clear to him while she dresses his wounds from the police beating; "You know, you cannot talk to the police otherwise you are dead" *(Dancehall Queen)*. Tafari refers to the danger encountered by inner-city residents who talk to the police regarding criminal activities. She states that

> (A)n unwritten but very well understood code of ethical behaviour is that those who have knowledge of criminal activities should remain silent or face the consequences of being identified as (police) informers. Those men, women or children who transgress this code virtually sign their own death warrants. (Tafari 2002: 229)

One of the reasons why informing the police of criminal activities might be a deadly pastime is the possible connection between the police and criminals. In the summary of a research project conducted by social scientists from the University of the West Indies, *They Cry 'Respect'! Urban Violence and Poverty in Jamaica* (1996), Horace Levy points to the awareness of inner-city residents regarding the connection between some criminals and the police. He writes that

> (A)nother factor is the conviction held by some that the police, even while they harass the innocent, well know who the real criminals are and are in league with them, even selling them guns and being involved in the drug trade. The fact that informants get to be known and eliminated by these criminals is traced to the police, who are roundly condemned for it. (Levy 1996: 42)

Even though the film does not establish a clear link between Priest and the police, Junior as an inner-city resident is aware of the possible connection between criminals and the police, so he knows the danger of talking to the police. The film plays on Junior's cultural knowledge regarding the possible link between the police and criminals in the way he expresses fright and anxiety when it comes to talking to the police.

After Priest demonstrates his forceful power to Junior by biting an innocent young man sitting in the bar in his ears where Junior is playing a game at a machine, Junior becomes terrified and runs out of the bar only to run straight into Priest who meets him at the other side of the bar. Priest puts a knife at Junior's neck and warns him about talking to the police. The police come unto the scene at the same moment when Priest is threatening Junior, but Priest is able to conceal the knife and convince the police that he and Junior are friends. After the police and Priest threatened Junior the viewing audiences see him wondering through the West Kingston gullies before he arrived home. When Marcia questions him as to his whereabouts for the last days, Junior becomes confused and closes his eyes stating that he does not want to see the police or Priest ever again. The character Junior feels alienated from the world and wants to close himself off and shield himself from the sight of Priest and the police. As Marcia points out to him, this is no way to live. In the light of the violence and alienation that Junior experiences he seeks to lose himself in darkness. He is unable to face the reality of losing his friend and cope with the violent threats from Priest and the police, he wants to hide in darkness, even if it is mental darkness. As Marcia states, "Junior does not work, bath or even eat" *(Dancehall Queen)*. Junior stops living his normal life, he even becomes alienated from his basic human needs and living conditions.

The emotional alienation that Junior suffers is due to the violent death of his friend Sonny that he witnessed and the constant threat of violence from Priest and the police. As Tafari writes: "(T)hose who control the state and its institutional apparatuses – particularly the security forces – have played active roles in the deployment of the discourse of violence in the inner-city communities" (Tafari 2002: 124). Junior is as much afraid of the police as of Priest. As one of the police points out to his colleague: "Junior just want some raas claat lick, and they are going to break him up till he remembers even his grandmother's birth date" *(Dancehall Queen)*. The police and Priest threaten Junior with psychical violence; the police want to use violence to force Junior to talk, Priest uses force to stop Junior from talking. The use of violence by the police and criminals in some urban communities as controlling device is clearly represented in the film.

Another theme of violence that the film addresses is the psychical force between Larry and Priest. After Marcia finds out that Larry is a "dangerous brother otherwise he would not have been able to run the Go-Go clubs," and that he is responsible for Sonny's death, she sees the possibility of getting rid of Priest and Larry at the same time. At first Marcia turns to the thug Chalice to "use his connection" to fix Priest.

Marcia comes to the conclusion that "no man can help her, so she will have to help herself" *(Dancehall Queen)*. Marcia in the guise of the dancehall mystery lady, 'the sexy bitch' gets Larry's male attention, she also starts to flirt with Priest after he threateningly asks her if she ever wonders why her brother is still alive. Marcia plays Larry and Priest against each other by informing Priest that "ghetto grape vine said it was some big man that contracted him to kill Sonny" *(Dancehall Queen)*. Marcia 'the sexy bitch' tells Larry that Priest is bothering her and when she points out to him that Larry is her man, and that he control things Priest said not for long, and said Larry is too old for a sexy girl like her *(Dancehall Queen)*. In the end Marcia arranged to meet both Priest and Larry at the same location without ever intending to be there herself. Both men fight each other, Larry shooting Priest in his shoulder and killing him with his own knife in the end. Marcia who is aware of the male discourse of violence is able to play both men against each other. Even though Marcia is a woman and objectified by Larry as 'the sexy bitch', and Junior is only alive because Priest likes "Marcia kind of fire" (*Dancehall Queen*), she is able to exercise her own power despite the male structures and discourse that opposes her as a woman. According to Tafari

> (H)owever, contrary to assumptions that these constituencies of social actors are unilaterally disempowered, women also undoubtedly exercise their own power despite structures and discourses that militate against their overall autonomy as a social category. (Tafari 2002: 237)

Marcia is able to get Larry's male attention and protection through her guise of sexy dancehall clothes, speech and attitude. Larry is willing to kill Priest because his male pride is insulted even though he told Marcia before that he normally does not use his gun. It is not only Larry's pride that is insulted, Larry is aware of the inner-city code of behaviour which demands that as a man he should be able to protect his woman. By killing Priest, Larry demonstrates to Marcia, Priest and himself that he is the one in command. As Tafari states, "to be a man who is *the man* or the phallocratic authority figure in the inner-city, is to be the protagonist who embodies the powerful status conferred by the possession of both the penis and the gun" (Tafari 2002: 260).

In the film Larry tells the mystery lady that even though he has a gun he never uses it, because he is too smart for that. Instead he delegates, Larry delegates the killing of Sonny to Priest the bad man who has "killed over ten people". I would like to suggest that only people with wealth and status are able to delegate to others. Larry, a wealthy landowner, has no problem in finding a 'rude boy' to take care of his problem with Sonny. If one examines the history of Jamaica one recognizes that delegation of violence has its roots in the history of plantation slavery. According to Orlando Patterson, one of the major features of Jamaican plantation slave history was the absentees landowners. The daily organizations and functioning of the Jamaican slave society were carried on by overseers; the brutality committed on the slaves was very often delegated to the African 'drivers'. Patterson argues that the drivers were estimated for the strength of their bodies and it was not unusual for the 'greatest villain' to occupy this position (Patterson 1969: 62). He continues stating that "on most estates it was not necessary for a white person to supervise the lashing of a slave by a driver" (Patterson 1969: 63).

One of the forms of alienation that the film refers to is the alienation, which Tanya undergoes, when she is forced by her mother, due to the family's economic dependency, to go along with Larry's sexual advances. Tanya, a teenager, would prefer her first sexual intercourse to be with someone her own age, not with a man old enough to be her father. Larry under the pretence of helping Marcia and her family financially is attracted to Tanya and wishes to have a sexual relationship with the young girl. Tanya informs her mother about Larry "feeling her up", but her mother tells her that "dozen of men tries to feel her up", and that she should "just go along with the program as much as possible" *(Dancehall Queen)*. As Marcia explains Larry's contribution takes care of most of the bills. The young girl is shocked at her mother's responses to her complaints regarding Larry's sexual advances. In the next scene with her mother Tanya accuses her mother of turning her into a whore. As she said, "she did not expect her first sexual experience to be with a man she does not love or a man old enough to be her father" *(Dancehall Queen)*. Marcia is shocked at her daughter's accusation as she said, "she was not doing all of this for herself. She just wanted to make sure that her daughters have food to eat, clothes to wear and some opportunities that she herself never had" *(Dancehall Queen)*. Carolyn Cooper points out that

> (S)omewhat surprisingly in *Dancehall Queen*, the woman is complicit in the sexual exploitation of her daughter. She functions as a pimp, procuring her daughter to Larry. Yet another layer of disguise: It is her concern for her family's economic well-being that precipitates the decision to sacrifice the daughter. But Tanya is devastated by Larry's predatory desire for her since she views him as a father figure. The enforced sexual relationship that Marcia engineers for her daughter is thus not only rapacious but also incestuous. Yet beneath the apparent heartlessness of the mother's action lies a somewhat pragmatic assessment of her daughter's options: Since there is a juvenile suitor in the offing and Tanya seems likely to become sexually active, Marcia figures that her daughter might as well get maximum economic returns on the sexual transaction. (Cooper 2004: 141)

The incestuous nature of Larry's relationship with Tanya is reinforced in the scene when we view Marcia and Larry sitting in the dark like parents waiting for Tanya who tries to sneak into the house after dark. Tanya is confronted by her mother and Larry who demanded an explanation as to where she has been since school was finished several hours ago. Larry asks Tanya why she is wasting his time, as he points out "when he makes an investment he expects to get returns" *(Dancehall Queen)*. Here it is clear that as far as Larry is concerned his economic support to Marcia and her family means he has a right to a sexual relationship with her teenage daughter. According to Tafari the practice of trading sex for material gain goes back to the slave culture where African women were often raped by European men, so trading sex for material was simple a case of making the best out of a bad situation (Tafari, 2002). Marcia in her poor and economic depressed condition is also forced to rely on one of the few economic opportunities open to some poor urban women in Jamaica. Marcia asks her daughter, as to what a young boy of her age can offer her. Tanya is shocked at her mother's linkage of sex with material gain. She indicates to her mother that there is more in life than money. Marcia wants to know if that is what they teach Tanya at school. As she said, "is it what they teach you at school? Well thank God you have a good education. I was not lucky like you, so I cannot think like you" *(Dancehall Queen)*. Tanya is alienated from her mother's view regarding sex. Rachel Mosely-Wood draws attention to the fact that Marcia tries to teach Tanya that there are no moral issues where economic survival is concerned and that as a woman her body is her primary and most basic economic asset (Mosely-Wood 2002: 204). Even though I agree with Mosely-Wood's comment, I think her argument holds true for Marcia the single mother raising two children alone. I do not think her argument holds true for Tanya the teenage daughter. There are generational, and educational gaps separating Tanya and Marcia. Tanya wants to avoid the limitation of her mother's view regarding sex. As Tafari points out:

> In fact sex-for-materiality-trade would not have become such an elaborate feature of social relationship if these actors had had access to the opportunities for upward social mobility enjoyed by their privileged counterparts on the other side of the poverty line. (Tafari 2002: 334)

Tanya attempts with her rejection of Larry's sexual advances to break out of one of her social class limitations of exchanging sex for material gain.[21]

Larry, who is well aware of Marcia's dependency on his economic support, threatens and withdraws his support after Tanya's rejection of him as a lover. Larry's exploitive connection to Marcia and her family is made clear; he further points out that he is going to see how Marcia and her family are going to manage without his contributions, with a demonstrative glance at Marcia. This cinematic dialogue calls to mind the film *The Harder They Come* where detective Ray Jones threatens to starve all the ganja traders if they do not disclose Ivan's whereabouts. In the exploitive relationship between the rich and the poor, one is forced not only to sell oneself, but also one's children. In the film *Dancehall Queen* the character Larry represents a member of the upper Jamaican social class who seems to feed off the poor. In the guise of helping Marcia and her family Larry pretends to be interested in supporting Tanya in getting a good education, but he is only after sexual gains with Tanya. He is also in a position to delegate violence against Sonny because his informing causes him to lose two

---

[21] I am not saying that upper class women does not exchange sex for material, but at the moment my attention is focused on poorer African Jamaican women.

bulldozers. The representation of Larry in the film could be compared with Ray Jones from *The Harder They Come*. Both characters are corrupt and both use their upper social class position to exploit the poor.

When Tanya rejects Larry as a lover he withdraws his financial aid to Marcia and her family. As he said, he is going to see how they manage without his help. Ray Jones too turns against the ganja traders in *The Harder They Come*, when they refuse to tell him where Ivan is hiding. The tactic of the wealthy is to starve the poor into submitting to their bidding. Both characters are aware of the economic displacement of the poor, and the willingness of the poor to turn against their daughters and one of their own social class members in order to survive. As Tafari states, "(O)ut of desperation, some mothers actually encourage their daughter's sexual exploitation – usually by older men – a material method of maintaining the family" (Tafari 2002: 320). The economic depressed condition of the poor is a leading factor in the alienation and violence experience by the poorer class living in the urban center as is represented in both films.

When one examines the film *Dancehall Queen* there are many aspects of the cinematic representation which might be connected not only to the movie *The Harder They Come*, but to Michael Thelwell's novelization of *The Harder They Come*. In his depiction of Isaac the mentally unstable character, Thelwell points to the social displacement and degradation that Isaac experiences at the religious seminary as possible reasons for his mental illness. Also in Patterson's novel *The Children of Sisyphus*, Solomon experiences mental displacement due to the social and cultural alienation, which he experiences at the religious seminary.

In the film *Dancehall Queen* Junior's mental displacement is caused by the threat of violence from Priest and the police. The theme of mental alienation is adressed and represented by novelists as well as filmmakers. In the colonial and post-colonial society of Jamaica one major form of alienation, which is represented by cultural artists, is mental displacement. Characters become mentally displaced when they are forced to cope with alienating violence or with life situations which demean the characters and their cultural history.

Both films *The Harder They Come* and *Dancehall Queen* deal closely with the rude boy culture even though the theme is dealt with differently. In *The Harder They Come* the audience sees Ivan's development from country boy to city slicker who is trying to cope with the exploitive urban conditions. In *Dancehall Queen* one does not get a close look at Priest's development into a rude boy. As a viewer of *The Harder They Come* one can feel a certain degree of sympathy and understanding for Ivan and his struggle to overcome the exploitive violent condition of the city and the music industry. As a viewer of the film *Dancehall*

Queen one is as much afraid of Priest as the character Junior. The character Priest represents the violent anarchy of the rude boy culture.

The dichotomy of the city and the country is represented in the film *Dancehall Queen*. When Junior becomes mentally unstable his sister brings him back to the country. Both Marcia and Junior represent the migration of the poor from the country to the urban space. In the film the tranquil quality of the country is contrasted against the danger of the city. Junior is brought back to the country to rest and recover his 'senses'. One could compare this to Michael Thelwell's pastoral depiction of Ivan's childhood in the country. In both cultural texts the dichotomy of the urban and country is well represented and contrasted. Ivan became nihilistic after he lost the stability of knowing that he has a place in the country to return to. Marcia and her brother survive and start to gain a level of success, maybe because they still have the opportunity to return to the country when life becomes too violent in the city.

Even though the country is represented as a place of rejuvenation, one has to keep in mind that Marcia was thrown out of this idyllic setting when she became pregnant as a teenager. Marcia, denied the security of her family and the country when she became pregnant with her first daughter at age fifteen, was forced to survive on her own. One can only speculate that without a man Marcia was forced to raise her first daughter on her own, Marcia seeks the protection of another man only to become pregnant again. As she said to her friend Winsome, "my two baby fathers are absent without leave" (*Dancehall Queen*). The sociologist Orlando Patterson points to the possible connection between the slave culture and the neglect of some African diasporic men with regard towards their offspring. He states that because African slave men had no legal control or rights over their partners, and given the fact that slave women could be raped by European men without any consequences, the African slaves could never be sure that the children of their partners were in fact their own; to African slave men and their descent "(…) best hope of satisfying their fundamental biological need to leave some progeny in the world would have been to plant their seed whenever and wherever they could" (Patterson 1998: 43). Patterson further points out that this feature encouraged the male reproduction behaviour of producing children without the means to support them. He writes that

(I)n every other known form of human society, from the most primitive to the most advanced, men's decision to take on the responsibility of fatherhood, and hence their age of marriage, is critically linked to their capacity to provide for their offspring (…) After two and a half centuries in which this linkage was forcibly severed, however, Afro-American male slaves, and their descendants, *like male slaves and their*

descendents all over the Americas, developed a reproductive strategy in which these two
aspects of life were no longer necessarily or normatively linked. (Patterson 1998: 43)

African diasporic men have never had the means or possibilities to support
their offspring during slavery, this negative feature of the slave culture still
influences some African diasporic men's attitude today towards their children.
Moreover the unwillingness or maybe incapacity of Marcia's two children's
fathers to support their children economically leads to Marcia's economic
dependency on Larry, who uses this dependency to exploit Marcia and her
daughter.

One can compare the alienation experienced by Marcia and her family to the
alienation experienced by young Richard Wright and his family when Wright's
father deserted his family. I am concluding that one of the contributing factors
for alienation as represented in African diasporic cultural texts is the desertion
of the family by the father.

In the film the negligence of Marcia's two children's fathers is thematized
and stereotypical. Not only are Marcia's two children's fathers "absent without
leave"; "Priest is a terrorist who has killed at least ten people"; "Larry is a
dangerous brother otherwise he would not have been able to run the Go-Go
clubs"; "Junior became worthless since they killed his friend". The representation of Marcia compared to the representations of the male characters is stereotypical. Even though Priest threatens Marcia with violence even putting a knife
to her neck, she is still able to stand up to him. Her brother Junior becomes
terrified and mentally displaced when faced with the aggressive violent threats
of Priest. Marcia even with the knife at her neck is able to cope, later she even
uses Priest's attraction to her to get rid of him. I am not denying the strength
and courage of the character Marcia in protecting and raising her family. I am
criticizing the representation of Marcia as a superhuman compared to the way
in which African Jamaican males are represented as savage, worthless or
mentally unstable. Belinda Edmondson traces the stereotype of the superhuman
Black Caribbean women and the insufficient Black male to the 19th century
Oxford historian Anthony Froude. She writes that "Froude's and other English
male travellers' supposed admiration for the self-sufficiency of Black women
cannot be taken at face value, however, since the purpose of these observations
was really to point out the *in*sufficiencies of Black men" (Edmondson in David
Scott, 2003). In the film *Dancehall Queen* the strength of the character Marcia is
used to demonstrate the deficiencies of most of the male characters. I am also
maintaining that many of these deficiencies are stereotypical in their representations. At the beginning of the film Marcia cannot imagine her survival without
Larry's or Junior's support. As she asks Tanya, "can you imagine life without
Larry", plus her comment to her younger daughter that Junior is the only man

in the house and without his support they would starve. The viewing audience sees that Marcia is able to find other possibilities, when Larry withdraws his financial support and when Junior 'deserts' her due to his mental illness. The film uses Marcia's strength and resilience to demonstrate the inability of African Jamaican men to take care of their children, or survive the pressure of the threat of violence. Given the historical stereotype of the Black male perpetuated during and after slavery, it is not surprising that Marcia points out when asked by the Rastafarian photographer if she has a man; she laughs ironically and answers, "me a man? They don't seem to be of much use now-a-days" *(Dancehall Queen)*.

The representation of Marcia as superhuman Black woman at the price of depicting African Jamaican males as insufficient is not the only 19th century stereotype that the film presents.

Olivine the 'browning'[22] is represented as the sexy and famous dancehall queen. When Marcia in the disguise of the mystery lady is invited on the stage along with Olivine to dance with Jamaican famous dancehall singer Beanie Man, she is later accused by Olivine's 'brown' friends of 'dissing' (disrespecting) the Queen. Even though the film does not verbally comment on the 'racial' difference between Marcia and Olivine, this is nevertheless visually obvious. Belinda Edmondson points out in her essay regarding Caribbean women and public performances that the 19th century English travel narratives always emphasized the physical beauty of the brown women, and laid the ground for the treatment of brown women in the Caribbean today. She writes that "In the contemporary Caribbean, images of brown women are ubiquitous: they adorn tourism posters and newspaper advertisements for glamorous items such as jewelry, and are habitual winners of the region's innumerable beauty contests (…)" (Edmondson 2003: 6). Olivine accepts the cliché of herself as better than Marcia. After she finds out the mystery lady's real identity Olivine declares to Marcia that they don't belong on the same stage. As she said when asked by the Mystery lady if she is nervous, "how I am supposed to be nervous, when my so-called competition is nothing but an ordinary street vendor. So you don't belong on the same stage with me" *(Dancehall Queen)*. When one bears in mind that street vendors are usually African-Jamaican, Olivine distinguishes her historical racial class position from that of the mystery lady – Marcia. Olivine thinks she has a right to be the sexy dancehall queen on the stage, but not Marcia. Edmondson writes that

---

[22] In the Jamaican context the concept of 'browning' means someone of lighter skin color, signifying mixed heritage of African and European ancestors.

> Part of the problem of female public performance is that there are different registers of signification accorded to different racial types, even as the society continues to underplay race and overplay class criteria by which such distinctions are made. (Edmondson 2003: 7)

Olivine is a browning, a light-skinned person of mixed African and European ancestry, a racial category usually associated with uptown, middle-class social standing. When one keeps in mind Edmonds comment regarding the different registers of signification according to the different racial types then one understands why Olivine thinks that Marcia does not belong on the same stage with her. Olivine feels then that she has a legitimate right to be on stage. Tafari points out that race and skin color can be read from diverse social points. She writes that

> (R)ace-colour can therefore be conceptualised as an ideological, political and cultural construct, as well as a socialised component of genetic composition, constituting a continuum of degrees of privilege. (Tafari 2002: 95)

Olivine and her 'brown' friends feel that Olivine should have the privilege of dancing on the stage without any competition from Marcia. As far as they are concerned Marcia's place is outside "selling soft drinks" (Dancehall Queen). In the eyes of Olivine Marcia's legitimate place as an African Jamaican is in the street selling but not dancing on the stage or even as a dancehall queen.

One major aspect of gender, which the film thematizes, is Marcia's insistence that without a man she is not able to cope with the hardships or challenges of her life. Marcia is convinced that she and her daughters will not be able to survive without Larry's financial support. She tells Tanya that without Larry's aid she will not be able to pay her bills. She also points out to Tasha her youngest daughter that Junior is the only man in the house and without his contribution they would starve. The viewing audiences see the character Marcia finding possible alternatives when Junior became temporarily mentally displaced, and when Larry stopped his financial support. Marcia also indicates to Priest that now that Junior is gone she does not have a man to take care of her. Even though Marcia seems despite all obstacles capable of taking care of herself and her family, she still insisted that she needs a man to be able to survive.

In the Jamaican patriarchal society many women even if they are de-facto head of their households insist on seeing the man as head of the household. In his cultural anthropological study of the male gender in Jamaica and other Caribbean countries, Barry Chevannes points to Dorian Powell's argument regarding Jamaican women's insistence of seeing men as head of household even if they are not. He writes that

Dorian Powell found that many Afro-Caribbean women were *de facto* head of household, but *thought* their husband were. Their reasons were all based on the idea that men are the head by virtue of their masculine gender. Here many women fall back on biblical creative myths and injunction. (Chevannes 2001: 219)

The film questions Marcia's unwillingness to come to terms at first with her own female agency. She has managed against all odds to raise her daughters on her own, but she still embodies the cultural ideology that she as a woman needs a man to survive. Maybe one of the reasons why Marcia insists on thinking that she needs a man to take care of her is the cultural context in which she is living. According to Horace Levy inner-city women are respected for working, but without a man, a woman can become victim of rudeness and sexual crimes. He states that

Women are expected to depend on men as a major source of their survival, even though they are also respected for working and earning a good income. A woman without a man can be target of both community disrespect and rape. Even though when there is a man, he has to be tough enough to provide his woman with the protection she needs. (Levy 1996: 37)

Summary

In the film *Dancehall Queen* diverse forms of alienation and violence are represented. Violence is used in the film to silence characters accused of informing. The use of violence is motivated by power mechanisms and economic concerns. In the film mental alienations are caused by police violence and the threat of violence from the rude boy or "bad man". The delegation of violence by the wealthy businessman can be traced back to the plantation slave culture where violence was delegated by the European descendant overseers or masters to the African descendant 'drivers'. Larry is able to delegate violence because of his social position as a wealthy businessman. As represented in the film the young girl becomes emotionally and socially alienated from her mother's social class practice of trading sex for material gains. The tradition of trading sex for material gains among the economically disadvantaged in Jamaican culture can be tied to the slave culture where women of African descent were often raped by European men; so trading sex for material gains was simply making the best out of a bad situation. It is also out of economic desperation that some mothers encourage their daughters' sexual exploitation by older men. The abandonment of Marcia and her children by the children's fathers is a major cause of alienation for her and her children as shown in the film. The desertion of children by some fathers as represented in the film can be connected to African

Jamaican men's attitude towards their children, an attitude influenced by the legacy of the slave culture where males of African descent never had the means or possibility to support their children but were nevertheless encouraged by the slave system to produce as many children as possible.

7.5. Christopher Browne's Film *Third World Cop*

The Jamaican film *Third World Cop* (2000), directed by Christopher Browne, and written by Susanne Fenn, Chris Salewicz and Christopher Browne, tells the story of Capone, a star crime fighter, who on his first day as a police officer stationed in the city of Port Antonio killed three of the most wanted men in a shoot-out "without any back-up". The character detective Boyd a.k.a. Capone, played by actor Paul Campbell[23], is transferred back to Kingston after four years in Port Antonio. On his first day in Kingston Capone also kills three men, which lands him on his first case in Kingston. Capone, a poor boy from the Dungle ghetto returns to his home district where he is reunited with Ratty, a former friend from youth, played by Mark Danvers[24]. Unknown to Capone at first, Ratty is now the 'right hand' of the notorious local Don Oney. "Oney, a 1970s political gun man who lost one of his arms in a shoot-out, migrated to the United States during the 1980s where he became involved in New York City streets organized drug trade; he served five years in Rikers Island prison where he became knowledgeable in computers. After serving his prison sentence Oney was deported back to Jamaica in the early 1990s. Back in Jamaica and the Dungle, Oney regains 'donship' and began trading in illegal drugs, prostitution, illegal gambling, exhortation, racketeering, and other forms of crime" (*Third World Cop*).

In the analysis of the film *Third World Cop* I will continue with my discourse on violence and alienation connecting these elements to the socio-economic, political and cultural history of Jamaica.

The film *Third World Cop* is an action film where gun violence is depicted with the main character killing all of his opponents by the end of the film. The film contains a number of night scenes, which give the film a dark cinematic feeling: The scene at the dance that Ratty 'puts on', and also the wharf where Ratty and his gang go to get the guns from the barrels. The film opens with a night scene of two people having sex in a semi-dark room. The light is turned on when Jacko enters with the two gunmen. There are other atmospheric cinematic shots in the film. When Capone is transferred back to Kingston the camera gives a wide colorful aerial shot of Kingston metropolis and the office of the ministry. Later when Capone goes patrolling in his car with his partner Fly the camera depicts downtown Kingston busy with people and we get a background shot of 'Courts', one of Jamaica's infamous furniture store where one can get furniture on lay-away plans. The next major cinematic scene is

---

[23] Played the role of Priest in the film *Dancehall Queen*.

[24] Also played the character Junior in *Dancehall Queen*.

Capone driving through the Dungle. Dilapidated zinc fences, young African Jamaican men sitting on different bridges at different gully squares. The football pitch that Ratty and his gang built is a dried dirt patch with three sides fenced with old rusty zinc.

The scene at the harbor where Capone and Ratty go fishing, here again one is confronted with the dilapidated gangways into the water where two children are sitting and fishing. The viewer sees a big ship dock in the harbor opposite his view, there is also a loaded cargo ship sailing by. This is one of the few scenes of possible tranquility in the cinematic representation of the inner city Dungle community. From close-up to aerial and wide angle shots, the film depicts the poverty in the Dungle with the diverse tropical building materials, wooden houses, and shacks made from rusting zinc.

In her text *born fi' dead* (1995), Laurie Gunst points to the connection between Jamaica's two political parties and some inner-city gunmen. Gunst traces the history of political violence in Jamaica and the migration of some of the major inner-city gunmen to the United States where they became involved in the street drug trade in New York City, Miami and other American cities. She writes that

> (T)he gunmen began migrating to America just after the 1980 election in Jamaica; by that time Kingston's top-ranking mercenaries had already begun trafficking in homegrown marijuana and transshipped cocaine. They soon branched out from Jamaica into the American market, and the money they made from the drug trade snapped the leash that had once bound them to their politician-patrons. The party leaders, menaced by an outlaw they could no longer control, turned the Jamaican police loose in the ghettos to execute their former paladins. This reign of terror sent posse men by the hundreds on the run to the United States. (Gunst 1995: xv)

The film in its representation of the characters Oney, Ratty and his gang, Not Nice, and Capone, fictionalizes the history of some of Jamaican urban inner-city communities and the violent experiences of people inhabiting these communities. I will demonstrate later in my analysis where I see parts of Jamaican urban people's violent cultural history as represented in the film. Before commencing with the analysis I will define a few concepts, which are relevant for my interpretation.

7.5.1. Deportee

A deportee is a citizen of another country who is expelled from his or her country of residence. In Jamaica the term deportee has come to connote

Jamaican citizens who are deported back to Jamaica due mostly to illegal drug activities abroad. Carolyn Cooper defines deportees as "Jamaican citizens who have fallen foul of overseas law enforcement agencies" (Cooper 2004: 52). Cooper also refers to the ironic and metaphorical use of the term in Jamaica to denote cheap second hand Japanese cars (Cooper 2004: 52).

Anthony Harriott, professor of sociology and lecturer in the Department of Government at the University of the West Indies Mona, points out in his study *Police and Crime Control in Jamaica: Problems of Reforming Ex-Colonial Constabularies* (2000), that deportation of Jamaican citizens from the US, England, and other Caribbean countries has to do with the crackdown on Jamaican posses abroad who are involved in drug trading. He refers to the increasing involvement of Jamaican drug gangs in the international drug trade and the use of deportation by some countries in combating the drug gangs. He writes that

> (D)eportation has become an effective measure for combating drug gangs; consequently, it is a useful indicator of the extent of internationalization of Jamaican criminal organizations. Deportation began in earnest in 1989. In 1987 and 1988, a total of 11 persons were deported, all from the USA. (…) By 1994, deportation increased significantly to 1,434, with 874 or 61 percent from the USA (…) The exponential increase in deportation after 1988 was associated with a crackdown on Jamaican gangs posses in the USA, where they had gained notoriety for their use of violent tactics to increase their market share of the drug retail trade. (Harriott 2000: 19)

In the film *Third World Cop* one of the characters is named 'Deportee', and Oney was deported back to Jamaica from the United States due to his involvement in organized drug trading in New York City. I will demonstrate the further relevance of the term deportee later in my analysis.

7.5.2. Don

According to the *Webster's New World Dictionary*, 'don' is a member of a university teaching staff, or a Spanish gentleman. A don is also a Spanish title used before a man's name. Today in Jamaican urban and popular culture the word don is used widely, but mostly as a title for notorious gunmen with sometimes political or narcotics-political connections. According to Donna P. Hope in her text *Inna di Dancehall: Popular Culture and the Politics of Identity in Jamaica*,[25]

---

[25] Even though Hope's text has been criticized by Jamaican cultural critic Cecil Gutzmore due to the inaccuracy of most major dates in the Jamaican dancehall culture, I think her definition of the terms "don" and "shotta" are correct.

> "Don" is a title of distinction afforded to men who are considered to be of high social, political and economic status in Jamaica. It is particularly used to denote status among men from the lower socio-economic levels and in the inner-city context. The term is commonly used in inner-city and dancehall slang and its definition draws significantly from the distinctive label given to Mafia overlords of the kind immortalized in the film *The Godfather*. The Jamaican term, however, is oriented around indigenous symbols of the ghetto gunman who may sometimes have political or narco-political linkages. Political dons are affiliated to one of the two major political parties of Jamaica (the ruling PNP or the opposition JLP) and generally oversee the running of garrison communities in Jamaica. (Hope 2006: 91)

Anthony Harriott states that dons are usually drug entrepreneurs and organizers of major income-generating crimes, and may also be able to acquire state contracts (Harriott 2000: 96). He also notes that in the inner-city communities where there is evidence of 'warlordism' the local dons usually rule. Harriott further calls attention to the existence of these communities beyond state jurisdiction and outside the reach of its fundamental institution, such as tax paying. He writes that

> (T)hese communities exist, to a large measure, outside the jurisdiction of the state, beyond the reach of its fundamental institutions, such as tax paying, and have neutralized institutions such as the local police. While the state structures have not been completely supplanted, these communities have proceeded to develop their own alternative institutions, such as the payment of tribute and protection tax, and an alternative justice system. (…) In many respects, it is an attempt to replicate the state system, but it operates on the inquisitional principle whereby a judge or panel of judges is responsible for the investigation of reported incidents. (…) Many readily report incidents to this institution rather than the police because there is a much reduced danger of reprisal from the offender and because the outcome is speedier and the service less costly. It is seen by many as being more effective than the police. (Harriott 2000: 110)

I will illustrate later where I see Oney the local don replacing the state institutions.

Horace Levy states in his study *They Cry 'Respect'! Urban Violence and Poverty in Jamaica*, that during the political violence of the 1970s and early '80s each set of men or "military crop" was charged with the defence of its own area and answered to one single leader who reported to the political directorate (Levy 1996: 14). This single leader is today known as the 'don'. Levy refers to the firm discipline of the don over his soldiers. According to him some of the earlier dons were Robin Hood figures that stole from the rich and gave to the poor, but he also points to the other less noble side of these dons. He writes that

(O)f course, there is another, less flattering view of the don, then and now, which emphasises, or at least takes into account, the negative traits. A don in this view is involved in the trade of drugs, a term used by community people to refer only, as we shall see, to hard drugs, mainly cocaine. He distributes guns. (Levy 1996: 14)

The cinematic representation of the characters Ratty and Oney can be traced to early and contemporary definitions of the don. I will refer to this later in my analysis of both characters.

7.5.3. Shotta

According to Donna P. Hope 'shotta' is the Jamaican Creole word for shooter. The term is often used in Jamaican dancehall culture. Hope refers to Christopher Charles' definition of the term "shottas as the gunmen in the informal party militias and the organized criminal gangs that are controlled by the don" (Hope 2006: 94).

Hope herself defines 'shotta' as "an independent inner-city gunmen who operates without the structural constrains of a defined gang" (Hope 2006: 94). I will show later in my analysis of the characters Ratty and Capone the relevance of the concept 'shotta'. I will also connect the term 'shotta' with the 'rude boy' concept of the late 1960s and early 1970s in Jamaican urban and popular culture.[26]

> The shottas are gun-toting men who are rank lowest on the continuum of the violent masculinities that exist in inner-city and garrison culture. In Jamaican dancehall and inner-city culture, the addition of the prefix 'top' or 'don' adds more seniority and respect to the title. (Hope 2006: 94).

7.5.4. Analysis

One of the first themes of violence that is depicted in the film *Third World Cop* is the violence between the police officer Capone and the criminals who killed his partner and tried to kill him as well. As mentioned above, the film starts with Capone having sex with a woman; the knocking on his door interrupts. The person outside is his partner Jacko. When Capone opens the door it is pushed forceful by two gunmen who come in with his partner. Capone is warned by one of the men holding the gun to his partner's head that it is him they came

---

[26] Hope also point out that "shotta" is a direct descendent of the rude boy.

for. Jacko tries to talk to the man holding the gun to his head, but the gunman shoots him in the head when he refuses to sit down. Capone, who has been reaching for his gun under his pillow, while his partner tries to talk to the gunmen, is able to shoot both gunmen that entered with Jacko. Capone's comment, to the murderer of his partner who is badly wounded but not dead, as he shot him at close range is "me a go send you home guilty of charge" (*Third World Cop*). Capone's comment makes it clear that as a police officer confronted with a murder he is the sole judge, jury and executioner. Harriott calls attention to the paramilitarism style of Jamaican police force, which originated during the harsh British post-emancipation period and after the famous 1865 rebellion lead by Paul Bogle. He also points to the excessive use of violence by Jamaican police force, he then connects this excessive violence by the police force today to the original intention of the ruling British government in creating the paramilitary police force in Jamaica. He states that

> Jamaica has a history of episodic political violence, but an even longer history of paramilitarism. The JFC developed in the context of the harsh post-emancipation period, the popular rebellion of 1865 and retrogression to Crown Colony government. It thus carries the historical baggage of being originally fashioned as an instrument of domination and continues to be associated with the excessive use of violence. (Harriott 2000: 80)

Capone in killing the second gunman demonstrates that as a police officer, confronted with deadly violence of the gunmen, he is willing to return this deadly force. He is not interested in arresting or saving the criminals' lives; he is more concerned with ascertaining his violent domination over the criminals.

The viewers see Capone in his next forceful confrontation with criminals on his first day working as a police officer in Kingston. As Capone's superior told him, "his talent is wasted in Port Antonio. They need more men like him on the front line in Kingston where the ministry has set up a special team to deal with organized crime, and she has recommended Capone for a position" (*Third World Cop*). She warns Capone before he leaves, that his method of crime fighting might be effective, but not always right.

Capone and his new partner Fly are riding around in a white 'deportee' car patrolling when Capone notices two young men getting out of their car. One young man enters a warehouse while the other sits on the car waiting. When the young man on the car sees Capone coming he runs into the warehouse calling "Police! Police!" Capone chases the young man into an abandoned warehouse where two other young men are packing out guns sent to Jamaica via the 'mother' church in charity barrels. When Capone identifies himself as police officer, two of the young men open gunfire at him. He easily kills these two young men. The third is hiding behind two barrels nervously putting his gun together. Capone makes no attempts to arrest the suspect, instead he gives him enough time to load his gun, then shoots him before he himself is shot. Harriott states that

> A distinction must be made between police violence as a necessary means for accomplishing a duty (as in making an arrest) and its use as punishment, often based on "factual" or intuitively established guilt. Procedural notions of democracy find a ready parallel in procedural law (just outcomes being linked to rights-protecting and power-checking procedures). From this perspective police interventions, especially in their reactive mode, ought to be essentially procedural. Yet the JCF had had an abiding indifference to procedural law and due process. Police interventions have become less procedural and more substantively concerned punishment. Police forces with this kind of punitive tradition tend to exhibit high levels of violence. (Harriott 2000: 80)

I am ascertaining that the film's representation of the character Capone, and his method of policing shows similarities with Harriott's characterization of the Jamaican police force. Capone demonstrates an indifference to "procedural law and due process," he deadly penalizes most of his violent offenders directly. I would also like to suggest that the film *Third World Cop* represents and draws attention to methods of the Jamaican police force.

I mentioned above that the film seems to represent certain personalities from the Jamaican garrison inner-city communities; the character Capone could be read as a cinematic representation of the 1970s Jamaican killer cop "Trinity". According to Laurie Gunst, Keith Gardner, named "Trinity" was a child of the ghetto, he had a brother who became an infamous outlaw. Trinity made it out via a career as police officer, but many of his youth friends did not. Gunst wrote, "Trinity was a child of the ghetto who got out, and his career led him to kill the grown men he'd once played with when they were all children in Trenchtown" (Gunst 1995: 123).

The representation of the character Capone's social background is similar to the police officer Trinity's social and class background. Like Trinity, Capone was born and raised in a poor garrison inner-city community. Both Capone and Trinity were able to make it out of their inner-city communities via careers as police officers. Capone like Trinity kills some of the grown men he once played with as a child. Capone kills Razor in the first shoot-out he had with Ratty and his gang, and he also kills Ratty at the end of the film. As Capone points out, since childhood his relationship with Ratty was that of brothers. Even though Trinity did not kill his notorious outlaw brother, he was killed by another police officer.

Trinity tells Gunst in their interview that he got his name from a spaghetti western (Gunst 1995: 123). I would like to suggest that the name Capone reminds one of the notorious violent gangster boss Al Capone. Even though the film does not give an explanation as to the roots of Capone's name, I am suggesting that he might have gotten his name from cinematic representations of 'Al Capone'. Gunst points to one possible root of gunmen in Jamaican inner-city communities taking their names and modeling themselves on Hollywood desperadoes: She writes in reference to many inner-city gangs and their taking of names from Hollywood films, that

> (T)he Vikings had taken their name from the movie starring Kirk Douglas, and one of their leaders, Glen Pusey, started calling himself "Dillinger," after his favorite American outlaw; thus began the time-honored tradition of gunmen modeling themselves on Hollywood desperados. The outlaws vied with each other for the distinction of killing top ranking from opposing gangs. (Gunst 1995: 124)

Trinity also discusses with Gunst the impact that westerns and gangster movies have had on Jamaica's cult of badman-ism. Gunst herself refers to "sufferers stories about Trinity showing up at dance halls dressed all in black, with a brace of pistols on his hips like gunfighter" (Gunst 1995: 124).

In the film when Ratty and Capone are reacquainted Ratty invites Capone to be his security at the dance he is having the next day. Capone too shows up at Ratty's dance dressed all in black, and wearing a bullet belt, even though he only carries two guns. I think one could still see some similarities between the fictionalized police character Capone, and the real life police officer Trinity. The film uses real life characters as bases for fictional characters.

When Ratty gives the two youths the 'tool'-guns as Oney commanded him to do, he tells them that it is "a bran new nine, and it is the wickest hand gun ever made" (*Third World Cop*). He refers to the fact that it is the same gun used by the White boy who plays the police officer in the action film. Ratty here assumes that the youths are aware of the film he is talking about. Laurie Gunst draws attention to the connection between Jamaican gunmen and some violent Hollywood films. She writes:

> But long before the posses began migrating to America, they were learning bad-guy style from Hollywood. These island desperados are the bastard offspring of Jamaica's violent political 'shitstem' (as the Rastafarians long ago dubbed it) and the gunslinger ethos of American movies. They are a Caribbean cultural hybrid: tropical bad guys acting out fantasies from the spaghetti westerns, kung fu kill flicks, *Rambo* sequels, and *Godfather* spin-offs that play nightly in Kingston's funky movie palaces and flicker constantly (…) I was captivated by this crazy synthesis between Hollywood and Jamaica's Johnny-Too-Bad renegades. (Gunst 1995: xv)

It is not only Gunst who is captivated by the influence of American violent movie culture on Jamaican inner-city violence. Perry Henzell commented on the influence of American western and gangster movies on his 'rude boy' characterization of Ivan in the film *The Harder They Come*. I demonstrated this in my analysis of the film above.

In my examination of the character Ratty I will focus on elements of violence and alienation that are represented in the film. Ratty is the right hand man of the Don Oney and "someone who takes care of the little people" *(Third World Cop)* in his poor inner-city community. Ratty builds a football pitch for the youths in his community, he puts on talent contests, shows and dances; he is also selling guns that Oney imported from the United States. Ratty is the young man that Capone "took under his wings when his older brother Lion, Capone's best friend was killed by gangs across from the Gully, and the reason Capone decided to become a policeman – so that he could take revenge." Ratty is now the 'top shotta'. Even though he talks about peace, he is selling guns. Imani Tafari points to the importance of football as an alternative to violence in some inner-city communities. She states that "(T)herefore, this is one mechanism that provides an important arena for encouraging the development of alternative notions of (hegemonic) masculinity to the dominant theme of violence" (Tafari 2002: 233). I would like to draw attention here to the contradictions of the character Ratty. Even though he seems to look for alternatives to violence in his community by building a footfall pitch, he is still selling guns, which are responsible for much of the violence taking place in his community.

When Capone visits Ratty at home after they were reacquainted a day before, he finds out that Ratty's mother is very sick and dying. Capone notices the number of medicines that Ratty's mother is taking, and the high costs of these medicines. He also notices diverse gun magazines, plus the same gun manual that he found with the three young men whom he had a shoot-out with on his first day as police officer back in Kingston. Capone is surprised and after leaving Ratty's house he returns to confront Ratty. At first Ratty tries to deny his involvement with the guns, but then he tells Capone to come into business with him. "The two of us can run things, build the neighborhood, there is still money to be made" *(Third World Cop)*. Capone refuses Ratty's offer, telling him that guns only lead to destruction. Ratty tells Capone that the police also use their guns to kill, and asks what is constructive in that. Capone tries to 'reason' with Ratty. As Ratty points out, "no one care about people in the ghetto, government don't care, investors don't come down here, he cannot even get a job because of his address in the ghetto" *(Third World Cop)*.

In Jamaica many inner-city communities are deprived of government services such as garbage disposal, the right to vote freely, because only communities that are politically homogeneous have access to the limited state resources, which are given on patron-client basis (Harriott 2000: 96). Harriott points to community stigmatization for many inner-city residents, which makes it difficult for young men to find jobs; this can be used as a justification for crimes. He writes that

> (M)ost males express little hope of viable jobs as their skill levels are low, and community stigmatisation further reduces their chances of acceptance by prospective employers (with the exception of some state agencies where their political connections provide the necessary entrée). Such exclusion from viable legitimate opportunities in the private sector and reduced access to state resources provided justification for the most predatory forms of illegality. (Harriott 2000: 96)

Horace Levy also mentions that even though it might sound simple, area stigma is a pivotal feature contributing to the violence in some inner-city Jamaican communities. Regarding area stigma he writes that

> (I)t is pivotal because it effectively prevents the people from this area from walking that much desired and badly needed road to survival and indeed self-fulfillment – employment, which has to be outside, since few jobs are available inside their communities. (Levy, 1996)

The stigma placed on certain Jamaican inner-city communities functions similar to the stereotyping of different African diasporian people due to 'race' and class. The area stigma like the stereotype places restrictions on people's identity and limits their chances of finding alternatives to their social problems.

It is not only stigmatization, and lack of state resources, that some inner-city communities have to undergo, but also the daily struggle to stay alive. Harriott refers to the doctrine of survivalism, which takes literal meaning in some inner-city communities in Jamaica. He states:

> The concept of survivalism implies rules and beliefs about social life and what constitutes appropriate behaviour. Here, the people are confronted with stark evidence of precariousness of their existence in the highly visible cases of social failure – the friend who met violent death at the hand of a rival gang or the police, mentally ill persons who have been abandoned by family and society, the hopeless crack addict, and the destitute street people of all ages who were once members of the community. In these conditions criminality is increasingly seen as a form of social struggle. And as unvarnished market relations permeate most aspects of social interaction, giving greater impetus to competitive individualism, the society is perceived as operating on the principles of social Darwinism – whereby all are fair game, and one may resort to any means in the pursuit of one's goals. (Harriott 2000: 101)

The character Ratty, faced with social failure of his community, does not see any other possibility for getting out of the inner-city besides criminality. As he tells Capone while they are fishing before Capone finds out about his involvement with the guns, "he always dream of getting out of this dirty ghetto Dungle, build a bigger and better life, and by the hook or the crook" *(Third World Cop)*, he intends to fulfill his dream. The viewers see Ratty talking to Oney telling him that there is money to make of the dances, but Oney tells him that it is peanuts compared with the plans he has for the guns. Without Oney's backing and approval Ratty cannot put on dances; he works for Oney and as Oney said "he is in charge and everyone has to do what he says." Levy too refers to the difference made by many Jamaican inner-city residents between marijuana – "herb" – and "hard" stuff, mainly cocaine and crack (Levy 1996: 30). He also connects the violence in some Jamaican inner-city communities with the drugs. He states that "(T)he violence and crime of the communities studied are interwoven with the trade in and, to some extent, the use of *drugs*. The link between them is guns, which now arm the violence, raising its level and widening its criminal reach" (Levy 1996: 29). In the film Oney is arming his neighborhood because he plans to start dealing in cocaine. The representation of violence in the film can also be traced to Oney's involvement with drugs.

When Capone goes with his partner Fly and two other police officers to arrest Ratty, Ratty shoots one police officer, while making his escape. He also later shoots Deportee, one of his gang members, because he informs Oney and Not Nice, the corrupt police officer, where the gang is hiding out. This he learned from Capone when he offered him a deal if Ratty helps him to catch Oney with the guns.

After Not Nice raided and killed a member of Ratty's gang, Ratty kills Deportee, then he calls Capone to accept his offer for a deal. In exchange for Ratty giving detailed information as to the where the guns are hidden and the reason why Oney is arming the neighborhood, Capone arranges with his superintendent that Ratty will receive a new identity and be sent to Antigua till the trial. On their way to the airport Capone, his partner Fly, and Ratty are stopped by a police roadblock. The police-blocking the street is Not Nice and another corrupt officer. Soon after Oney drives up in his car with his bodyguard he curses Ratty for his informing, Oney tells him "informer fi dead". Ratty immediately accuses Capone of betraying him. To prove that this is not the case Capone gives Ratty one of his two guns. Capone, Fly and Ratty are able to defend themselves against the shooting from Not Nice and his colleague, and Oney and his bodyguard. After Not Nice, his partner, and Oney's bodyguard are killed plus Oney arrested even though he tries to run away, Ratty refuses to give Capone back his gun. Capone tells Ratty that they made a deal, but as

Ratty says, "if he informs on his people in the ghetto, then he cannot return to them; he will take the trip to Antigua then come back as a bigger hero" *(Third World Cop)*. Ratty is alienated from his friend Capone. Even though Capone tries to help Ratty, Ratty does not feel that he can afford to trust Capone as a police officer. Ratty is aware of the ghetto's code of honor, which sees informers as the worst enemies in league with the police. As Harriott writes:

> In the community setting, the informer is labelled an instrument of the most threatening out-group (the police). In this dualistic world inhabited by insiders, friends and enemies, members of Party A and Party B, poor and 'rich', the informer and enemy – the worst expression of bad faith. The essence of bad faith is the attempt to escape the self – in this case, the identity as a member of the community and the duties and responsibilities associated with this identity, including the duty to protect one's own. The informer is, according to this logic, pretending to be something he is not and refusing to choose himself (as a member of the community). In becoming an informer he dons an identity mask. From this perspective, it is not sufficient to simply unmask the informer; he or she must be punished by death. The stigmatisation of informants, as a defensive tactic tat cuts the sources of information to the police, is thus usually very successful. (Harriott 2000: 108)

Even though Ratty was willing to trust Capone at the time he made the deal with him, after the road-block with Not Nice and his colleague Ratty comes to realize that Capone is no longer one of his people. In the beginning when Capone is reunited with Ratty and former friends, Ratty tells Deportee to "don't test, him a one a we" *(Third World Cop)*. With the interference of Not Nice, Ratty questions Capone's integrity. He seems to come to the conclusion that even if he is willing to trust Capone because of their friendship from youth, Capone is now a police officer, working for the same government which has caused many of his social alienations. Even if Capone is trustworthy the rest of his colleagues and the state is not as far as Ratty is concerned. This forces a social bonding for the character Ratty with the rest of the 'sufferers' like himself. As he tells Capone, "for everything there is a season", and for Ratty this is now the season where his good friend becomes his deadly enemy. An enemy he needs to kill, because his own 'survival' depends on it.

"For everything there is a season, a time for love and a time to for hate. A time for peace and a time for war" *(Third World Cop)*. Ratty is quoting from the biblical chapter Ecclesiastes. According to the *The African Heritage Study Bible* the Book Ecclesiastes gives a glimpse into the life of one who had the means to pursue happiness through any avenue. By quoting from the Book of Ecclesiastes Ratty is referring to the injustice of life and he is aware of how good people suffer despite their goodness and that the wicked prosper in their wickedness. With these words he shoots at Capone, but Capone is faster with his gun. Capone accuses his dead friend of "being a fool". As he said "you could have live, but instead you choose to die" *(Third World Cop)*. I would like to suggest that for Ratty, resident of one of Jamaica's deprived inner-city communities, one of the few choices that he has is death. Ratty is aware that he could never return to his former community and the respect which he enjoys if he takes Capone's offer. He would have to completely displace himself from everyone and most of his life experiences. The film calls attention to what one dancehall artist calls the "scarce comodification of opportunity" for young urban African diasporic males in the Jamaican society today. It would appear from the representation of the film that a few of the limited opportunities open to young inner-city males are police careers or criminal careers – maybe become 'shotta police officer' or just 'top shotta'. The high unemployment of young males in Jamaica has strongly influenced the violence in many communities in the urban centers in Jamaica. When Capone drove his car through the Dungle on his first day working in Kingston, the viewers see young men of all ages standing on street corners. (Even though the film might be playing on stereo-types regarding African diasporic men in general, at the moment I will interpret this simply as cinematic depiction of urban unemployment.) Levy points to the high rate of over 75 percent unemployment in some of Jamaica's violent urban communities which the university team had examined, and draws attention to the fact that inhabitants readily acknowledge the influence of unemployment on crime in their communities. Levy writes that

> The unanimous view, repeated over and over by everyone, was that without work, crime would forever flourish. Clearly there was recognition of the devastating impact on character and personality of the absence for lengthy periods of gainful employ-ment. Impact on the community was well understood. For all, employment is basic. (Levy 1996: 56)

Even though Levy is referring to the particular communities he examines in his report, his statement is still relevant for my interpretation of the situations depicted in the film.

In the film the character Not Nice is represented as a corrupt police officer who is working together with Oney. When Capone, on his first day stationed in Kingston, and Fly returned to the police station after killing the three young men in the shoot-out, Not Nice asks Capone how many birds he killed. Capone answered that he killed three, Not Nice arrogantly smiles and tells Capone "that is not even half a bag" *(Third World Cop)*. The reference by Not Nice to the young men Capone killed as birds dehumanizes the criminals. Levy eplains in his report of certain Jamaican urban communities that some police officers use the concept "bird land" to refer to certain inner-city communities in Kingston

(Levy 1996). Harriott also mentions the dehumanization of criminals in Jamaican society. He writes that

> (T)he frightening threat of crime to society is coupled with the dehumanisation of the criminals as part of a special dangerous class of nonpersons habituated in the use of violence, who may be pursued without regard for the law. As they are presumed to be creatures of a culture of violence who understand only the language of violence, this (it is argued) is the only effective form of discourse. (…) A sort of "social cleansing" is seen as necessary for the survival of the society. (Harriott 2000: 64)

Not Nice dehumanizes the criminal, and feels he has a right as a police officer to cleanse the society of these criminals (one might asks the question who is going to 'cleanse' the Jamaican society of police like Not Nice). When Capone and Not Nice are instructed to "capture or kill members of 'dutty' gang, Ratty gang" *(Third World Cop)* as Capone's and Not Nice's supervisor said, "we are not in the boys scouts" *(Third World Cop)*. The police supervisor already degrades Ratty and his gang as dirty, for him Ratty and 'dutty' means the same thing. Not Nice tells Capone, "me a go spare the government the court house charge, me a go send all ah them goa Dove Cot" *(Third World Cop)*. Not Nice is referring to one of Kingston's well-known cemeteries in the urban center. As far as Not Nice is concerned it does not make any sense to spend tax payers' money on court fees, it is less costly to the government to just execute the gang without trial, because as far as he is concerned, they are guilty already without trial. After Not Nice is given the address of where Ratty and his gang are hiding out by Deportee and Oney, he arrives with his corrupt partner and another police officer just as Capone enters the room and calls out "Police!" Not Nice kills the police officer, then his partner kills one of the gang members. Not Nice also wanted to kill the other member of the gang that was there. When Capone defends the gang member, Not Nice asks Capone if he did not see the gang member killed the police officer. Capone who had jumped on the gang member and knocked him unconscious when he entered the room refuses to cooporate with Not Nice telling him, "no you did. Don't fuck yourself" *(Third World Cop)*, while he points his gun at Not Nice and continues to defend the member of the gang. The willingness of Not Nice to murder his fellow officer and put the blame on the gang member calls attention to the brutality of the police against criminals and the instrumentalization of policemen by the dons. Not Nice wants Ratty and his gang dead not only because he is a police officer fighting dangerous criminals with deadly force; but because he is working for Oney too, and Ratty and his gang have become useless to Oney and must be killed. By killing the police officer and blaming it on one of the gang members Not Nice substantiates to the public the danger of Ratty's gang. Another reason for the character Not Nice killing his colleague could be the director's intention to comment on the internal violence in the Jamaican police force itself. Harriott points to the high rate of offending and violent criminality among the Jamaican police forces, he indicates that it is higher than the crime rate of the society as a whole. Harriott writes that

> Increasingly, police violence is not just directed at citizens but also at colleagues internally. In 1993, 13 percent of all internally initiated disciplinary charges were based on violence of this sort [Charge Book JCF; Table 3.1] This pattern of police offending is an intensification of the pattern for the society as a whole. The society is caught in a contradictory situation in which its most violent offenders are charged with "keeping the peace". (Harriott 2000: 59)

The character Oney is the don in the Dungle ghetto; he is importing guns from America because he plans to "start dealing with the Columbians" *(Third World Cop)*. According to Ratty "he is planning on moving into the cocaine trade big time, so he is arming the neighborhood" *(Third World Cop)*. Oney is also jealous of the respect Ratty gets from the community. As he said, "Ratty should stop focusing on social work, building football pitch, and taking away all the glory from the community, it is him Oney, who looks after youths around the neighborhood" *(Third World Cop)*. When Ratty tells Oney that lots of money can be made from the dances, Oney replies that that this is only small change compared with his plans for the guns.

Ratty's and Oney's conversation is interrupted by a young man who "has a job to pull, and needs some tools" *(Third World Cop)*. Oney informs the youth that he and his friends could have the "tools", but "he gets one third of anything the youth get". When the youth shows is displeasure at Oney's demand, Oney asks the youth if he thinks that the "tools" grow on trees. The youth then conceals his displeasure and accepts Oney's offers saying "that is cool, godfather, you just call the shots me we lick them" *(Third World Cop)*. As I mentioned before with the description of the don, he is the man in control of his community. In the film Oney is willing to give the youth the "tools", the gun that he needs for his robbery. Oney sets the price. The dialogue between Oney and the youth in this scene remains one of someone with a good idea who goes to an investor to get his financial backing for a project. The young man wants to start 'working', even though it is criminal work, and he needs a bank or some-one to invest in his talent and ambitions. As Ratty points out above, "govern-ment and investors don't come down here", so Oney fulfills with criminal exploitation the needs of his community. Harriott points to the failure of some state institutions to and the alternative institutions which have developed in some inner-city communities. He also comments on the formal economy failure to generate legitimate income, which aids the flourishing of the underground economy. He notes that

> As the formal economy continues to decline relative to the informal, and the state remains feeble and incapacitated in opening viable legitimate income-generating opportunities for young people, the underground and the institutions and skills associated with it may be expected to continue to flourish. This will result in deeper criminal embeddedness in the communities and, consequently, a greater disjuncture between informal internal community control and formal external police controls. (Harriott 2000: 111)

It is not only guns that Oney provides for the youths of his community. On Capone's first day back in the Dungle, he chases a young man named Skinny that the Reverend said helped him with the barrels. When Capone caught the young man who attempted to run away from him, he found a ratchet knife and some marijuana. Capone asks Skinny if Oney gave him 'weed' to sell, he said yes. Oney supplies the necessary means for young men in his area to make a living, even though it is illegal. In one scene Oney is sitting in his club *Sadam's* where a number of young women are auditioning for jobs as 'go-go' dancers. The lack of legitimate income generating opportunities for young people in the Dungle forces them to turn to Oney, who is able to capitalize on these people's needs to survive in the inner-city communities. Oney supplies the young men with guns to carry out their robbery, gives them 'weed' to sell and provides women with jobs as 'go-go' dancers or prostitutes. As Capone ironically points out when he first looks at Oney's police record, "he is a real business man" (*Third World Cop*). In the garrison community represented in the film residents are alienated and violated due to the lack of social institutions and lack of gainful employment. I would also like to assert that this is also contributing to the contemporary violence in Jamaica today.

In the film it is oftentimes difficult to distinguish between the violence of the police and violence of the criminals. As stated above Not Nice kills one of his own colleagues with the main reason being to claim that one of the gang members did it. When Capone, Ratty, and Fly are confronted with the roadblock from Not Nice, his corrupt partner, and back up from Oney and his bodyguard, Capone and Ratty are able to function almost naturally as partners in shooting their way out of the middle. Capone tells Ratty to cover him when he goes after Not Nice. Ratty also covers Fly, so that he is able to run after Oney. Here in this cinematic scene it is very difficult to separate the police from the criminals. As Gunst said while she reflects on the police officer Trinity, "I thought about the affinity between cops and criminals, how like each other they finally became" (Gunst 1995: 124). When one examines the film *Third World Cop*, one is compelled to agree with Gunst that there is a true affinity between police and criminals in Jamaica. I would like to suggest that this might be one of the reasons for the high rate of killings between police and gunmen in Jamaica. As one recording group put it, "Police and thieves in the streets, killing the nation with there guns and ammunition" (Junior Murvin).

The first time Capone is reunited with his friends from youth, he is greeted as 'shotta' Capone. One could see the character Capone as a metaphorical 'top shotta' even though he is not working for any 'don' or maybe the government what could also be metaphoric seen as the 'top don'. Capone is able to kill all the criminals and police who confront him with violence. Besides his partner Fly and Oney, who is arrested, Capone is the only one from all 'gunfighters' left. Even though Ratty's gang members refer to him as the 'top shotta', he is no match for Capone. In the final scene Ratty tries to kill Capone, one sees Capone preparing his gun, but he let Ratty shoot first. Trinity describes to Gunst what it was like to be in a shoot-out, he points to the timing that is decisive in a shoot-out. He said:

> (T)here is a feeling of high that you get. Your adrenaline is running and your heart is beating fast, because you don't know what is going to happen in a split second, between the moment when the guy reaches for his waist and all hell breaks loose. You don't want to shoot him before you know, because you haven't seen the gun yet, but you don't want to wait either, because just a split second will decide whether you are going to die. (Gunst 1995: 124)

In the cinematic representation of the shoot-out between Capone and Ratty, Capone too waits and make sure that he sees Ratty's gun; even letting him shoot first and diving out of the way of Ratty's bullet before shooting him. The film fictionalizes Jamaican real police and criminals violent life experiences. The film tries to depict and comment on the violence and alienation in some Jamaican inner-city communities.

In the film the character of Deportee is played by the famous Jamaican dancehall artist and infamous badman Desmond Ballentine a.k.a. Ninjaman – Don Gorgon. Deportee does not like the police and is suspicious of Ratty's relationship with Capone. When Capone and Ratty are confronted at the Wharf where the gang went to get the guns from the barrel, both Ratty and Capone are surprised to see each other. None of them shoots, but Deportee pushes Ratty out of the way and starts shooting at Capone. Later he wants to know from Ratty and the rest of the gang how Capone knows so much of what is going on. Deportee suggests that there might be an informer in the group. When Deportee mentions the word 'informer' all the gang members pull their gun to defend their honor. Ratty points out that maybe because they left the barrels on the side Capone could have figured out what is going on. Deportee questions the respect that Ratty has for Capone. As one the members points out, "him come back again with him same idiot attitude" *(Third World Cop)*. According to Imani Tafari the deportees have added another feature to the gang wars in Jamaica's inner-city communities. She points to the displacement of some of the deportees in the Jamaican society due to the fact that some deportees grew up in the metropolis and are Jamaicans only by affiliation (Tafari 2000: 141). Deportee also tells Oney that Ratty must be with his police friend when he asks him where Ratty is after Deportee enters Oney's bar *Sadam's*. Later when Oney wants Ratty dead, because he feels Ratty is getting too big and because Capone tells him that Ratty offered him a partnership in the "business runnings", it is Deportee whom he tells to "dust" Ratty. Oney also offers Deportee to form his own 'posse' in preparation for his plans to start dealing with the Colombians. Regarding the deportees Tafari writes that "(T)heir frustration at being displaced from their familiar surroundings has resulted in their performance of acts of violence and rivalry with local commandos, exacerbating the already existing tensions" (Tafari 2002: 141). In Jamaica the difficulties of some of the deportees to fit into the Jamaican cultural norm is very well known. The famous reggae dancehall artist Buju Banton made a song criticizing the egoistical nature of deportees for not sending anything they earned abroad back home. When some are deported they arrive back home in Jamaica with only the clothes on their back. (The Jamaican film *Shotta* also thematizes the subject.) The Jamaican society is highly dependent on the remittances sent to Jamaica by Jamaicans living abroad; the deportee's failure to live up this standard is sharply criticized. Regarding Buju Banton's famous song, Carolyn Cooper writes, "furthermore, the violation of the common decency of sending remittances to less fortunate relatives 'a yard,' the deportee failed to maintain ties of kinship (…)" (Cooper 2004: 54). The film plays on some of the above mentioned negative characteristics of the deportee. The character Deportee is alienated from Ratty and the rest of his gang members. He is always ready to misjudge his colleagues and even willing to kill Ratty and take his place on Oney's side.

The film *Third World Cop* comments on the diverse elements of violence in some Jamaican inner-city communities. One aspect of violence that is represented throughout the film is violence caused by gangs. One of the first introductions to the gang violence in the film is the young boy sitting on a bridge with two friends holding a chocolate box in the form of a heart. When Capone on his first day back in the Dungle, stops to ask the three young men for Skinny who the Reverend told him helped with the barrel, he sees the young man with the box. Capone asks what is inside the box, the young man shows him the middle finger with a gold ring on it. The young man points out to Capone that it is the finger of his older brother, nineteen years old, who was killed by gunmen across the gully last week. Capone's best friend Lion, Ratty's brother was also killed by the gang across the gully. Rita, a young woman who used to be in love with Capone, indicates to Capone, when he asks her who is the man Oney is taking to at the dance, that it is the don from across the border, and that few years ago no one could walk down a certain street due to gun shots from different gangs. Levy refers to gang violence which is referred to as "war" and points out that those fighting the war are called "soldiers" or sometime "warriors". He states that

> (T)he war is between gangs representing different areas, defending each its own territory, attacking those from other areas who cross the line of demarcation, or who clash with their members in some way, as well as preying to an increasing extend on the residents in their own sections. (Levy 1996: 17)

Even though one could claim that Jamaica has always been a violent place for Africans and their descendants with a history of violent plantation slavery and brutal post-emancipation oppression of the majority of the population, today when one examines the violence of the last twenty years in Jamaica one comes to appreciate the heavy influence of political violence in the formation of inner city gangs or 'posses' as they are sometimes called in Jamaica.

Laurie Gunst in her study on the Jamaican criminal underworld recounts her conversation with an old Jamaican inner-city resident named Chronicles who traces the gang violence in Jamaican inner-city communities to the formation of the two party political system. Chronicles points to the different stages that the violence went through. He draws attention to the 1930s when one party supporter would throw bricks and bottles to break up the opposition meeting or bringing brooms to party meetings. According to Chronicles things started to change in the 1960s when guns came in (Gunst 1995: 66). The two party system has always played divide and conquer with the poor inner-city residents of Jamaica. Chronicles shows that the violence has always been there and explains why politics is so important to people living in the inner-city communities of Jamaica. He said, "(Y)et the violence was always there, the PNP and the JLP playing divide and conquer with us sufferers. You may be surprised by how much politics means to us in the ghetto, but the reason is because we know that if our party loses, we will starve" (Gunst 1995: 66). Even though the violence in the film is not directly connected to political violence I would like to stress the influence of political violence on the development of the gangs.

Another reason for the violence in some Jamaican inner-city communities that the film represents is the trade of illegal drugs such as cocaine. In the film one reason Oney is importing the guns is due to the fact that he plans on moving into the cocaine trade "big time".

The deadly combination of cocaine and guns can be seen as two of the major factors influencing alienation and violence in Jamaica's inner city according to the representation of the film and contemporary violence in Jamaica today. The ill effects of hard drugs and guns, plus high unemployment, and lack of necessary social resources, are all contributing factors which keep the violence and alienation as a constant disturbing factor of the Jamaican society since independence. In his novel *The Children of Sisyphus* Orlando Patterson also represents the Dungle and the violence and social alienation confronting the inhabitants of this community. After over thirty years the Dungle still remains in the film *Third World Cop* a place of violence and alienation; it is a place to flee at any price as both Dinah and Ratty to do, but they are both killed in the end. According to both of these cultural texts it is only death that awaits any African Jamaican who tries to escape the violence and alienation off the 'ghetto Dungle'. Ivan too is killed when he tries to change his life of poverty.

Summary

In the film *Third World Cop* diverse forms of alienation and violence can be observed. The excessive violence used by the Jamaican police force can be connected to the paramilitaristic style of the Jamaican police force, which was created by the British colonial rulers as an instrument of domination. The internal violence of the police force represented in the film can be tied to the instrumental use of some police by criminals. Violence and social alienation can also be connected to community stigmatization, which reduces the chance of finding jobs for many young people. I pointed out that community stigmatization functions similar to the stereotyping of African diasporian people due to race and class. The high rate of unemployment in Jamaican inner-city communities also influences the violence in the urban center. The use of guns by drug dealers trading in cocaine and crack to control their area ("turf") also plays a major role in the violence represented in the film and in the Jamaican society. In the film there are a number of references to gang violence. The gang violence in Jamaica can be tied to the formation of the two party political system where party supporters would throw bricks or bottles.

8   Conclusion

In my thesis I showed how the concept of diaspora can be used to connect African American and Jamaican cultures. I emphasized in how far Euro-centric ideologies laid the foundation to empirical definitions of race of the eighteenth and nineteenth centuries. I further argued that these discourses on human species have an ongoing influence on how Africans and their descendants are represented in the so-called New World cultures of the United States and Jamaica. I drew attention to the ambivalence of race in the Jamaican society even though race is important, but it is hidden by British influenced discourse of class.

In my interpretation of Frederick Douglass' autobiographical text I pointed to the inhuman treatment of Douglass and the other slave children. Douglass does not know who his father is or his date of birth, but all the White children know their fathers and their date of birth. Douglass himself compares his and other slaves' existence to animals. I called attention to the dehumanizing system of slavery, which equated Africans and their descendants as property instead of human beings. Douglass' family relations are displaced and he and the rest of the slaves are emotionally alienated from normal family relations due to the system of slavery. I showed how violence was used on the slaves for capricious reasons and pointed out with the support of Patterson's arguments on the facet of power, which allows one human being to dominate another. I also used Patterson's arguments on the daily use of violence in any given slave society because of the low motivation of the slave regarding work to further prove the embeddedness of violence in the American slave system.

In Richard Wright's autobiographical text *Black Boy* I showed how Wright represents the traumatic effects of living under the political, economical, social and cultural oppressions of Jim Crow laws for himself and other African Americans. Wright and other African Americans living in the South and North were confronted with the limitations on their movements as well as on their identities. I pointed out how the system of slavery with its negative influences continues to determine Wright's family relations. Wright's own father neglected and abandoned his family. I argued with the support of Patterson's sociological arguments that Wright's displaced family relation can be tied to the system of slavery where African descendant males were encouraged to have children without the necessary means of taking care of them. Wright also represents the violence that was used against him by European Americans when he tried to become an optic apprentice in the South. Violence was also used against Douglass when tried to learn calking in the shipyard in Baltimore. Douglass and Wright, even though they were living in different centuries, experience similar violence from European Americans when they tried to learn trades that could improve their economic situations.

In Toni Morrison's novel *Song of Solomon* I showed how Morrison presents Jake being killed by European Americans because of his prosperous farm. The use of violence against African Americans by European Americans for monetary gains and social control continues to condition African Americans cultural artistic representations of why African Americans were lynched during the nineteenth and twentieth centuries. The continued discourse on the use of violence on African Americans during the first post-emancipation century represents the traumatic effects that these memories still hold for some African Americans.

In my interpretation of Spike Lee's film *Bamboozled* I pointed to how the director represents the cultural trauma that the stereotypical images of the minstrelsy culture continues to have on some African Americans today. I called attention to the excessive use of violence by the Mau-Maus rap group to protest against the demeaning images of African Americans identities in *Mantan: The New Millennium Minstrel Show*. I mentioned how Lee criticizes African American media artists who do not question how their representations of stereotypical images of African American identities aid to their own disempowerment in the American society. I pointed to the cinematic depictions of the character Dela's emotional and socio-cultural alienations because on the one hand he is confused by his own search for middle-class creative identity, and on the other hand he has internalized the negative stereotypical images and limitations placed on African American identities by the mainstream media.

In Henzell's film *The Harder They Come* and Thelwell's novel of the same title I used Fanon's arguments to show how violence is used by the main character to achieve his goal and protest against his feelings of alienation. The colonizers' ability to divide the natives against each other and therefore against themselves is another experience of alienation for the main character in both cultural texts. The use of violence by the oppressive forces represented in the form of the police is used to control and keep the native in subordinate position. In Thelwell's novel the main character becomes alienated and violent when he lost the security of knowing he has a place to return to in the country. Moreover the dichotomy of country and town which turns the movement from country to town/city into an experience of displacement provided yet another basis for the alienation for the protagonist.

In the novel *The Children of Sisyphus* I argued with the support of Fanon's comments regarding how the Creole language – the mother language of colonial/post-colonial children – is used to negate Blackness. I referred to how

Brother Solomon became mentally displaced while studying at the Church of England theological seminary. I argued that Patterson draws attention to the stereotype beliefs that education is not for Africans and their descendants because they do not have the brain capacity. This is a stereotypical condition based on the Europeans' scholarly discourses on race as I pointed out in my chapter on race at the beginning. The use of stereotypes along with violence to limit African diasporian cultural existences is well represented in both African American and Jamaican cultural texts. I also showed how the character Mary thinks her daughter can only do well at school because she inherited the brains from her father. I called attention to the fact that Mary, a prostitute who really does not know anything about the father of her child, gives all the credits for her daughter's educational success to this man because he is White. I pointed out that Mary and Big White Chief along with Hagar in Morrison's novel suffer from 'insidious trauma'. I used Jill Matus' concept of 'insidious trauma' to refer to the violence that is done to these characters' souls because they have internalized the stereotypical limitations placed on their African descendant identities by Europeans and their descendants for economic, social and cultural and moral control. One sees how the European definition of race based on cultural ideals of the eighteenth and nineteenth centuries and the American popular culture of minstrelsy have aided in constructing and fixing negative images of African diasporians. Some of these images have unfortunately been internalized by some African diasporians who became traumatized and violated because of the constant negation of their selves that is demanded of such mental oppressions.

In the film *Dancehall Queen* I commented on the significance of race in deciding what occupation one is expected to carry out in the confrontation between the characters Marcia and Olivine. Olivine's statement to Marcia that she does not belong on the same stage with her but outside selling soft drinks can only be understood when one is aware that most street vendors in Jamaica are African Jamaicans, so the reference of Olivine – the 'browning' – that Marcia does not belong on the stage with her has to be read in a cultural historical manner to understand how race conditions Olivine's comment. I supported my interpretations with Belinda Edmondson's arguments on the different racial registers that condition public performance even though race is underplayed.

In the film *Third World Cop* I referred to the paramilitary style of the Jamaican police force, then with the support of Anthony Harriott's arguments, I drew attention to the original intention of the British colonial powers in creating a paramilitary police force in Jamaica. I pointed to excessive use of violence by the Jamaican police force and showed how this violence by the police is used not only against criminals but also against each other. I also drew attention to how the 'community stigmatization' in Jamaican urban society prevents some African Jamaicans from finding gainful employment. The community stigmatization can be compared to stereotypes because they both fix African diasporians identities in the so-called New World societies of the United States and Jamaica.

In my thesis I showed that the process of enslavement is always a violent and alienating experience. In the American and British slave systems ideological arguments were constructed to dehumanize the Africans and their descendants so that the system of slavery would be morally accepted. Africans and their descendants became culturally traumatized by the consequences of the ritualized degrading images of their identities and the violence used to force African diasporians to accept the dehumanizing class position in both societies. The process of having to prove their humanity after slavery and emancipation has caused many African diasporians in the United States and Jamaica to become alienated from – and violated by – the society they live in.

9   Bibliography

Andrews, William, Harris, Trudier, Smith Foster, Frances (eds). *The Oxford Companion to African American Literature.* Oxford: Oxford University Press, 1997.

Augier, Roy, Smith, M. G., and Nettleford, Rex. *Report on the Rastafari Movement in Kingston Jamaica.* Kingston: Institute of Social and Economic Research, 1960 (7th edition 1988).

Austin-Broos, J. Diane. *Jamaica Genesis: Religion and the Politics of Moral Order.* Chicago: The University of Chicago Press. 1987.

Aylmer, J. Kevin. *Towering Babble and Glimpses of Zion: Recent Depictions of Rastafari in Cinema.* in: Murrell, S. Nathaniel, Spencer, D. William, Mcfarlane, A. Adrian (eds.). *The Rastafari Reader: Chanting Down Babylon.* Kingston: Ian Randle Publishers, 1998.

Baker Jr., Houston A. *Long Black Song: Essays in Black American Literature and Culture.* Charlottesville: The University Press of Virginia, 1972.

Baker, Houston A., Diawara, Manthia, and Lindeborg, Ruth H. *Black British Cultural Studies: A Reader.* Chicago: The University of Chicago Press, 1996.

Baldwin, James. *Notes of a Native Son.* London: Michael Joseph, 2nd impress. 1964

Barrett Sr., Leonard E. *The Rastafarians.* Boston: Beacon Press, 1977.

Bell, Bernard W. *The Afro-American Novel and Its Tradition.* Amherst: The University of Massachusetts Press, 1987.

Bennett Jr., Lerone. *Before the Mayflower: A History of Black America.* New York: Penguin Books, 5th edition 1982.

Bhabha, Homi K. *The Location of Culture.* London and New York: Routledge, 1994.

Bone, Robert. *Richard Wright.* In: *Pamphlets on American Writers,* Nr. 74. Minneapolis: University of Minnesota Press, 1969.

Brathwaite, Edward K. *History of the Voice.* London and Port of Spain: New Beacon Books, 1984.

Bryer, Jackson R., Duke, Maurice, Inge, M. Thomas (eds.). *Black American Writers. Bibliographical Essays, Vol. 1. The Beginnings Through the Harlem Renaissance and Langston Hughes.* London: The Macmillan Press, 1978.

Burgum, Edwin Berry. *The Art of Richard Wright's Short Stories.* In: *Five Black Writers: Essays on Wright, Ellison, Baldwin, Hughes, and Jeroi Jones.* Gibson Donald (ed.). New York: New York University Press, 1970.

Campbell, Jane. *Mythic Black Fiction: The Transformation of History.* Knoxville: The University of Tennessee Press, 1986.

Camus, Albert. *The Myth of Sisyphus and Other Essays.* New York: Vintage Books, 1959.

Cham, Mbye (ed.). *EX-ILES: Essays On Caribbean Cinema.* Trenton: Africa World Press, Inc., 1992.

Christian, Barbara. *Black Feminist Criticism: Perspectives on Black Women Writers.* New York: Pergamon Press, 1985.

Chevannes, Barry. *Rastafari: Roots and Ideology.* Syracuse: Syracuse University Press, 1994.

_____ (ed.). *Rastafari and Other African-Caribbean World Views.* New Brunswick: Rutgers University Press, 1995.

_____ *Learning To Be A Man: Culture, Socialization and Gender Identity in Five Caribbean Communities*. Kingston: The University of the West Indies Press, 2001.

Childers, Joseph, and Hentzi, Gary (eds.). *The Columbia Dictionary of Modern Literary and Cultural Criticism*. New York: Columbia University Press, 1995.

Collins, Patricia Hill. *Black Feminist Thought: Knowledge, Consciousness, and the Politics of Empowerment*. (2nd ed.) New York: Routledge, 2000.

Cooke, Michael G. *Afro-American Literature in the Twentieth Century: The Achievement of Intimacy*. New Haven: Yale University Press, 1984.

Cooper, Carolyn. *Noises in the Blood: Orality, Gender, and the "Vulgar" Body of Jamaican Popular Culture*. Durham: Duke University Press, 1993.

_____ *Sound Clash: Jamaican Dancehall Culture at Large*. New York: Palgrave Macmillan, 2004.

Cotterell, Arthur. *A Dictionary of World Mythology*. New York: G. P. Putnam's Sons, 1980.

De las Casas, Bartolomé. *A Short Account of the Destruction of the Indies*. Ed. Griffin, Nigel. London: Penguin Books, 1992.

Dent, Gina, and Wallace, Michele. *Black Popular Culture*. New York: The New Press, 1983 (edition 1998).

Diawara, Manthia (ed.). *Black American Cinema*. New York: Routledge, 1993.

Dookhan, Isaac. *A Post Emancipation History of the West Indies*. Essex: Longman, 1988 (9th edition 1997).

Dyson, Michael Eric. *Reflecting Black: African American Cultural Criticism*. Minneapolis: University of Minnesota Press, 1994.

Edmondson, Belinda. *Public Spectacles: Caribbean Women and the Politics of Public Performances*. In Scott, David (ed.). *Small Axe: A Caribbean Journal of Criticism*. Bloomington: Indiana University Press, 2003.

Emanuel, James A., Gross, Theodore E. (eds.). *Dark Symphony: Negro Literature in America*. New York: The Free Press, 1968.

Evans, Mari (ed.). *Black Women Writers 1950–1980: A Critical Evaluation*. New York: Anchor Books, 1984.

Eyerman, Ron. *Cultural Trauma: Slavery and the Formation of Africa American Identity*. Cambridge: The Press Syndicate of the University of Cambridge, 2001.

Fabre, Genevieve, O'Meally, Robert (eds.). *History & Memory in African American Culture*. New York: Oxford University Press, 1994.

Fanon, Frantz. *Black Skin White Masks*. New York: Grove Press, 1967.

_____ *The Wretched of the Earth*. New York: Grove Press, 1963.

Felder, Hope Cain (ed.). *The Original African Heritage Study Bible. King James' Version*. Iowa Falls: World Bible Publishers, 1998.

Fishburn, Katherine. *The Problem of Embodiment in Early African American Narratives*. Westport. Greenwood Press, 1994.

Ford, Nick Aaron. *The Ordeal of Richard Wright*. In: *Five Black Writers*. Donald Gibson (ed.). New York: New York University Press, 1970.

Fuchs, Cynthia. *Spike Lee Interviews*. Jackson: University Press of Mississippi, 2002.

Furman, Jan. *Toni Morrison's Fiction*. Columbia: University of South Carolina Press, 1996.

Garlington, S. W. *"An Ugly, Yet Factual Portrait". The African*. In: *Richard Wright Critical Reception*. John M. Reilly (ed.). New York: Burt Franklin & Co., Inc. 1978.

Gates Jr., Henry Louis. *Figures in Black: Words, Signs, and the "Racial" Self.* New York: Oxford University Press, 1987.

_____ (ed.). *The Classic Slave Narratives: The Life of Olaudah Equiano, The History of Mary Prince, Narrative of the Life of Frederick Douglass, Incidents in the Life of a Slave Girl.* New York: Mentor Publish by the Penguin Group, 1987.

Gilroy, Paul. *The Black Atlantic: Modernity and Double Consciousness.* London: Verso, 1993.

_____ *Against Race: Imagining Political Culture Beyond the Color Line.* Cambridge: The Belknap Press of Harvard University Press, 2000.

Gray, Obika. *Radicalism and Social Change in Jamaica, 1960–1972.* Knoxville: The University of Tennessee Press, 1991.

Griffin, Farah Jasmine. *The African American Migration Narrative.* New York: Oxford University Press, 1995.

Gunst, Laurie. *born fi dead: a journey through the Jamaican posse underworld.* Edinburgh: Payback Press, 1995.

Hakutani, Yoshinobu, and Butler, Robert (ed.). *The City in African American Literature.* Madison: Fairleigh Dickinson University Press, 1995.

Hall, Stuart (ed.). *Representation: Cultural Representations and Signifying Practices.* London: Sage Publications, 1997 (7th edition 2003).

Harding, Wendy, and Martin, Jacky. *A World of Difference: An Inter-Cultural Study of Toni Morrison's Novels.* Westpoint: Greenwood Press, 1994.

Harriott, Anthony. *Police and Crime Control in Jamaica: Problems of Reforming Ex-Colonial Constabularies.* Kingston: University of the West Indies, Mona, 2000.

Hart, Richard. *Slaves Who Abolished Slavery. Volume 1: Blacks in Bondage.* Kingston: University of the West Indies, 1980.

_____ *Slaves Who Abolished Slavery. Volume 2: Blacks in Rebellion.* Kingston: University of the West Indies, 1985.

Hebdige, Dick. *Cut 'N' Mix: Culture, Identity and Caribbean Music.* London: Routledge, 1987.

_____ *SubCulture: The Meaning of Style.* London: Methuen & Co. Ltd, 1978.

Heinze, Denis. *The Dilemma of "Double Consciousness": Toni Morrison's Novels.* Athens: The University of Georgia Press, 1993.

Henderson, Carol E. *Scarring the Black Body: Race and Representation in African American Literature.* Columbia: University of Missouri Press, 2002.

Hope, Donna P. *Inna di Dancehall: Popular Culture and the Politics of Identity in Jamaica.* Kingston: University of the West Indies, Mona, 2006.

Hügli, Anton (ed.). *Philosophielexikon: Personen und Begriffe der abendländischen Philosophie von der Antike bis zur Gegenwart.* Hamburg: Rowohlt, 1991.

Israel, Joachim. *Der Begriff Entfremdung: Makrosoziologische Untersuchungen von Marx bis zur Soziologie der Gegenwart.* Hamburg: Rowohlt, 1972.

Jackson, Blyden. *A History of Afro-American Literature Vol. 1: The Long Beginning 1746–1895.* Baton Rouge: Louisiana State University Press, 1989.

_____ *The Waiting Years: Essays on American Negro Literature.* Baton Rouge: Louisiana State University Press, 1976.

Jordan, Margaret I. *African American Servitude and Historical Imaginings: Retrospective Fiction and Representation.* New York: Palgrave Macmillan, 2004.

Kemayo, Kamau. *Emerging African Survivals: An Afrocentric Critical Theory.* New York: Routledge Press, 2003.

Kent, E. George. *Blackness and the Adventure of Western Culture.* In: Bloom, Harold (ed.). *Modern Critical Views: Richard Wright.* New York: Chelsea House Publishers, 1987.

Lane, Layle. *The Call.* In: *Richard Wright Critical Reception.* John M. Reilly (ed.). New York: Burt Franklin & Co., Inc., 1978: 155–156.

Lentricchia, Frank, and McLaughlin, Thomas. *Critical Terms for Literary Study.* Chicago: The University of Chicago Press, 1990. (2nd edition 1995).

Levy, Horace. *They Cry 'Respect'! Urban Violence and Poverty in Jamaica.* Kingston: University of the West Indies, Mona, 1996.

Lotter, Konrad, Meiners, Reinhard, Treptow, Elmar (eds.). *Marx-Engels Begriffslexikon.* München: C.H. Beck, 1984.

Mack, Douglas R. A. *From Babylon To Rastafari: Origins And History Of The Rastafarian Movement.* Chicago: Research Associates School Time Publications, 1999.

Margolies, Edward. *The Letters of Richard Wright.* In: Lloyd W. Brown (ed.). *The Black Writers in Africa and the Americas.* Los Angeles: Hennessey & Ingalls, Inc, 1973.

Massood, Paula, J. *Black City Cinema: African American Urban Experiences in Film.* Philadelphia: Temple University Press, 2003.

Matus, Jill. *Toni Morrison.* Manchester: Manchester University Press, 1998.

McCall, Dan. *The Example of Richard Wright.* New York: Harvest Book, 1969.

McFarlane, Adrian A., Murrell, Nathaniel S., Spencer, William D. (eds.). *The Rastafari Reader: Chanting Down Babylon.* Kingston: Ian Randle Publishers, 1998.

McKay, Nellie, Earle, Kathryn (eds.). *Approaches to Teaching the Novels of Toni Morrison.* New York: The Modern Language Association of America, 1997.

Mitchel, Angelyn (ed.). *Within the Circle: An Anthology of African American Literary Criticism from the Harlem Renaissance to the Present.* Durham: Duke University Press, 1994.

Morrison, Toni. *The Bluest Eye.* New York: Vintage Press, 1970.

_____ *Song of Solomon.* New York: Vintage Press, 1977.

_____ *Tar Baby.* New York: Signet Book, 1981.

_____ *Playing in the Dark: Whiteness and the Literary Imagination.* Cambridge: Harvard University Press, 1992.

_____ *Unspeakable Things Unspoken.* In: Mitchell Angelyn (ed.). *Within the Circle.* Durham: Duke University Press, 1994.

_____ *Rootedness: The Ancestor as Foundation.* In: Evans, Mari (ed.). *Black Women Writers 1950–1980: A Critical Evaluation.* New York. Anchor Books, 1984.

Mosely-Wood, Rachel. *Looking at Women: Representation of Women in Selected Examples of Popular Culture in the Caribbean.* Unpublished Doctoral Thesis – Doctor of Philosophy at the University of the West Indies, Mona, 2002.

Nelson, Emmanuel (ed.). *African American Autobiographers: A Source Book.* Westport: Greenwood Press, 2002.

_____ *The Art of Richard Wright.* Carbondale: Southern Illinois University Press, 1969.

Nettleford, Rex. *Mirror Mirror: Identity, Race and Protest in Jamaica.* Kingston: Kingston Publishers Limited, 1998.

Owens, Joseph. *Dread: The Rastafarian of Jamaica.* Kingston: Sangster's Book Ltd, 1976.

Patterson, Orlando. *The Children Sisyphus*. Essex: Logman,1964.

_____ *The Sociology of Slavery: An Analysis of the Origins, Development and Structure of Negro Slave Society in Jamaica*. Rutherford: Fairleigh Dickinson University Press, 1969.

_____ *Slavery and Social Death: A Comparative Study*. Cambridge: Harvard University Press, 1982.

_____ *Rituals of Blood: Consequences of Slavery in Two American Centuries*. New York: Basic Civitas Books, 1998.

Peach, Linden. *Modern Novelists: Toni Morrison*. New York: St. Martin Press, 1995.

Petesch, Donald A. *A Spy in The Enemy's Country: The Emergence of Modern Black Literature*. Iowa City: University of Iowa Press, 1989.

Powell, Kevin, *Who's Gonna Take the Weight? Manhood, Race, and Power in America*. New York: Three Rivers Press, 2003.

Reed, Ishmael. *The Reed Reader*. New York: Basic Books Publishers, 2000.

Redding, Saunders. *The Alien Land of Richard Wright*. In: *Five Black Writers*. Donald Gibson (ed.). New York: New York University Press, 1970.

Reilly, John M. (ed.). *Richard Wright: the Critical Reception*. New York: Burt Franklin & Co., Inc, 1978.

Russell, Sandi. *Render Me My Song: African American Women Writers from Slavery to the Present*. New York: St. Martin's Press, 1990.

Scott, Jr., Nathan A. *The Dark and Haunted Towers of Richard Wright*. In: *Five Black Writers*. Donald Gibson (ed.). New York: New York University Press, 1970.

Sherlock, Philip, and Bennett, Hazel. *The Story of the Jamaican People*. Kingston: Ian Randle Publishers, 1998.

Smith Foster, Frances. *Witnessing Slavery: The Development of Ante-bellum Slave Narratives*. Westport: Greenwood Press, 1979.

Smith, Valerie. *Self-Discovery and Authority in Afro-American Narrative*. Cambridge: Harvard University Press, 1987.

_____ (ed.). *New Essays on Song of Solomon*. Cambridge: Cambridge University Press, 1995.

Sontag, Susan. *Regarding the Pain of Others*. New York: Farrar, Straus & Giroux, 2003.

Stepto, Robert B. *From Behind the Veil: A Study of Afro-American Narrative*. Chicago: University of Illinois Press, 1979.

Stolzoff, Norman C. *Wake the Town & Tell the People: Dancehall Culture in Jamaica*. Durham: Duke University Pres, 2000.

Tate, Claudia. *Psychoanalysis and Black Novels: Desire and the Protocol of Race*. New York: Oxford University Press, 1998.

Tafari-Ama, Imani. *Blood, Bullets and Bodies: Sexual Politics Below the Poverty Line – The Political Economy of Violence, Power, Gender and Embodyment in Jamaica's Inner City*. Maastricht: Shaker Publishing, 2002.

Tafari, I Jabulani. *A Rastafari View of Marcus Mosiah Garvey: Patriarch Prophet Philosopher*. Kingston: Great Company Ja-Ltd, 1996.

Thelwell, Michael. *The Harder They Come*. London: The X Press, 1980.

Thiong'o, Ngugi. *Homecoming: Essays on African and Caribbean Literature, Culture and Politics*. Westport: Lawrence Hill and Company, Publishers, Inc., 1973.

Toll, Robert, C. *On With The Show: The First Century of Show Business in America.* New York: Oxford University Press, 1976.

Turner, Graeme. *Film as Social Practice.* London: Routledge, 1988 (2nd ed. 1993).

Walker, Melissa, *Down from the Mountaintop: Black Women's Novels in the Wake of the Civil Rights Movement, 1966–1989.* New Haven: Yale University Press, 1991.

Wallace, Michele. *Dark Designs & Visual Culture.* Durham: Duke University Press, 2004.

Waller, Nicole. *Contradictory Violence: Revolution and Subversion in the Caribbean.* Heidelberg: Universitätsverlag Winter, 2005.

West, Cornel. *The Cornel West Reader.* New York: Basic Books, 1999.

_____ *Beyond Eurocentrism and Multiculturalism. Volume II – Prophetic Reflections: Notes on Race and Power in America.* Monroe: Common Courage Press, 1993.

Widmer, Kingsley. *The Existential Darkness: Richard Wright's The Outsider.* In: *Five Black Writers.* Donald Gibson (ed.). New York: New York University Press, 1970.

Wright, Ellen, and Fabre, Michel (ed.). *Richard Wright Reader.* New York: Harper & Row, 1978.

Wright, Richard. *Uncle Tom's Children.* New York: Signet, 1936 (7th edition 1947).

_____ *Native Son.* New York: Vintage Press, 2000.

_____ *12 Million Black Voices.* New York: Thunder's Mouth Press, 2002.

_____ *Black Boy: American Hunger.* New York: Harpers Perennial, 1991.

_____ *Joe Louis Uncovers Dynamite.* In: *Richard Wright Reader,* ed. Ellen Wright and Michael Fabre. New York: Harper & Row, 1978.

_____ *Blue Print for Negro Writing.* In *Richard Wright Reader,* ed. Ellen Wright and Michael Fabre. New York: Harper & Row, 1978.

_____ *White Man Listen.* New York: Anchor Books, 1964.

_____ Introduction. In: Drake, St. Clair, and Cayton R. Horace. *Black Metropolis: A Study of Negro Life in a Northern City.* Chicago: University of Chicago Press, 1993.

Yearwood, Gladstone L. *Black Film as a Signifying Practice: Cinema, Narration and the African American Aesthetic Tradition.* Trenton: Africa World Press, 2000.

Zips, Werner. *Afrikanische Diaspora: Out of Africa Into New Worlds.* Hamburg: Lit Verlag, 2003.

9.1. Filmography

Browne, Christopher. *Third World Cop.* Jamaica: Palm Pictures, 2000.
Henzell, Perry. *The Harder They Come.* Jamaica: Art House Productions Ltd., 1972.
Lee, Spike. *Bamboozled.* USA: New Line Production. Inc., 2000.
Letts, Don, Elgood, Rick. *Dancehall Queen.* Jamaica: Island Jamaica Film in association
      with Hawks Nest Productions, 1997.

9.2. Discography

Stephens, Tanya. *Rebelution.* Jamaica: VP Records, 2006.
Various. *The Harder They Come.* Jamaica: Island Records Ltd., 1972.

Afrika und ihre Diaspora

hrsg. von A.o. Prof. Dr. Manfred Kremser und A.o. Prof. Dr. Werner Zips (Universität Wien)

Michaela Schäfer
Weißes Gold malischer Frauen oder: Was Entwicklung bedeuten kann
Karitébutter auf dem Weg in die Welt – vom „traditionellen" Fett zum Eliteprodukt
Die Karitébutter oder das *Weiße Gold der Frauen* ist eines der vielen afrikanischen Produkte, das sich *auf den Weg in die Welt* macht. Längst ist sie nichts rein „Lokales" und „Weibliches" mehr, denn die Nachfrage nach Karitébutter oder nach Karitémandeln kommt aus allen möglichen Richtungen. Interesse zeigt die Industrie genauso wie die afrikanische Diaspora oder die gebildete europäische Elitekundin. Durch eine genauere Betrachtung *herr*schaftlicher Praktiken der Entwicklung werden hier lokale und globale Implikationen sich verändernder Produktions- und Vermarktungsformen aufgezeigt.
Bd. 8, 2010, 216 S., 19,90 €, br., ISBN 978-3-643-50136-3

LIT Verlag Berlin – Münster – Wien – Zürich – London
Auslieferung Deutschland / Österreich / Schweiz: siehe Impressumsseite

Martina Könighofer
The New Ship of Zion
Dynamic Diaspora Dimensions of the African Hebrew Israelites of Jerusalem
The New Ship of Zion explores the dynamic Diaspora dimensions of the African Hebrew Israelites, a spiritual movement of African Americans who have traced their roots to Zion. With the successful establishment of thriving model communities in Israel and Ghana they have built up a framework for repatriation to the motherland. The resulting constructions of ethnic and cultural identity are the subjects of this book. It also sheds light on the ideological concepts of other communities that travel the same waters as the New Ship of Zion, such as the Rastafarians.
Bd. 7, 2008, 144 S., 19,90 €, br., ISBN 978-3-8258-1055-9

LIT Verlag Berlin – Münster – Wien – Zürich – London
Auslieferung Deutschland / Österreich / Schweiz: siehe Impressumsseite

Erwin Ebermann (Hg.)
Afrikaner in Wien
Zwischen Mystifizierung und Verteufelung. Erfahrungen und Analysen
Die mangelnde Integration der 6500 afrikanischen Zuwanderer Wiens erklärt sich durch auch gegensei-
tige Vorurteile, Ingroup-Denken und das Scheitern der Vermittler. Die Autoren aus Afrika und Öster-
reich beschreiben Herkunft, Leben, Erfahrungen und Akzeptanz der Afrikaner am Arbeitsplatz, bei der
Wohnungssuche, bei der Exekutive und in Freundschaft und Liebe. Sie stützen sich auf langjährige Er-
fahrungen, Umfragen unter 154 Afrikanern und 702 Wienern sowie Ergebnisse realer Bewerbungen für
Arbeitsplätze und Wohnungen. S. a. http://www.afrika-wien.at „ . . . sollte im ganzen deutschsprachigen
Raum gelesen werden" (Franz Nuscheler, Direktor des Instituts für Entwicklung und Frieden, Duisburg)
Bd. 3, 3. Aufl. 2007, 440 S., 28,00 €, br., ISBN 978-3-8258-5712-7

LIT Verlag Berlin – Münster – Wien – Zürich – London
Auslieferung Deutschland / Österreich / Schweiz: siehe Impressumsseite

Patric Kment
Afíríkà yèyé mi! – Meine Mutter Afrika!
Reafrikanisierung, kulturelle Expansion und Transformation der Òrìshà-Religion Trinidads.
Geschichte und Grundlagen der Veränderungsprozesse einer afroamerikanischen Religion im
Spannungsfeld von Eklektizismus, Synkretismus und Reafrikanisierung
Die Orisha-Religion auf Trinidad war immer wieder Gegenstand internaler und externaler Veränderungs-
prozesse. Die Geschichte dieser ursprünglich westafrikanischen Religion auf Trinidad ist daher eine Ge-
schichte der Transformationen: Orisha ist in seiner gegenwärtigen Form nicht nur das Resultat von Unter-
drückung und christlicher Missionierung, Orisha wird ebenso als der kreative Versuch einer autonomen
Wiedervergesellschaftung von afrikanischen Ethnien in der Diaspora und somit als aktive kulturelle Expansion in afrikanische und „fremde" kulturelle Sphären und Weltbilder verstanden.
Bd. 4, 2005, 232 S., 24,90 €, br., ISBN 3-8258-7262-9

LIT Verlag Berlin – Münster – Wien – Zürich – London
Auslieferung Deutschland / Österreich / Schweiz: siehe Impressumsseite

Werner Zips (Hg.)
Afrikanische Diaspora
Out of Africa – Into New Worlds
Afrika und ihre Diaspora sind miteinander durch ein Geflecht von historischen, sozialen, kulturellen, po-
litischen und vor allem emotionalen Beziehungen verbunden. Gewalt, Verschleppung und Versklavung
bestimmten die längste Zeit über die aufgezwungene Entfremdung zwischen dem Motherland und den in
alle Welt verstreuten Töchtern und Söhnen Afrikas. Ihre Erinnerung an und Identifikation mit Afrika wur-
de vielfach gebrochen, aber niemals ausgelöscht. Darin liegt der geschichtliche Anknüpfungspunkt für das
heutige Streben nach Rückbesinnung, Neubeginn und Wiedervereinigung. In einem Symbol des afrikanischen Königtums fand die Suche nach den eigenen Wurzeln ein sprechendes Zeichen: dem rückwärtsge-
wandten Vogel Sankofa, der sich aus der Vergangenheit pickt, was er für die Bewältigung der Gegenwart
braucht, um seine Zukunft zu verbessern. Diese Hoffnung konzentriert sich auch in einer Momentauf-
nahme: der Umarmung des jamaikanischen Poeten Mutabaruka mit dem ghanaischen Master Drummer
Ghanaba auf dem Boden der einstigen Sklavenburg von Cape Coast. Die Beiträge zu diesem Buch belegen
auf vielfältige Weise das dynamische world wide web des kulturellen Austausches zwischen Afrika und
ihrer Diaspora.
Bd. 1, 2. Aufl. 2008, 472 S., 29,90 €, br., ISBN 978-3-8258-3971-0

LIT Verlag Berlin – Münster – Wien – Zürich – London
Auslieferung Deutschland / Österreich / Schweiz: siehe Impressumsseite